First Follow Nature

First Follow Nature

PRIMITIVISM
in English Poetry 1725-1750

MARGARET MARY FITZGERALD

OCTAGON BOOKS

A DIVISION OF FARRAR, STRAUS AND GIROUX

New York   1976

Reprinted 1976

OCTAGON BOOKS
A DIVISION OF FARRAR, STRAUS & GIROUX, INC.
19 Union Square West
New York, N.Y. 10003

Library of Congress Cataloging in Publication Data

FitzGerald, Margaret Mary, 1916-
    First follow nature.

    Reprint of the ed. published by King's Crown Press, New York.

    Originally presented as the author's thesis, Columbia University, 1947.

    Bibliography: p.
    Includes index.
    1. English poetry—18th century—History and criticism.
    2. Primitivism in literature. I. Title.

[PR565.P75F5   1976]   821'.5'093   76-12089
ISBN 0-374-92748-0

TO MY MOTHER

and to the memory of

MY FATHER

Preface

First follow Nature, and your judgment frame
By her just standards, which are still the same.

ALEXANDER POPE offered that advice to critics as a guide
to the framing of their literary judgments, but his contemporaries, and he himself (in other contexts) appealed to the
authority of Nature for guidance in matters more weighty than
the turn of a phrase or the composition of an epic. To Pope's generation "first follow Nature" was a rule, not merely of literature,
but of life itself.

Part of the fascination which Nature held for men of the early
eighteenth century expressed itself in their repeated desire to go
"back to nature," or to live "according to nature." The phrase
"back to nature" suggests at once that strain in human speculation
which modern writers have named "primitivism." But whether the
reader pictures eighteenth-century dreamers looking back towards
a lost age of gold (chronological primitivism), or searching in contemporary life for a lost age of innocence (cultural primitivism), he
should remember that such dreamers felt they were trying to recapture a more "natural" mode of existence. The ideal "back to
nature" cannot be summed up merely in terms of regrets for
Arcadia or of dreams of idyllic retirement. The problem remains
of what constitutes the Nature to which the idealists are retreating.
Is such a Nature synonymous with order, restraint and temperance,
or with variety, freedom and profusion? Faced with the ever-
growing complexity of this problem of primitivism, the reader is
in a mood to appreciate Professor Lovejoy's reminder that "the history of primitivism is in great part a phase of a larger historical
tendency . . . the use of the term 'nature' to express the standard
of human values, the identity of good with that which is 'natural'
or 'according to nature.'"

In the past, works on primitivism in the literature of a given period have tended to restrict themselves to special aspects of the subject. Alan D. McKillop's *The Background of Thomson's Seasons*, for instance, and Lois Whitney's *Primitivism and the Idea of Progress in English Popular Literature of the Eighteenth Century* are primarily concerned with chronological and cultural varieties of primitivism. The present study, *First Follow Nature*, is to my knowledge the first attempt to examine a given portion of literature in the light of the wider implications of the concept.

I have tried to untangle the strands of primitivism in English poetry between the years 1725 and 1750. The reader may well challenge the arbitrary limitations "poetry," and "1725–1750." Justification may, I think, be offered for both. First of all, a study of this kind must necessarily be limited in its scope: in the last analysis, its value rests on the thoroughness with which the chosen field has been covered. Next, since poetry was an important, even a preferred eighteenth-century vehicle of ideas, the poets should offer a fair sampling of eighteenth-century opinion in regard to primitivism. Finally, the years 1725–1750 have their own special significance, marking as they do the important transition period between the elegant neo-classicism of the Age of Anne, and the dawning romanticism of the later eighteenth century.

Periodicals, miscellanies, collections of verse, works of separate poets of these twenty-five years yielded me about two thousand passages of non-dramatic poetry relating to various aspects of primitivism. Throughout the reading of those verses, good, bad, mediocre, and execrable, I held to the idea that the goal of the search was not merely the discovery of what Colley Cibber thought of Royal George, nor what an anonymous scribbler praised in "heavenly" Caroline, but that the end of the work lay in reaching a better understanding of the climate of opinion in which the poets great and small alike composed their verses—such an understanding as would ultimately make more clear the contribution of the major writers of the period, would point out wherein they reflected, discarded, improved upon, certain important ideas current in their time.

At first, faced with scores of passages, I thought the achievement of that end, or indeed of any end, a lost cause. Gradually however, out of the legions of third rate odes, the miles of pedestrian couplets, the myriads of mock heroics, certain patterns began to emerge. As the poets discussed their dreams of the past, their fears of the present, their judgments on literature, art, morals, it became possible for me to see certain broad divisions in the trends of their opinions. These divisions have dictated the structure of this book.

The first section of this study surveys the strains of chronological and cultural primitivism to be found in the poets' verses. Here appear the topics most frequently discussed by the modern critic, and most familiar to the general reader. The material in this section adds little to the familiar picture, but it does, I hope, serve to show the relative strength and persistency of such conventional ideals as those of the golden age, of pastoral bliss, of rural retirement, and of the poor but contented citizen.

The second section of the book deals with the poets' use of Nature as a guide to their literary, aesthetic, and ethical judgments, and applies the *vivere secundum naturam* as a touchstone for interpreting poetic quarrels (all loud with appeals to Nature) that raged about landscapes, literature, and rules of life during the second quarter of the eighteenth century.

Last scene of all, the Epilogue, brings together those conclusions indicated throughout the book about the primitivism of the major writers, Thomson, Young, Akenside, Pope, Gray, and the Wartons, pointing out which phases of primitivism interested each of these authors, and in what manner each outstripped or fell behind his fellow poets in his treatment of the subject.

When, in 1935, Professors Lovejoy and Boas published the first volume of *A Documentary History of Primitivism and Related Ideas*, they implied in their preface that any complete treatment of the idea of primitivism must necessarily be a cooperative enterprise. Their own *Primitivism and Related Ideas in Antiquity* was intended as the first of a series of volumes, others of which, it is to be hoped, will still appear. Even then however, there will, as they suggested, be need for many other "special monographs on particular episodes" in the history of primitivism. Some of the gaps have already been filled in by such studies as Professor Boas' *The Happy Beast*

in French Thought in the Seventeenth Century in which he discussed a specific philosophical offshoot of the concept during a
particular period, and Miss Whitney's study *Primitivism and the
Idea of Progress* which dealt primarily with those strains as they
appeared in English prose from 1750–1800. I like to hope that *First
Follow Nature* may rank as a contribution, however small, to the
general project.

I wish to express deep appreciation to the American Council of
Learned Societies for the grant of a fellowship which helped me to
continue my studies, and to acknowledge also the generosity of
the libraries of Yale and of Harvard in allowing me to use their
eighteenth-century materials. To Professor Ernest Hunter Wright
who advised and encouraged me in my undertaking, and to Professor Elliott VanKirk Dobbie who unsparingly and painstakingly
criticized the structure and arrangement of my manuscript, I am
most grateful. But above all, to Professor Marjorie Hope Nicolson
who has been unendingly patient, and kind, and firm, through all
my struggles with problems of organization and of writing, and
who has never failed to give me sorely needed guidance and inspiration, I owe a debt of gratitude that it is not possible I shall ever
be able to repay.

Contents

PART ONE

Primitivism

Chronological and Cultural

I

Chronological Primitivism

FROM Hesiod to Miniver Cheevey many men have thought, or have pretended to think, that their happiest days were in the past. The man in the street calls that longing regret for "the good old days," the philosopher terms it "chronological primitivism," but named or unnamed the tendency is a constant in human nature. Early eighteenth-century poets who sang the charms of vanished eras rather than those of Georgian England were only adding another chapter to a long and honorable tradition.[1]

The reader who follows their excursions into the past must be prepared for much that is conventional, much that is repetitious. Timeworn in theme, threadbare in verse, the poems that fail as literature are useful as documentary evidence. They form a partial history of the course of primitivism during the early years of the eighteenth century.

The poets' additions to the long tradition of primitivism blend easily into its venerable conventionality. They dreamed, as generations of writers before them had dreamed, of the classical Golden Age and of the lost beauty of Eden. Life and literature prompted their reminiscent longings. Memories of classical readings, recollections of journeys to Virgil's tomb and Horace's vine-crowned hills, the horror of men of their country and generation for the degenerate state of continental Europe,—all these were powerful motives for lamenting the vanished grandeur of Rome and Greece.

Of all regrets for bygone days, the poets' longings for past times of good government at home were most frequent and most impassioned. No single theme hallowed by tradition could compare in popularity with a subject that had nothing to do with Virgil or with *Genesis*, the burning theme of contemporary politics. Classic morals might adorn a plaint of modern degeneracy, but there was nothing like the fury of a scorned Tory to inspire golden pictures of blest eras before Sir Robert.

I

Despite their overwhelming preoccupation with the glories of the classic past, the poets of this period gave some time and some attention to chronological primitivism dealing with Christian themes. At least occasionally they meditated on the lost delights of Eden, regretted the joys of the patriarchal age, and criticized the evils of modern Christianity.

Members of a generation which rocked with wordy quarrels about the essential qualities of human nature,[2] the verse writers were curious about the psychological effects of the fall of man. They looked back to Eden, not so much to deplore man's sins as to survey his pristine powers of intellect. Man exiled from Paradise had lost his perfect balance of reason and passion and had become a depraved creature, a fugitive from the Creator, bereft of perfect love and of heaven on earth.[3] Some shadow of Eden's peace remained to him in rural life, but most of the pleasures of that vanished garden were

> Delights that ne'er to guilty man return,
> Delights that guilty man could never boast,
> Since the blest age of innocence was lost.[4]

Among those lost blessings man's superior mental endowments seem to have impressed the poets most. They remarked the clarity of vision and calm of passion which Adam had possessed before the fall, his simplicity, his innocence, his intuitive knowledge, "where truth was almost felt as well as seen, (perception half) and scarce a mist between." [5] His unmarred nature had a perfect harmony of parts:

> Sound was the body, and the soul serene;
> Like two sweet instruments, ne'er out of tune,
> They play their several parts.[6]

But that early perfection of humanity had changed:

> alter'd now, and falln's he is,
> Immers'd in flesh, and dead within;
> Dead to the taste of native bliss,
> And ever sinking into sin.[7]

In man's altered state his runaway passions rushed the individual and society towards ruin:

> When Man in Nature's Purity remain'd,
> By Pain untroubled, and by Sin unstain'd. . . .
>   In the pure Splendor of substantial Light,
> The Beam divine of Reason bless'd his Sight. . . .
> Nor dar'd the Body, passive Slave, controul
> The sov'reign Mandates of the ruling Soul.
>
>   But soon by Sin the sacred Union broke,
> Man bows to Earth beneath the heavy Yoke;
> The darkling Soul scarce feels a glimm'ring Ray;
> Shut in gross Sense from our immortal Day. . . .
> Material Objects Heav'n-born Souls possess;
> Passions enslave, and servile Cares oppress:
>   Fraud, Rapine, Murder, Guilt's long direful Train,
> Distracted Nature's anarchy maintain. . . .
> While Order's Rule must be inforc'd by Pains.[8]

In describing man's first state, the poets consciously or unconsciously echoed their century's bitterly-fought controversy over the nature of man. Eighteenth-century answers to the perennial question "What is man by nature?" had ranged in sentiment from stoic pride in reason to hedonistic trust in sense. By depicting man's fall from grace as punished by his corresponding fall from reason and his enslavement to passion, the poets who looked back to Eden had clearly taken sides with the advocates of reason as the standard of human conduct. Their position was perfectly in line with Christian belief as to man's fallen nature: their difference lay in their concentration of interest upon the psychologoical effects of the fall of man, rather than upon its spiritual significance.

The patriarchal age, like the Garden of Eden, had a special

charm for poets of the early eighteenth century. They varied their discussions of the fall with psychological overtones; they loaded their patriarchal scenes with sociological implications. Interest in the patriarchs was part of their concern with the origins of society. Seventeenth-century debates over the patriarchal sanction of royal power had awakened repercussions that lasted beyond their time.[9] Sir Robert Filmer's *Patriarchia*, arsenal of arguments for the Stuart supporters, had so popularized the ideal of patriarchal society that in a later day such divergent characters as the deist statesman Bolingbroke and the dissenting journalist Defoe could both describe the patriarchal age as the golden era of mankind. That same golden ideal of patriarchal society served eighteenth-century poets at once as a pattern of pastoral peace and as a blueprint of a perfect social order.

James Thomson was easily the best of the poets who felt the emotional appeal of the patriarchal age.[10] Peace, simplicity, absence of toil, and absence of ambition cast a gentle grace over the patriarchal scene which he wove into the tapestries of the Castle of Indolence:

> What time Dan Abraham left the Chaldee land,
> And pastured on from verdant stage to stage,
> Where fields and fountains fresh could blest engage.
> Toil was not then. Of nothing took they heed,
> But with wild beasts the silvan war to wage,
> And o'er vast plains their herds and flocks to feed:
> Blest sons of nature they! true golden age indeed! [11]

The same idyllic charms doubtless blessed the quiet vale to which Thomson's Knight of Industry retired after his diligent labors, "replete with peace and joy, like patriarchs of old." [12]

Thomson loved the aesthetic appeal of the patriarchal state; Pope admired its excellence as a social system.[13] The latter's picture of the happy era mingled the vegetarianism of a classical Golden Age with the simplicity of the patriarchal.[14] From the point of view of primitivism, Pope's state was a mixture of primitivism and progress, since his ideal included not only an original state of ordered simplicity, but a later improved state to which man had introduced various arts and crafts. A state of Nature successively simple and complex implied a norm of Nature that included the ideals both of regularity and of irregularity. The same confusion between opposed meanings of "Nature" that complicated Pope's patriarchal state clouded the issue in countless eighteenth-century controversies about man and society.

The benevolent, obedient, humane citizens of Pope's ideal community are excellent examples of the naturally good human being that was his generation's answer to Hobbes' insistence on the innate selfishness of mankind:

> Nor think in Nature's state they blindly trod;
> The state of Nature was the reign of God:
> Self-love and Social at her birth began,
> Union the bond of all things, and of Man.
> Pride then was not; nor Arts, that Pride to aid;
> Man walk'd with beast, joint tenant of the shade;
> The same his table, and the same his bed;
> No murder cloath'd him, and no murder fed.[15]

The confusion of the term "Nature" and the concept of the naturally benevolent human being were two interesting phenomena of primitivism that recurred in many connections throughout the eighteenth century.[16]

Between them Pope and Thomson covered whatever the poets of their time had to say on the patriarchal age either as a state of pastoral happiness, or as a model social order. Different as were the sources of their admiration for that blissful era, both poets would probably have given assent to the lament of an obscure contemporary:

> But long has man forgot such simple ways,
> Truth, unsuspecting harm! the dream of ancient days.[17]

The sentiment might serve as a refrain to every phase of chronological primitivism.

Some poets, not venturing into the remote past of the patriarchal age or the remoter happiness of Eden, sought in earlier periods of the Christian era for models of virtue that would shame eighteenth-

century evils.[18] Saintly hermits and humble clerics had adorned
the early Church: modern Christians were another matter.[19] As
the bitterest of the censures acidly explained:

> When Christ was betray'd to Pilate, the Praetor,
> In a dozen apostles, but one prov'd a traytor!
> One traytor alone, and faithful eleven;
> But we can afford you six traytors in seven.[20]

But the minor voices of complaint sounded thin and superficial
beside Wesley's passionate protests against the religious apathy
of his generation. The reformer whose efforts to reawaken spiritual fervor among his countrymen constituted the major chapter
in eighteenth-century English Protestantism infused his poetry
with evangelical zeal. Again and again he prayed for divine help
to restore himself and his generation to their "primitive estate" of
grace. He sought vainly among contemporary Christians for the
successors to the Christians of "golden days," the men of apostolic
times whose followers seemed "vanished from the sons of men."
He remembered with longing the courage of the Smithfield
martyrs, and the zeal of early Protestants who "could not bear thy
Romish foe." [21] He saw in the English Church of his time:

> Leaders, who turn the lame out of the way,
> Shepherds, who watch to make the sheep their prey,
> Preachers, who dare their own report deny,
> Patrons of Arius' or Socinus' lie,
> Who scoff the gospel truths as idle tales,
> Heathenish priests, and mitred infidels! [22]

Sad in tone and passionately sincere, Wesley's verses reproved as
much in sorrow as in anger:

> The service which our fathers paid,
>   The faith Thou didst in them approve,
> Of this we now have shipwreck made,
>   And lost our hope and left our love.[23]

His prayers for a return to primitive Christian charity were kin in
message to his plea:

O, let us find the ancient way
Our wandering foes to move,
And force the heathen world to say,
See how these Christians love.[24]

The little that early eighteenth-century poets had to say on Christian themes of chronological primitivism foreshadowed other and more popular phases of the general subject. The pastoral background of patriarchal scenes is very like the idyllic pictures of rural life which brighten many a page of cultural primitivism. The contrast between fallen man exiled from Eden and the good man in the state of Nature recurs again and again as part of the rival claims of reason and passion as guides to human life. The added zest which contemporary evils give to traditional discussions (in this case the ills of eighteenth-century Christianity) breaks out with triple violence in political denunciations which express admiration for former ages in direct proportion to their contempt for the Walpole ministry.

II

A far stronger strain of chronological primitivism finds expression in the poets' admiration for the classical past. Eighteenth-century writers succumbed to the lure of the classical Golden Age just as readily as had every generation of poets since the Renaissance. If the charm of that happy era suffers in their pedestrian imitations, the blame is the imitators', not the models'. The want of skill in many of their classic echoings need not matter to us, since our concern is rather with the particular aspects of the age of gold which they chose to remember, than with their deviations, if any, from their literary memories.

The Golden Age of antiquity had been a sunshiny era wherein war was not, nor trade, nor commerce, nor wealth—a halcyon period that had degenerated all too soon into an iron age of avarice, cruelty, and conflict. Like poets before them and poets after them, eighteenth-century writers loved the Arcadian innocence and gentle unworldliness of the Golden Age. They liked to recount its virtues, to remember that innocence and unselfish love marked the age "when time was young," that then swains had no guile, and nymphs no greed, and mankind no ambition:

> Happy the world in that bless'd age,
> When beauty was not bought and sold,
> When the fair mind was uninflam'd
>   With the mean thirst of baneful gold.[25]

"While yet the world was young," man lived at peace with every creature on the earth. Nature fed her children "with lavish hand": her sons lived long and happily, free in life and love.[26]

Sometimes the poets added a touch of "hard primitivism" to their pictures of the golden time,[27] but in the main they were content to stress the charm of that long ago world, its gentle serenity and undiminished ease:

> This was the life of the Saturnian age,
> Which shines so splendid in the poet's page;
> When goddesses descended from above
> To teach the infant world to live and love:
> When uncorrupted reason only reign'd
> With truth and virtue o'er the happy land.
> Then the kind earth bedeck'd with nature's pride,
> The wants of men spontaneously supply'd;
> Like Paradise of old, untill'd the plain
> Pour'd forth her fruits, and swell'd the springing grain;
> The cluster'd vine adorn'd the fertile field,
> The liquid honey from the oak distill'd:
> The swain around him looking with surprize
> Saw without toil a plenteous harvest rise.[28]

James Thomson outdid his contemporaries in depicting the lavish life of the age of gold. In the course of his revisions of the *Seasons* he discarded his most luxurious description of the Golden Age, but we can still enjoy his picture of a bounteous time wherein

> spontaneous harvests waved
> Still in a sea of yellow plenty round.

> The forest was the vineyard, where, untaught
> To climb, unpruned and wild, the juicy grape
> Burst into floods of wine.[29]

Peace within man, and plenty without: the gold of the happy age had no alloy—except impermanence.

Consciousness of that impermanence shadowed some of the poets' Arcadian pictures. They could not forget that the Saturnian era of peace and plenty, "and good things more than ten times twenty," [30] had given way to succeedingly worse conditions, until modern times showed mankind wholly possessed by ambition, treachery, and greed.[31] Neither rich nor poor had present comfort:

> This pines, and dies neglected at the door;
> While gout and fevers wait the loaded mess,
> And take full vengeance for the poor's distress.[32]

Love was no longer bought with gentle words: the arrows of the love-god must now be tipped with gold:

> Few are the maids that now on merit smile,
> On spoil and war is bent this iron age:
> Yet pain and death attend on war and spoil,
> Unsated vengeance and remorseless rage.[33]

Just as James Thomson had loved the beauty of the golden age, so he mourned the tragedy of its passing:

> But now those white unblemished minutes, whence
> The fabling poets took their golden age,
> Are found no more amid these iron times,
> These dregs of life! Now the distempered mind
> Has lost that concord of harmonious powers
> Which forms the soul of happiness; and all
> Is off the poise within. . . .
> Convulsive Anger storms at large; or, pale
> And silent, settles into fell revenge.
> Base Envy withers at another's joy,
> And hates that excellence it cannot reach.

Desponding Fear, of feeble fancies full,
Weak and unmanly, loosens every power.
Even Love itself is bitterness of soul,
A pensive anguish pining at the heart.[34]

Thomson and his fellows might confine their interest in man's early happiness to nostalgic glances towards time's golden dawn, but Joseph Warton was not content merely to dream of a Golden Age from the vantage point of an eighteenth-century study. He wanted not simply to look back, but to go back to halycon times. Like his fellow poets, Warton conjured up a vision of an early age without war or wealth, but unlike them he actually urged eighteenth-century men to throw off the restraints of civilization and return to the forests, the meadows, the flower-filled fields:

Yet why should man, mistaken, deem it nobler
To dwell in palaces, and high-roof'd halls,
Than in God's forests, architect supreme!
Say, is the Persian carpet, than the field's
Or meadow's mantle gay, more richly wov'n;
Or softer to the votaries of ease
Than bladed grass, perfum'd with dew-dropt flow'rs?
O taste corrupt! that luxury and pomp,
In specious names of polish'd manners veil'd,
Should proudly banish Nature's simple charms! [35]

Thomson, despite the skill that gives his Arcadian pictures a charm that others so often sought vainly to achieve, was the conventional dreamer of an Age of Gold. Warton, even when writing on so traditional a theme, was slipping away from his contemporaries, drifting out from safe neo-classical shores towards the uncharted deeps of romanticism. Impatient with mere wishing for the past, tired of civilized life, longing for "Nature's simple charms," he was setting out on the course that was to lead many a later poet "beyond the sunset, and the baths of all the western stars . . ."

III

The poets did not confine their reminiscent longings to legendary ages of gold: for purposes of rousing degenerate moderns to a sense of their fallen estate, memories of the historically great served even better than regrets for Arcadia.

When they sought in history a reasonable facsimile of the Golden Age, the great days of the ancients were a natural answer to their quest. To men who had long soared with Cicero on towering flights of rhetoric, conquered Gaul (probably with a vindictive thought of modern Gallia) with Caesar, crossed the Alps with Hannibal *via* Tacitus, stormed Latium with Virgil and wooed Lydia with Horace, who had studied ontology with Lucretius and morals with Epicurus, the ancients were elder brethren affectionately known and infinitely revered.

It was natural and conventional for such poets to contrast their fellow men with the giants of ancient times, and to find their contemporaries wanting. Beyond question the ancients seemed wiser, sturdier, better than their modern descendants.[36] Ancient sportsmen, masters of the whirling chariot and the wrestler's toils, put to shame the "slim race of modern beaus"; ancient women were bred to glory, modern women to ignorance and frivolity.[37] As one critic ungallantly reminded the fair,

> No more such generous sentiments we trace
> In the gay moderns of the female race;
> No more, alas! heroic virtue's shown,
> Since knowledge ceas'd, philosophy's unknown.[38]

It was as citizens, rather than as private individuals, that the poets most sharply attacked the moderns. Nor is it surprising that ancient political integrity should stir the writers, for "corruption" was the political warcry of their generation. To Opposition poets overwhelmed with a sense of the baseness of their own times, the Roman republic seemed a model of virtue: before hallowed visions of SPQR, Parliament and its pocket boroughs shrivelled into a mob of tawdry intriguers.

The corrupt and selfish modern fared ill in comparison with the honorable citizens of the classical world. The happy past was bribeless: modern senators sold their votes.[39] "Dethron'd is virtue, in her stead reigns gold."[40] Greeks and Romans were fired to perish for their country's good, but eighteenth-century Englishmen preferred comfort to country.[41]

Many poets (Thomson and Swift among them) were busy pointing out how far their fellow citizens had fallen from the ancient ideal of public service, but for a really detailed list of eighteenth-century political evils the reader must go to an anonymous writer who entitled his poem *Liberty*, apparently to illustrate his country's lack of that blessing:

> When careful statesmen for their country reign'd,
> And men to serve each other was [sic] ordain'd;
> When Caesars fought, and Catos bled for Rome,
> And soldiers strove for glory to o'ercome;
> No thoughts of plunder dar'd their courage on,
> They us'd their captives as they'd use their son.
> But now, in chains, for liberty we treat.
> Now man for riches, not for honour's priz'd,
> And vertuous souls, with poverty, despis'd.
> Those who are doom'd [sic] the nation's chief support,
> Are bred in luxury, and maintain'd at court:
> Soft ease and plenty crown their daily boards,
> They reap the fruits which Nature, kind, affords. . . .
> The coach o'er looks the peasant with his flail,
> And stars outshine the ragged in a jail.[42]

And so on and on in an ever-darkening list of evils.

After such remonstrances eighteenth-century statesmen should have mended their ways, but since the great men's interests were practical rather than poetic, they left the reward of virtue to the ancients, and went on pocketing their more substantial gains in the form of pensions and payrolls.

It was a foregone conclusion that in literature as well as in statecraft the ancients far outstripped their modern rivals. The English version of the battle of the ancients and the moderns had fought its main campaigns around the citadels of science. When the smoke cleared, leaving the moderns in possession of the field, it was the field of scientific achievement, not the field of literature of which they remained the victors. In literary realms the names of Homer and Virgil still served to conjure with, and the rules of Aristotle had yet to go down before the defenders of Shakespeare's "native woodnotes wild."

Poetic praises of classic literature made up in number what they lacked in variety. The ancient poet was purer than the modern, the ancient playwright more moral.[43] In skill as in virtue the classics bore off the palm.[44] Theocritus was the true model for the pastoral: Homer and Virgil showed weak modern bards an example of matchless genius.[45] Let men read Homer himself, for that beggar'd poet "yet was, in noble verse, a richer prince Than all his wealthy dull translators since." [46]

The most amusing and original expression of esteem for classical writers took the form of a letter purporting to be from Horace in the Elysian fields to his imitators in England. The Roman chides:

> Pert meddling bard! must I arise
>   From bliss each year, and fix my name
> To gossip tales, and patriot lies,
>   To St. John's worth, and Walpole's shame? [47]

He loses his customary urbanity to protest with more vigor than elegance:

> The crown, and verdant wreath I gave
>   To Drusus' brow, shall ever bloom;
> Those heap'd by thee upon their grave,
>   Shall stink around each patriot's tomb.

Horace in Elysium sounds like an angry Whig.

More important than their creation of a pseudo-Horace with Whig sympathies was the poets' praise of the ancients not for perfection of form, but for fervor of inspiration. Where the reader might reasonably expect a series of neo-classical appreciations of Virgil's skill and Horace's elegance, he finds instead paeans to the poetic fire and soaring pinions of the wild free muse of the ancients. Here is a small but definite indication of that growing strain in eighteenth-century criticism that prized the "grace beyond the reach of art" above docile imitation of traditional techniques.

The fire of the ancients had been their greatest gift: the moderns failed to match the men of old because their poetic inspiration was cold and weak:

> When Graecians liv'd, auspicious times!
> Glory inspir'd the sacred rage:
> How faint the Muse in Albion's clime
> Now glimmers in th' enervate page! [48]

Glory inspired the wild, free classic muse: the modern age was content "with senseless rapture all, and empty song":

> Ev'n those the knowing and the virtuous few,
> Who noblest ends by noblest means pursue,
> Forget the Poet's use; the powerful spell
> Of magic verse, which Sidney paints so well.
> Forget that Homer wak'd the Grecian flame,
> That Pindar rous'd inglorious Thebes to fame,
> That every age has great examples given
> Of virtue taught in verse, and verse inspir'd by Heaven. [49]

That concept of poetic excellence had little in common with the critics of reason, decorum, restraint, deliberate polish. The "magic verse" of Sidney, the "Grecian flame" of Homer, the power of Pindar speak a language strange to neo-classical ears. [50]

To some of the poets that language of poetic fire seemed familiar enough. They mourned the Gothic night that darkened the world since the day that the muses fell, and

> foul barbarian hands
> Their mysteries profan'd, unstrung the lyre,
> And chain'd the soaring pinion down to earth. [51]

The unchaining of those soaring pinions was to carry the poetry of the next century far beyond neo-classical themes and traditions.

Poetic tributes to ancient statecraft and literature clearly attest the firm hold which Grecian glory and Roman grandeur had on early eighteenth-century imaginations. If the writers had not the burning fervor with which the romantics were to hail the "Isles of Greece," still they did possess a sturdy and sensible respect for the wisdom that had made Athens immortal and the efficiency that had rendered Rome impregnable. Being human, and therefore especially resentful of personal injuries, the poets returned most frequently to the attack on eighteenth-century political evils, loading their salvos against contemporary corruption with ammunition from classical storehouses. Being human, and therefore variable, some of the poets even at this early date replaced sober esteem for classic style with lively enthusiasm for the poetic fire of the ancients.

IV

Reflections on the poor estate of modern Greece and Rome inspired the most eloquent poetic laments for the passing of ancient grandeur. Whether the plaint was a melancholy *sic transit,* or whether it was a warning to Britain to guard her greatness, the theme was always of solemn import.

Luxury, the bane of empire, had wrecked the Greek and Roman states. Thomas Warton hailed Sparta's courage and Plato's thought:

> Greece! how I kindle at thy magic name
> Feel all thy warmth, and catch the kindred flame.
> Thy scenes sublime and awful visions rise
> In ancient pride before my musing eyes.[52]

But he remembered sadly that wealth and pleasure had spelled the ruin of Grecian glory:

> No more her groves by Fancy's feet are trod,
> Each Attic grace has left the lov'd abode.
> Fall'n is fair Greece! by Luxury's pleasing bane
> Seduc'd she drags a barbarous foreign chain.[53]

And he exhorted England, "Britannia watch! O trim thy withering bays . . . Yet oh! beware Lest thou the fate of Greece, my country, share." [54]

Luxury had ruined Rome as well as Greece. The poets agreed in blaming the state of modern Rome on the nation's progressive moral decay. No one of them granted the Romans any achievements in modern times. Even poets writing from Rome in the shadow of the masterpieces of the Renaissance had eyes only for the ruins of the ancient world.[55] To their gloomy eyes Rome's fall, like Lucifer's, was irrevocable.

Thomson's stately praises of classic Roman greatness are typical of his fellow poets' feelings:

> A land in all, in government and arts
> In virtue, genius, earth, and heaven reversed.
> Who but these far-famed ruins to behold,
> Proofs of a people, whose heroic aims
> Soared far above the little selfish sphere
> Of doubting modern life.[56]

Her legions were the servants of Rome and of liberty; her senate, a tribunal of demigods, "all head to counsel, and all heart to act"; her people, lovers of liberty, "inexorable, firm, just, generous, brave." [57] But neither the swords of her soldiers, the statutes of her lawgivers, nor the courage of her citizens saved Rome's imperial might:

> The queen of nations rose; possessed of all
> Which nature, art, and glory could bestow—
> What would you say, deep in the last abyss
> Of slavery, vice, and unambitious want,
> Thus to behold her sunk? [58]

While Thomson meditated Rome's grandeur as an empire, John Dyer remembered the happy Augustan days when poetry was revered by the meanest hind, a blessed age far from the strife of modern times when "nature's stores are shut with cruel hand, and each aggrieves his brother." [59]

He revered the simple hardihood of the first Romans, their few desires, their sturdy characters. In those days men "content Feasted at Nature's hand, indelicate, Blithe in their easy taste." [60] It was the Romans of later times who riotously spent the wealth of their conquests, sold liberty itself to pamper their artificial tastes, and brought upon their country the terrible day of reckoning:

> Sudden the Goth and Vandal, dreaded names,
> Rush as the breach of waters, whelming all
> Their domes, their villas; down the festive piles,
> Down fall their Parian porches, gilded baths,
> And roll before the storm in clouds of dust.[61]

Grim as were Dyer's and Thomson's pictures, it remained for Joseph Trapp to sound the most doleful lament for fallen Italy:

> Health and delight in every balmy gale
> Are wafted now in vain: small comfort bring
> To weeping eyes the beauties of the spring.
> To groaning slaves those fragrant meads belong,
> Where Tully dictated, and Maro sung.
> Long since, alas! those golden days are flown,
> When here each science wore its proper crown:
> Pale Tyranny has laid their altars low,
> And rent the laurel from the Muse's brow . . .[62]

Oppression and Ruin, Black Desolation and War rend the unhappy land:

> To the soft oaten pipe, and past'ral reed,
> The din of arms, and clarion's blast succeed:
> Dire shapes appear in every op'ning glade;
> And Furies howl where once the Muses stray'd!
>   Is this the queen of realms, for arts renown'd?
> This captive maid, that weeps upon the ground?
> Alas! how chang'd! dejected and forlorn!
> The mistress of the world become the scorn!
> Around stand Rapine, Horror, and Despair;
> And Ign'rance, dark ally of barb'rous War.[63]

Joseph Trapp's scorn for modern Italy was a natural feeling for a man of his century and country. A certain distrust of foreigners, a native prejudice against Catholicism,[64] pride in England's prosperity and politics as contrasted with the economy and statecraft of the continent, combined to sharpen his condemnation of modern Roman society. His idyllic treatment of ancient Rome was also natural, for like most men of his generation, Trapp was personally devoted to the classics, and the pastoral scenes of the ancients offered ample pictures of the Italian countryside of old, resonant with the music of reed and pipe.

Emotion rather than reason inspires Trapp's and Dyer's desolate insistence on gloom and ruins. Something approaching romantic ardor fires a few of the poetic celebrations of ancient grandeur. For the rest, moralizing applications of ancient errors to contemporary conditions and comfortable sentiments of national complacency [65] in expressions of sympathy for modern Greece and Rome restore the conventional neo-classical balance. Alike removed from insular self-approval and from graveyard grimness, James Thomson's tributes to the grandeur of the classic past best represent contemporary sentiment.

V

Stronger than aesthetic interest in a nebulous Golden Age, more persistent than academic interest in the faded bays of Rome, was the poets' devotion to the glories of England's past. Ranging the centuries from Boadicea to Queen Anne, the writers held up to contemporary English manners, morals, politics, literature the overpowering example of Britain's former greatness. They shamed the men of letters with the memory of Milton and Shakespeare, the men of state, by the glories of Cressy and Agincourt.

Sometimes the poets were content to look with reverent eyes on the monuments of an earlier day and to dream proudly of the past. Windsor was a

> Mansion of princes, and fit haunt of gods,
> Who frequent shall desert their bright abodes,
> To view thy sacred walls with trophies hung:
> Thy walls by British Arthur first renown'd,
> The early seat of chivalry and fame . . .[66]

The remains of an ancient castle reminded the passer-by of happier times when within that "friendly gate, The Stranger hospitable Rites receiv'd, The Rich were honour'd, and the Poor reliev'd." [67] Not the passing of time but rather the incompetence and knavery of men had destroyed the grandeur of the happy past. The fate of an ancient country seat leveled by the extravagance of its modern owners was emblematic of the degeneration of eighteenth-century Englishmen from the standards set by their forbears:

> And see the good old seat, whose Gothic tow'rs
> Awful emerge from yonder tufted bow'rs;
> Whose rafter'd hall the crowding tenants fed,
> And dealt to Age and Want their daily bread;
> Where crested knights with peerless damsels join'd,
> At high and solemn festivals have din'd;
> Presenting oft fair Virtue's shining task,
> In mystic pageantries, and moral mask,
> But vain all ancient praise, or boast of birth,
> Vain all the palms of old heroic worth!
> At once a bankrupt and a prosp'rous heir,
> Hilario bets,—park, house, dissolve in air. [68]

On that theme of modern degeneracy, the poets made many and varied protests.

Modern learning and literature were decayed: men must look to earlier days for examples of wisdom and genius. "In former times" learning blessed England; now dulness and ignorance covered the land. Oxford itself, a prey to flattery, admitted within its walls the "raw young squire," encouraging him "to spoil a plowman and to ape a gent." [69] The grand tour had ruined "the good old way" of educating Englishmen at home. [70] Growing ignorance and folly justified the dire prediction:

> The dark'ning age declines apace:
> With tears I think upon the race
> Our future progeny must breed,
> And fear, our grandsons will not read. [71]

Learning drooped and the muses fled.[72] Oxford saw faction rage within its confines where once Sidney, Raleigh, Hampden, Locke had made its name illustrious.[73] The University of Aberdeen, beset by bitter days, looked back to better times when worthy men planted "the various tree of knowledge," and "soft and serene the kindly seasons roll'd, And science long enjoy'd her age of gold." [74]

Not only learning in general, but poetry in particular had become debased. Formerly, satire had reformed men: now it merely affronted them.[75] Panegyric served "to varnish crimes." [76] The age disdained manly thought and wit.[77] Patrons gave ear only to the most arrant flattery.[78] Once matters went very differently:

> Fam'd were the bards of old, untainted days!
> When only merit felt the breath of praise. . . .
>   But now, sad change! no more the poet's theme
> Tastes thy chaste waters, Hippocrene's stream.
> His breast no more the sacred sisters urge,
> Of truth the patrons, and of vice the scourge:
> Venal, he seeks the court, and shuns the lawn,
> On pride to flatter, and on pow'r to fawn.[79]

The "godlike Sidney" [80] and the renowned Milton, "great pattern to succeeding times," [81] had given way to the starving modern bard who shivered in his garret little consoled that his poetic predecessors fared much more comfortably:

> Alas, poor Devil! who must bear the curse
> Of poetry, when every age grows worse. . . .
> Not so Johnson [sic] did his genius rack,
> He kept it briskly up with malmsey sack;
> Champaign and Burgundy he could allow,
> But poets then were scarce to what they're now.[82]

Dramatic poetry as well as non-dramatic suffered from the general degeneracy of the age. Men yawned at *Cato's* moral strictures and preferred puppets, and pantomime, and the *Beggars' Opera* to the rules, the humor, the taste, and the wit that had formerly improved the British stage.[83]

Despite the romantic gleam of Sidney's name, or the passing praise of Milton for his unfettered verse, most of the evocations of England's literary past were conventional moralizings [84] designed to reprove modern writers for their wickedness and frivolity.

On questions of manners, morals, and politics poetic reproofs increased in fervor and frequency. Nostalgia for earlier, simpler, homespun times underlay their impatience with the pretty race of contemporary coxcombs, and their resentment of the pert patter of contemporary manners.

Pope voiced the common contempt for pretty beaux, but his protests against contemporary manners were only part of a general chorus of poetic criticism.[85] The complaints covered many themes. Frivolity had turned the once sensible, sober town of Bath into a fashionable resort where

> flamboys scour the streets by night!
> Chairs ply, dice sound, and bullies fight;
> Fops lisp o'er coffee, women tattle,
> Lords woo, rakes swear, and coaches rattle;
> Balls, equipages, noise and pother,
> Bath!—'tis one London chang'd for t'other.[86]

The new habit of tea-drinking seemed to the poets another evidence of national decline. The nut-brown ale of Merrie England, sacred to Robin Hood and to many a storied hero, had given way to "Indian slops," and the writers resented the change.[87] Coincident with the decline in ale for breakfast was the decline of the breakfast itself. The modern generation refused the stout fare of their forebears, and as punishment for their squeamish tastes had wan complexions and woeful temperaments:

> Our grandsires thus (says antient lore,)
> Improv'd their time in days of yore. . . .
> The swains robust regal'd their souls,
> With native cheer and home-brew'd bowls:
> Then British fields cou'd well afford

> To spread a plenteous, healthful board;
> E'er foreign gout had reach'd our land;
> Or cooks had poison'd half the land;
> E'er Indian slops (in China toys,
> Unworthy of our girls and boys,)
> Had giv'n each rosy British fair
> A pallid look and languid air . . .[88]

Not alone poor appetites, but poor manners marked the sad decline of the younger generation. The boys were pert, the girls frivolous. Ladies wore mannish riding habits: men were affected beaux. Novels, ombre, and quadrille had lured women from domestic arts, and shallow wit had turned men from intelligent conversation.[89]

Not in manners alone had Britain failed: her moral decline was sadder than her fall from courtesy:

> We're apt to storm and make a mighty pother,
> And say each age is viler than the other;
> But we've the happiness, or rather curse,
> To think no age than this can e'er be worse:
> For man is rais'd to such a pitch of evil,
> That could they meet him, they'd debauch the devil.[90]

Noblemen were wicked, churchmen proud, all men avaricious: the virtue of former days had given way to knavery and stupidity.[91] Modern men had added to the number and variety of their forefathers' vices: they had disgraced their honorable sires:

> Bid Britain's heroes, awful shades! arise,
> And ancient honour beam on modern vice:
> Point back to minds ingenuous, actions fair,
> 'Till the sons blush at what their fathers were:
> Ere yet 'twas beggary the great to trust;
> Ere yet 'twas quite a folly to be just;
> When low-born sharpers only dar'd a lie,
> Or falsify'd the card, or cogg'd the dye;
> Ere lewdness the stain'd garb of honour wore,
> Or chastity was carted for the whore;

> Vice flutter'd, in the plumes of freedom drest;
> Or public spirit was the public jest.[92]

Those forefathers would disown their descendants, a generation that had reached the last extreme of wickedness:

> Well—we have reach'd the precipice at last;
> The present age of vice obscures the past.[93]

As usual, the poets lamented loudest the corruption of modern men.[94] Over and over they bewailed the evil power of gold in their generation. The rural scenes loved by their ancestors were now despised for wealth. Rural life itself, once blameless and innocent, had degenerated to a scene of treachery and violence.[95]

Love and justice were pawns in the money mart. Love belonged to the highest bidder.[96] Titles and wealth secured the interest of the world when "intrinsick worth" was left to suffer undefended. The mighty might do as they pleased, money would buy them a pardon.[97] "If great, ne'er stick at vice,—who dare defame? The vicious poor alone can merit shame." "Love, honor, merit, all things now are sold." [98] The poor man was always guilty, for the judge heard only "the soft persuasive rhetorick" of bribes.[99] The court divine who knew Machiavelli better than his Bible was loaded with pluralities, while "the poor curate in his tatter'd gown," remained "the page's jest, the sport of ev'ry fool." Heaven itself was sold for gold.—"But there is no salvation for the poor." [100]

The climax to poetic outbursts against contemporary corruption was, of course, Pope's *Epilogue to the Satires*. Believing "nothing is sacred now but villany," he included all England in the terrible indictment:

> Hear her black trumpet through the land proclaim,
> That not to be corrupted is the shame.[101]

Denunciation could go no farther.

Pope's attack is a bitter summary of the charges of the minor poets. The year of his denunciation, 1738, marked the height of the opposition to Sir Robert Walpole's "corrupt" administration: it reminds the modern reader that the verses denouncing the power of wealth (many of them the anonymous jibes of behind-the-scenes hack writers) were not mere poetical exercises, but were rather energetic attacks against a political machine whose efficiency was insured by its success in vote buying.

Most of the mourners of the degenerate age were Tories. Pope, Ramsay, Johnson, and Thomson (a Tory on occasion) lent their illustrious names to a list that included many a minor or anonymous versifier. Great poets and small painted a gloomy picture of modern England and a glorious picture of her valiant past. Various scenes of that lost grandeur sprang to life under their pens [102]— Boadicea's reign, the days of the Druids, Eliza's sea supremacy, Marlborough's victories, and of course, the "never-fading honours" of Cressy and Agincourt. Sad for England that the modern descendants of such heroes were helpless and indecisive knaves:

> See where the once fam'd empress of the main,
> By pirates robb'd, from vengeance does refrain. . . .
> The British Lions quite degen'rate drown,
> See themselves robb'd, yet lie supinely down . . .[103]

In place of Elizabeth's might, her conquests, her dominion of the seas, modern England had only:

> Treasures immense, rais'd on the people's woe,
> A peaceful army, and a fleet for show,
> A nation's debt unpay'd, a hireling band,
> The station'd locusts of a groaning land.[104]

Contempt abroad was matched by oppression at home. The wrath of a generation of out-of-place poets and of their Opposition patrons, plus no doubt some patriotic anger at a venal régime, broke out in Pope's defiant:

> Yes, the last pen for Freedom let me draw,
> When Truth stands trembling on the edge of law
> Here, last of Britons; let your names be read;
> Are none, none living? let me praise the dead;
> And for that cause which made your fathers shine
> Fall by the votes of their degen'rate line.[105]

Poetic appeals to England's glorious past testify to the growing spirit of nationalism which accompanied England's gains in wealth and in prestige during the early eighteenth century. The number and intensity of the protests illustrate the zeal which a contemporary motive can lend to an abstract theme. Poets have discovered that the surest way to appeal to English hearts is to remind them, not of Cato and Cicero, but of Elizabeth; not of Caesar, but of the Black Prince.

Idealization of England's past is the strongest ripple on the smooth stream of chronological primitivism during the early eighteenth century. Except for that deepening strain of nationalism, the current runs quietly. Already the principal poets are settling into the positions which they will hold throughout most of the discussions of primitivism. Thomson, representative of the greatest number of primitivistic themes, but fairly conservative in his sentiments: Pope, confined to philosophical or political topics: Joseph Warton, more emotional and more radical than his contemporaries, and more interested in the exotic aspects of primitivism. Only Edward Young, who figures so largely in other phases of the subject, has as yet scarcely appeared on the primitivistic scene.

The poets who turned backward in their dreaming were but trying, as men of every generation had tried, to forget present griefs in visions of a golden past. Whether they looked to the vales of Arcady or to the England of Queen Anne, they sought the same blessings—harmony, peace, virtue. When they looked for those qualities, not in an earlier era, but in a different way of living, their search for the good life among noble savages, rural swains, and country gentlemen, added to the ever-widening stream another current—the current of cultural primitivism.

Cultural Primitivism

MAN'S desire to "get away from it all" motivates his cultural primitivism.[1] Periodically tiring of the complexities of civilization, he dreams of a simpler way of life.[2] The city man wants "five acres and independence." The rich man (in literature at least) wearies of wealth's responsibilities and envies the lot of his poorer neighbor. The adventurous spirit longs for the pioneer days of rugged frontiersmen, the timid soul for the sunlit safety of a South Sea Isle. One and all are attempting to accomplish the same end—that is, to find a less intricate design for living.

As cultural primitivists early eighteenth-century poets make no pretence of hardihood. Pleasure, not pioneering is their watchword, and although now and then a more venturesome writer will admire the rugged simplicity of a far-off people, for the most part the poets, with due regard for their floury wigs and flowered waistcoats, hail relaxation and enjoyment as the chief blessings of an ideal community.

Although by the seventeen-nineties the vogue of cultural primitivism had ranged from the country gentleman to the noble savage, with the latter skyrocketing in popularity as the century progressed, the first fifty years of the century show traditional subjects strongly entrenched, and the more exotic aspects of cultural primitivism decidedly in the minority. The early poets have little to say about the noble savage or about hard and soft extremes of life on foreign shores: they are content with such stock themes as pastoral life, rural retirement, and the innate superiority of the man of humble means.

I

These nations then seem to me to be so far from bar-
barous, . . . The laws of nature govern them still,
not as yet much vitiated with any mixture of ours; . . .
to my apprehension, what we now see in those natives
does not only surpass all the images with which the
poets have adorned the golden age, and all their inven-
tions in feigning a happy state of man, but moreover the
fancy, and even the wish and desire of philosophy it-
self.[3]

—*Montaigne,* Of Cannibals

Ever since ancient times men had been trying to give the noble
savage a local habitation and a name.[4] Classical writers had seen
him in the person of sturdy Germanic tribesmen, or in the gentle
inhabitants of the Hebrides, or the legendary dwellers of the
Islands of the Blest. Later men had continued to dream that the
age of gold still lingered in some remote portion of the world, that
the earthly paradise, the vanished Atlantis, the isle of Avalon, yet
awaited the intrepid explorer over the verge of some lost horizon.
From Tacitus and his hardy Teutons[5] to Montaigne and his
Brazilian cannibals,[6] the tradition of the noble savage stubbornly
persisted.

In seventeenth-century England, heroic plays[7] with their innocent and wronged savage rulers helped keep alive concepts of the
noble savage drawn from the ancients and from Montaigne. The
heyday of the faultless barbarian, so far as Englishmen were concerned, arrived in the last forty years of the eighteenth century,
when the voyages of Captain Cook and Captain Wallis[8] filled the
land with tales of a South Sea paradise, and when the visits of such
varied types of savage as the tropical Omai and the Labrador Esquimaux afforded England a first hand view of the children of
Nature.[9]

Since it was not until the second half of the eighteenth century
that the noble savage appeared in English literature in his full trap-

pings of innocence and nobility, poetry between 1725 and 1750 introduced him only in passing. As early as this, however, he was a type not unknown to the English public. Men had seen him in currently-acted heroic tragedies, had read his virtues in Montaigne and Aphra Behn. They had recognized him in Defoe's man Friday, and in Steele's Yarico: they had perhaps seen his real counterpart in the four Indian Kings who had visited England in 1710.

Addison had used the visit of the savages as an excuse for satirizing society under the time-honored device of a letter from a visiting foreigner to his homeland, but eighteenth-century men did not have to rely on Addison's prose for an account of the four kings: they could have gone and looked at the Indians for themselves. Many of them doubtless did, and could say with Mr. Spectator: "When the four Indian kings were in this country about a twelvemonth ago, I often mixed with the rabble and followed them a whole day together, being wonderfully struck with the sight of every thing that is new or uncommon." [10] Philosophy as well as literature spurred men's interest in the noble savage, for the simple barbarian was the living exponent of life according to Nature (however "Nature" might be interpreted).[11]

This child of Nature, unstudied and untaught, was the virtuous extreme opposed to the child of civilization, corrupted by custom and complexity. In the poetry of the period, Alexander Pope's "Lo, the poor Indian" passage [12] best summed up the essential qualities of the noble savage. Pope's poor Indian was a true child of Nature. Innate convictions assured him of the existence of God and the immortality of the soul, hence he practised automatically that natural goodness and natural religion dear to the hearts of eighteenth-century deists. He found a divine spirit in the clouds and winds much as the Shaftesburian virtuoso had found it in the Moralist's [13] exuberant apostrophe to Nature. He was the traditionally uncorrupt savage, the antithesis of the avaricious Christian whose "thirst for gold" belies his professions of piety. The poor Indian was fixed so fast in that eighteenth-century concept, the chain of being,[14] that even in heaven he never aspired to the glory of the pure spirits —even in eternity he knew and kept his place.

Resonant with philosophical overtones, Pope's Indian included and went beyond the characteristics of noble savages offered by lesser poets. The minor writers leaned towards emotionalism rather than intellectualism in their occasional stories of savage and sincere heroines betrayed by shipwrecked European adventurers. Doubtless the sad tales of *Inkle and Yarico* [15] and of *Avaro and Amanda* [16] drew the tribute of a tear from a generation that wept itself into hysterics over Pamela and Clarissa.

Sometimes interest in the colonies mingled with interest in the noble savage. One magazine verse reminded settlers in the new world to aid the "neighb'ring blameless Indian" and neither to demand nor to force subjection from him.[17] Another anonymous piece celebrated with enthusiasm:

> Fidenia . . . a very beautiful Negro girl, aged 16, from James River in Guinea, who, by every superior accomplishment, seems far beyond any of her kind. She learnt the English tongue in three months time, and in four, read the Spectators and Tatlers with inimitable grace. She has endear'd herself to a grateful master, by her fidelity and affection tho' he has been much censur'd for his regard to her. He was in danger of drowning in the great bay of C——; and 'tis impossible to express the tender concern she show'd, in her way, on that occasion.[18]

Fidenia was not the noble savage in her desire for and her skill in acquiring civilized knowledge, but she belonged to the type in her native kindness of heart and transparent sincerity: beauty and innocence marked her kinship to the ideal of the savage child of Nature:

> See! with what majesty she walks!
> What modesty adorns her mien!
> How simply innocent she talks,
> Inchanting slave! my Indian queen! [19]

While Fidenia, like her literary sisters Amanda and Yarico, was the daughter of soft tropical climes, "the happy savage," the hero of a short poem, was the son of a fierce desert land, content despite the harshness of his surroundings, and preferable in his freedom from vice to his more comfortable civilized brothers. His happy state represented an extreme view of human nature: it placed natural goodness on a par with the instinctive wisdom of the beast:

> O happy he who never saw the face
> Of man, nor heard the sound of human voice!
> But soon as born was carry'd and expos'd
> In some vast desart, suckled by the wolf,
> Or shaggy bear more kind than our fell race;
> Who with his fellow brutes can range around
> The echoing forest: his rude artless mind
> Uncultivated as the soil—he joins
> The dreadful harmony of howling wolves,
> And the fierce lyon's roar. . . .
> Happy the lonely savage! nor deceiv'd,
> Nor vex'd, nor griev'd—in ev'ry darksome cave,
>   Under each verdant shade he takes repose.
> Sweet are his slumbers—of all human arts
> Happily ignorant, nor taught by wisdom,
> Numberless woes; nor polish'd into torment.[20]

The later eighteenth century was to weep and wail over wronged savages, but even the earlier eighteenth century showed signs of becoming emotional over the persecuted children of Nature. In the seventeen-forties Joseph Warton was beginning to add feeling to his treatment of the noble savage. His "dying Indian" departed from life in a grandiloquent soliloquy: [21] his savage in "The Revenge of America" railed at his conquerors with marked absence of traditional Indian stoicism:

> What woes, he cry'd, hath lust of gold
> O'er my poor country widely roll'd;
> Plunderers proceed! my bowels tear,
> But ye shall meet destruction there;
> From the deep-vaulted mine shall rise
> Th' insatiate fiend, pale Av'rice!
> Whose steps shall trembling justice fly,

Peace, order, law, and amity!
I see all Europe's children curst
With lucre's universal thirst:
The rage that sweeps my sons away
My baneful gold shall well repay.[22]

Just as in chronological primitivism Warton had gone to the extreme of suggesting that men desert urban life for a wild existence in the forest, so in cultural primitivism he went so far as to wish that he himself might live like the simple Indian of his song:

O who will bear me then to western climes,
(Since Virtue leaves our wretched land) to fields
Yet unpolluted with Iberian swords:
The isles of Innocence, from mortal view
Deeply retir'd, beneath a plantane's shade,
Where happiness and quiet sit enthron'd,
With simple Indian swains, that I may hunt
The boar and tiger through savannahs wild,
Through fragrant deserts, and through citron groves?
There, fed on dates and herbs would I despise
The far-fetch'd cates of luxury, and hoards
Of narrow-hearted avarice; nor heed
The distant din of the tumultuous world.[23]

Warton was alone in his desire for savage companionship—his fellow poets had no wish to view the child of Nature at such close range.

Interesting sidelights of the poets' brief allusions to the noble savage are relatively few. A little contemporary color in the form of colonial references, a great deal of soft primitivism in gentle background scenes, a troop of barbaric heroes, guileless, innocent, and brave, and the poetic story of the noble savage of this period is told.

The most interesting trend is symbolized by the contrast between Pope's noble Indian and Warton's. Pope's description had been cool, reserved, rich in philosophical implications: Warton's was warm, enthusiastic, vibrant with emotional overtones. From disinterested commentary on "lo, the poor Indian" to casual comradeship with "simple Indian swains" is a long and important step. It marks a change from the vogue of reasoning about the noble savage as an illustration of philosophical tenets, to the fashion of lionizing him as an heroic and appealing individual. Again somewhat ahead of his generation, Joseph Warton in his sympathy with the great-hearted Indian of literary tradition foreshadows the sensibility which was later to drown rationalizings of savage goodness in a tidal wave of sentimental tears.

II

When they went far afield for their ideal modes of life the poets were torn between the delights of tropic paradises and the vigorous virtues of hardy arctic lands.

James Thomson's often quoted lines beginning "Bear me, Pomona" [24] might serve as a good guide to tropical primitivism. They had the lush scenery, the lazy, dreamy atmosphere, the completely toil-less life which were to be repeated again and again throughout the century in passages of soft cultural primitivism. But the citron groves of the familiar passage were not the only places where Thomson found unbought ease of life. His picture of the Niger and its tributaries was in the same vein:

> His brother Niger too, and all the floods
> In which the full-formed maids of Afric lave
> Their jetty limbs, and all that from the tract
> Of woody mountains stretched thro' gorgeous Ind
> Fall on Cormandel's coast or Malabar;
> From Menam's orient stream that nightly shines
> With insect-lamps, to where Aurora sheds
> On Indus' smiling banks the rosy shower—
> All, at this bounteous season, ope their urns
> And pour untoiling harvest o'er the land. [25]

Other poets had little to add to Thomson. Armstrong's picture of green shades and golden oranges, of melons and cocoa, and fountains "edged with racy wine," match in mood and in skill his fellow poet's passages.[26] Minor writers now and again rang changes on the conventional theme. Occasionally they celebrated the happy climes of classic tradition:

> I wander far thro' classic shades renown'd;
> O'er Helicon, thy hallow'd walk, and thine
> Green Ida, seat of desolated Troy:
> Eternal names in antiquated song.
> O! lead me where the cypress high embow'rs
> With pleasing shade, where thick'ning groves surround,
> The Lotus and the all-obscuring pine.
> To fruitful Chios, or th' Arvisian shade,
> Plenteous of chearing Bacchus; or thy shore,
> Kind Latium, let my loosen'd fancy range:
> Praeneste, Mother of the genial Vine,
> Cool Bajae, and Peligni, rich in streams,
> And Cuma, nam'd of rest and sweet repose.[27]

When visions of colonial empires stirred the poet's muse, Jamaica's simple charms inspired mild and gentle verse, and India's incredible wealth provoked splendid arrays of rhetoric.

> But 'tis more grateful to the muse's toil
> To sing the riches of the fertile soil:
> Her mountains teeming with the precious store,
> Of diamond quarries and of golden ore.
> There spring the glitt'ring gems which monarchs wear,
> And sparkling lustres which adorn the fair.
> The silk-worms form the wardrobe's gaudy pride;
> How rich the vests which Indian looms provide. . . .
> Be now her vegetable wealth survey'd;
> Too large a theme the coco's ample shade;
> A tree of wond'rous use in India grows,
> Which every needful benefit bestows. . . .
> Here tea's rich shrubs their valu'd leaves unfold,
> And hence gay vessels form'd of porcelain mould.
> In its wild woods the parrot builds her nest,

With plumage of the gayest tinctures drest.
Sweet docile bird, whose imitating tongue,
In words distinct repeats its mimic song.[28]

Whether in India or Jamaica, on the banks of the Niger, or in
the shades of Helicon, the writers were seeking the same delights,
warmth, and beauty, and lazy tropical leisure. That they seldom
sought such exotic retreats reminds the reader that the South Seas,
the happy hunting ground of all cultural primitivism, remained yet
unexplored. Exotic cultural primitivism flourishes under geographical stimulus, whereas rural retirement and the pastoral themes owe
their growth to the stimulus of literary tradition. Even at this early
date, however, the poets were alive to the charm of far corners
of the earth, especially far corners which had been or which might
be of use to British colonial interests. Popular imagination wanted
only reports of Tahiti and its storybook natives for verses to run
riot with the color and charm of exotic scenes, and the guileless bliss
of exotic peoples.

Very different from the equatorial jungles of soft tropical scenes
were the wild and icy regions which the poets celebrated when
they preferred hardihood to comfort. Thomson, varied, if not always consistent in his tastes, admired the sturdy happiness of the
snow-bound Grisons,[31] the strong sons of Scandinavia,[32] the "plain
harmless native" [33] of the Hebrides, the valiant inhabitants of Baltic
shores.[34] All his admiration for hardy simple folk fired his tribute
to the sons of Lapland:

They ask no more than simple Nature gives;
They love their mountains and enjoy their storms,
No false desires, no pre-created wants,
Disturb the peaceful current of their time,
And through the restless ever-tortured maze
Of pleasure or ambition bid it rage.[35]

And so on through a list of heroic qualities. The Laplanders' industry, simplicity, honesty and courage were typical of the virtues which made men feel that a harsh and primitive life might be
an enviable one.

Thomson's fellow-poets went far afield for their hard primitivism. Horace's "wild-born Scythians" and nomadic Getes,[36] and Virgil's Corycian swain, whose "mind was royal in a low estate," [37] represented the classical note in the discussions. Geographical rather than literary influences motivated praises of the Scottish Highlands, Siberia, a nameless country "on the verge of arctic skies," and "Kilda's race." [38] In all the bleak regions the hallmark of virtue was the absence of arts "that polish and deprave." [39] Thomas Warton, varying his scene of hard primitivism with some gothic details, described a "banished lord Amid Siberia's unrejoicing wilds"

> Who pines all lonesome, in the chambers hoar
> Of some high castle shut, whose windows dim
> In distant ken discover trackless plains,
> Where Winter ever whirls his icy car;
> Where still-repeated objects of his view,
> The gloomy battlements, and ivied spires
> That crown the solitary dome, arise . . .[40]

Even such a lord, though certainly no primitive countryman, was accounted fortunate because his exile freed him from "the splendours of the gaudy court," "its tinsel trappings, and its pageant pomps." [41]

Most original, and in its sturdy nationalism most touching of all poetical tributes to simple, hardy living, was the challenge of a Scotch rebel, "written by a Highlander on the day before he was taken." Its martial ring and its mocking defiance evoke echoes of the stubborn and independent daring that fought for the lost cause of the Stuarts:

> Ye think our highlands bleak and bare,
> O' Phoebus bounty ha' na share;
> And that, because for north we come,
> We're glad to leave our native home.
> But much mista'en, ye little ken
> Each bonny strath, and verdant glen,
> Where violets blow, and hawthorns bloom,

And gardens fine supply the room:
And Cowdenknows and Yarrow side,
As much the blithsome Scotsman's pride,
Who near these pleasant places dwells,
As Windsor Castle, or Versailles.
    'Tis true that we are unco' poor,
Our lords and lairds live on your store,
But sare each earns whate'er he gets,
They're yere ane tykes and turn yere spits,
While we at hame, wi mickle care,
Rut thro' our lives wi little gear:
Yet now and then the piper plays,
And Scottish slaves forget their waes,
Sing theyr ald sangs, and are as canty
As English clowns wi aw their plenty.[42]

Poverty and tyranny might oppress a highlander's life, but the violets and hawthorns blow for him in the springtime, and "now and then the piper plays."

The poets were not very daring in their hard primitivism. The only variants to their conventional sentiments were the contemporary ring of the Scotsman's defiance, and the gothic battlements of Thomas Warton's Siberian wilds. Collins' tribute to Kilda's race (written in 1749, although not published until much later in the century) might stand as a summary of all the virtues of primitive hardihood:

Go, just as they, their blameless manners trace!
Then to my ear transmit some gentle song
    Of those whose lives are yet sincere and plain,
Their bounded walks the rugged cliffs along,
    And all their prospect but the wintry main.
With sparing temp'rance, at the needful time,
    They drain the sainted spring, or, hunger-prest,
Along th' Atlantic rock the undreading climb,
    And of its eggs despoil the Soldan's nest.
Thus blest in primal innocence they live,
    Suffic'd and happy with that frugal fare

Which tasteful toil and hourly danger give.
Hard is their shallow soil, and bleak and bare;
Nor ever vernal bee was heard to murmur there! [43]

The poets' scenes of hardihood were all far away; there was no hard primitivism in their pictures of national life. The next century was to praise the hardworking ploughman, the sturdy shepherd, even the tired factory worker, but the early eighteenth century preferred to take its country life from the pastoral, its city life from its satirists, and its hard primitivism from other countries.

III

And high above our heads waved many a poplar, many an elm tree, while close at hand the sacred water from the nymphs' own cave welled forth with murmurs musical. On shadowy boughs the burnt cicalas kept their chattering toil, far off the little owl cried in the thick thorn brake, the larks and finches were singing, the ring-dove moaned, the yellow bees were flitting about the springs. All breathed the scent of the opulent summer, of the season of fruits; pears at our feet and apples by our sides were rolling plentiful, the tender branches, with wild plums laden, were earthward bowed, and the four-year-old pitch seal was loosened from the mouth of the winejars. [44]

—*Theocritus*, Idyl 7

Soft primitivism of the pastoral variety had a far journey from the groves and woodlands of the Sicilian shepherds to the fog-swept countryside of the English poets, but the tradition of life which took its tone from Theocritus survived the ravages of time and of transplanting. [45] In an alien climate, among an alien people, it forged a literary fashion strong enough to banish any lingering doubts of suitability and reasonableness, and to inspire many a neo-classical writer to find his rural themes rather in the vales of Arcady than in the lanes of England.

Theocritus' descriptions had had elements of realism, but the tinge of the Golden Age which overlay the simple lives of his shepherds fascinated his imitators until, lacking the first-hand experience of their model, they transformed his scenes of country life into an ideal picture of a land where youth and beauty and light and music ruled eternally in a realm that never grew old.

The charm of the pastoral carried over into fields other than that of the idyl. It penetrated the Georgic in those passages of that genre which were not devoted to didactic accounts of rural occupations. It pervaded the pastoral romance, carrying into prose a charm originally poetic. It inspired the pastoral lyric, echoing the cry of many a passionate shepherd to his love.

Englishmen had long cherished the classical pastoral,[46] reading and re-reading the *Eclogues* of Virgil and those parts of his *Georgics* which celebrate the joys of country living. They had enjoyed also the native pastoral, made dear to them in the dreamy passages of *Arcadia*, the *Shepherd's Calendar*, and the *Faerie Queene*. Each succeeding century English writers had adopted the form, and had poured into it the particular spirit of their generation. Eighteenth-century poets carried on that perennial interest in the pastoral, analysing it as a literary type, and imitating it after the models furnished by Theocritus, Virgil and Spenser.

We are not concerned with eighteenth-century pastoral theory, nor with formal eighteenth-century examples of the genre. Our task is to mark the persistence with which short poems in praise of the country adopt the language, the atmosphere, the idealized view of rural life inspired by the pastoral. The peculiar grace of such idyllic scenes had been summarized by Steele, when he described the effects of pastoral poetry:

> It transports us to a kind of fairy-land, where our ears are soothed with the melody of birds, bleating flocks, and purling streams; our eyes enchanted with flowery meadows and springing greens; we are laid under cool shades, and entertained with all the sweets and freshness of nature.[47]

Every urban society that becomes tired of its own sophistication turns longingly towards some ideal country of peace and simplicity and natural beauty. Eighteenth-century poets, writing from the noisy, smoke-filled London that enchanted and exhausted them, deafened by the street cries without, and the coffee-club chatter within, fled for mental quiet to pictures of pleasant pastoral scenes that had no counterpart in the reality of English rural life.

The country swain of their pieces had an ideal existence.[48] He slept on the hillside with his full scrip beside him. He watched the progress of the spring, enjoyed the fragrant breezes, and filled the country glades with his music. He had health and innocence, a clear conscience, and a contented life. Fountains and flowery meads and murmuring streams made up his countryside:

> The labours of the country yield delight.
> The shepherd on the broomy heath, or down
> Open and wild, or verdant valley, guides
> His fleecy charge; he works, he meditates,
> He walks, he reads; his Bible now, and now
> His flock attends; or dials quaintly carves
> Upon the russet plain, or lies between
> Two sloping hills (romantick seat!) his crook,
> His scrip, his faithful Lightfoot by his side.[49]

The joyous life of the shepherd was typical of the happiness of other rural workers.[50] In the poets' descriptions at least, the country girl spent her days admiring the "smooth mirror of the chrystal stream," and the ploughman passed his whistling duets with nightingales:

> To Philomela's voice attunes his note
> Melodious, and in emulation sweet
> (Love both inspires) They soothe the raptur'd plains.[51]

Fittingly enough, such fortunate folk had dwellings as charming as their pastimes.[52] Vine-covered cottages buried in honeysuckle, fields of wild roses for gardens, acres of corn, were a few of their blessings. In complacent content the "happy rustics" could boast cheerfully:

> In these shades with delightful tranquillity,
> Free from envy, care, and strife,

> Blest with innocence, health, and agility,
> O, how sweet's a rural life! [53]

"Sweet is the rising" expressed the attitude of many of the pastoral shepherds and swains.[54] Their daily work, when it was work at all, was a pleasure to them. They ran to meet it, "skipping o'er the mead," or marched out to cope with its problems sturdily confident in their prowess. The even tenor of their lives was free from strife and even from the passing frictions of everyday living. They were happy, sincere, simple-hearted, gently amicable even in their disagreements:

> If in disputes the rival swains engage,
> Their emulation never swells to rage;
> They take the judgment of a neighb'ring friend,
> And in a song their short contentions end;
> Each image is expresst with decent care,
> No sour reproach is heard, no wounds appear,
> No words immodest violate the ear.[55]

Of all the poets, James Thomson best combined in his works the themes of easy rural life and of Arcadian beauty. His "merry-hearted" shepherds slept on the downy moss,[56] while "the floating shade of willows grey" guarded their slumbers.[57] He recreated in glowing terms the spring sowing of the husbandman,[58] the summer scythe of the mower,[59] the rural gaiety of a sheep-shearing,[60] the village fireside with its games and gambols.[61] So far Thomson had only done better what his fellow poets could scarcely do well, but in addition to these pleasant scenes which, after all, have some reality in the happier aspects of rural living, Thomson portrayed another type of country,—the magic country of the *Castle of Indolence*,[62] which preserved the purely idyllic charm of the pastoral tradition far removed from any trace of the realities of everyday. Scene after scene in the first part of the poem conjured up the fairytale country which Thomson, following Spenser, created. His theme "the best of men have ever loved repose" [63] might be classic, and he might follow it with a reference to Scipio, but Thomson's "pleasing land of drowsyhead" [64] belonged to no classic tradition.

It was a romantic countryside vaguely beautiful and beautifully dim. It had no time, only "a season atween June and May": [65] no geography, but "it was, I ween, a lovely spot of ground." [66] It blended all the gracious sights and sounds of classic pastoral tradition and gave them something more, the spirit of the native English pastoral, the spirit of romance:

> Join'd to the prattle of the purling rills,
> Were heard the lowing herds along the vale,
> And flocks loud-bleating from the distant hills,
> And vacant shepherds piping in the dale;
> And now and then sweet Philomel would wail,
> Or stock-doves plain amid the forest deep,
> That drowsily rustled to the sighing gale;
> And still a coil the grasshopper did keep:
> Yet all these sounds yblent inclined all to sleep.[67]

Thomson's never-never land is the only contribution of merit that the poets make to this phase of cultural primitivism. Their pastoral pieces are pretty conventions, pleasant but unimportant. What importance they have lies in the fact that their sunny atmosphere brightens other scenes of cultural primitivism. It warms the retirement of the country gentleman, consoles the poor man's traditional innocence, in short, makes its cheerful way into almost all the poets' descriptions of English rural life, robbing them of every hardship, and of all semblance of reality.

IV

The love of retirement has, in all ages, adhered closely to those minds, which have been most enlarged by knowledge or elevated by genius.[68]
—*Johnson*, Rambler, *No.* 7

While noble savages, tropic paradises, arctic wastes, and pastoral scenes might afford early eighteenth-century poets glimpses of better ways of life, their favorite concept of living was embodied in the ideal of rural retirement. They had found the theory advanced on many a classical page: [69] they had known the pleasant reality in the form of visits to patrons' estates. They cherished the aura of exclusiveness that surrounded dignified withdrawal to a country home. Even as subjects for rhyming, the traditional retreats were convenient: they had been hallowed by the tributes of the ancients: celebrating them required little effort and no originality.

Rural retirement, as the poets sought it, was essentially "soft primitivism," for their dreams of country retreats were built upon ideals of comfort that belonged rather to wishful thinking than to practical reality; their retired haunts looked after themselves, produced food, shade and shelter on demand, and offered an easy, carefree mode of existence in the best pastoral manner.

Their chosen retirements included—any country retreat as a classical setting for inculcating virtues, a comfortable country retreat after the best Horatian model, and a contemplative rural solitude after the pattern of the English classicist, Milton. Often there is a mingling of classic retirement with Miltonic shades, a shadowing of the serene solemnity of the ancients with the meditative mood of *Il Penseroso*. Often both types of retirement have the object, not of comfort alone, or of contemplation, but of literary inspiration as well. Miltonic retirement is easily the most popular type of retreat, a not unnatural fact in view of Milton's tremendous influence and prestige during the eighteenth century.

The poets belonged to an era which recognized rural retirement as the prerogative of specially blest temperaments. Addison had warned: "It has been from age to age an affectation to love the pleasure of solitude, among those who cannot possibly be supposed qualified for passing life in that manner." [70] Forty years after Addison, the subject was still of interest: Samuel Johnson reminded his countrymen that "men overwhelmed with the pressure of difficult employments, harassed with importunities, and distracted with multiplicity, or men wholly engrossed by speculative sciences" were temperamentally suited to a life of seclusion, and that "such examples of solitude very few of those who are now hasting from the town, have any pretensions to plead in their own justification, since they cannot pretend either weariness of labour, or desire of knowledge." [71] The poets, in theory at least, satisfied Johnson's requirements. They sought the country for peace, for wisdom, for simplicity of life—that is, they sought it in verse: in actuality, the majority of them went right on living in London close to the booksellers, the coffee houses, and if they were fortunate, the court.

> *I do recommend retirement to you, but only that you may use it for greater and more beautiful activities than those which you have resigned; to knock at the haughty doors of the influential, to make alphabetical lists of childless old men, to wield the highest authority in public life—this kind of power exposes you to hatred, is short-lived, and, if you rate it at its true value, is tawdry.* [72]

—Seneca, Moral Epistles

The poets had nothing to add to the classic theme that wisdom and virtue are the fruits of a retired life. They echoed dutifully Cicero's enthusiasm for agriculture as the ideal occupation of the retired gentleman, recalled Cato's preference for the plough to the sword, and remembered Horace's devotion to the muse-haunted groves.

In pursuit of moral excellence, they willingly listened to Virgil's invitation:

> O leave the noisy town! O come and see
> Our country cots, and live content with me! [73]

The noise of the city was only an external source of annoyance. More serious still was the threat of urban living to the virtuous life. [74] Avarice, ambition, the pride of courts, the scorn of the great, possessed the town:

> No, no, 'tis vain in this turbulent town,
> To expect either pleasure or rest;

'Tis hurry and nonsense still tying us down;
'Tis an overgrown prison at best.[75]

Town life was a "hurricane" wherein conscience and peace were exchanged for doubtful successes in society or statecraft.[76] The country's humble plains were better than the gay town's shining towers and guilty pleasures. The city housed fops and courtiers and rich opportunists who "know no virtue but a good estate." It was the haunt of scandal and pride and hypocrisy: the man was wise who bade

Adieu to all the follies of the town,
Where noise and hurry all enjoyment drown,
Where vice o'er virtue has pre-eminence,
And nonsense gets the upper hand of sense.
Where honesty and honour are oppress'd;
Where but the name of virtue is profess'd,
Where virtue's self is grown a very jest.[77]

A taste for rural retirement marked the clear-sighted woman as well as the sensible man. "But still how good must be that fair-one's mind, Who thus in solitude can pleasure find!" [78] Such a sensible fair might be rewarded with the joys of rural love, sweet, sincere, and lasting, "such love as in these guiltless seats is known, Such as a state of innocence might own." [79] Still other pleasures awaited the rusticating belle. Thomas Warton, carrying over his own love of Nature to the conventional theme, promised her that she might

Count budding cowslips, or with lambkins play,
Sing with a nymph, or with a shepherd stray!
Then cast thee weary on the painted ground,
Where hazels cast a checquer'd shade around;
While issuing from a bud a bee shall come,
To bless thy slumbers with a drowsy hum.[80]

Of all the virtues which the town dwellers sought in country shades, perhaps the most eagerly looked for was peace.[81] Early in the period Dyer had found that "grass and flowers Quiet treads,

On the meads, and mountain-heads." [82] Not long after Dyer, Allan Ramsay told of Mercury vainly seeking peace in court, in church, in homes, until, as he despaired of his quest

> Just on the wing, towards burn
> A wee piece aff his looks did turn;
> There mistris Peace he chanc'd to see,
> Sitting beneath a willow tree. . . .
> Well, madam, said he, I perceive,
> That ane may long your presence crave,
> And miss ye still;—but this seems plain,
> To have ye, ane maun be alane.[83]

Dyer and Ramsay were but two who looked for Mistress Peace in solitudes. The other poets repeated endlessly that retirement was free from the cares of greatness, untroubled by the revenge, envy, distrust and sorrow that embittered life in courtly circles.[84] The honors of the mighty were ill pay for the pains which won them. A sensible man sought solitude himself and invited his friends to share it: "come, taste my Friend! the joys retirement brings, Look down on royal slaves, and pity kings." [85] The life of retirement was an ideal wide enough in appeal to charm such divergent personalities as an anonymous lady, a preromantic poet, and the great lexicographer. With varying degrees of skill they voiced the same ambition. The fair one moralized:

> I envy not the proud their wealth,
>   Their equipage, and state:
> Give me but innocence and health,
>   I ask not to be great.[86]

Samuel Johnson, weary of poverty and hack work, prayed:

> Grant me, kind heaven, to find some happier place,
> Where honesty and sense are no disgrace;
> Some pleasing bank where verdant osiers play,
> Some peaceful vale with nature's paintings gay . . .[87]

And William Collins longed for pastoral peace:

> I only seek to find thy temp'rate vale;
> Where oft my reed might sound
> To maids and shepherds round,
> And all thy sons, O nature, learn my tale.[88]

The pleasant theme of retirement had usually a solitary hero: he was most often one of three types. He might be a man who had achieved greatness and who deliberately left his honors to seek peace in seclusion:

> Oh! happy he, and amply blest by fate,
> Who free from noisy business and debate,
> The height of greatness modestly declines,
> And all his wishes to these shades inclines.[89]

He might, on the other hand, be a stoic gentleman who chose country solitudes to conquer his passions and perfect his reasonable equanimity:

> He who would know retirement's joy refin'd,
> The fair recess must seek with chearful mind. . . .
> But equal passions let his bosom rule,
> A judgment candid, and a temper cool,
> Enlarg'd with knowledge, and in conscience clear,
> Above life's empty hopes and death's vain fear.[90]

The two types are perennial: they might with equal ease be Lyttleton and Marlborough, or Cato and Horace.

The third seeker of rural quiet departed a little from the traditional concept. To stoic coolness and humble desire he added the popular eighteenth-century virtue of benevolence:

> Whose humble cottage limits his desires,
> Who with his little plot improves his mind,
> Benevolent to all, a slave to none . . .[91]

Amid the general run-of-the-mill sentiments even this slight deviation from traditional patterns is welcome.

In this, as in many phases of primitivism, Thomson's works offered the neatest and most poetic expression of "what oft was thought." His sketches of retirement combined the best of the idyllic atmosphere of pastoral simplicity with the most eloquent moralizing on the vanity of ambition:

> The best of men have ever loved repose:
> They hate to mingle in the filthy fray;
> Where the soul sours, and gradual rancour grows,
> Imbittered more from peevish day to day.[92]

He too was conscious of the security and tranquillity of country life: "thus safely low, my friend, thou canst not fall." [93] He put most graphically the mad and useless round of urban gaieties:

> The sons of riot flow
> Down the loose stream of false enchanted joy
> To swift destruction. On the rankled soul
> The gaming fury falls; and in one gulf
> Of total ruin, honour, virtue, peace,
> Friends, families, and fortune headlong sink.[94]

From brilliant halls and frenzied gaming tables Thomson would have men turn to "that simple life, the quiet-worshipping grove, And the still raptures of the free-born soul." [95]

In the hands of poets of less conventional temperaments, the hackneyed theme of rural retirement suffered some changes. John Wesley departed from his contemporaries' comfortable dreams of retirement: he sought solitude to repent and to commune with God, asking "some unfrequented wilderness" [96] as a sanctuary from the world's evil:

> Far in some lonely, desert place,
> For ever, ever would I sit,
> Languish to see the Saviour's face,
> And perish, weeping at His feet.[97]

Like Wesley, Edward Young looked on retirement, not as a traditional whim, but as a spiritual necessity. His early poem *Love of Fame* had discoursed conventionally, "give me, indulgent gods! with mind serene, And guiltless heart, to range the sylvan scene." [98] But two decades later in the *Night Thoughts*, Young had a differ-

ent message. His manner had become gloomier, his tone more
solemn as he marked the wise man's retirement to cypress shades
to "visit his vaults and dwell among the tombs":

> We see, we hear, with peril; safety dwells
> Remote from multitude; the world's a school
> Of wrong, and what proficients swarm around!
> We must, or imitate, or disapprove. . . .
> From nature's birth, hence, wisdom has been smit
> With sweet recess, and languish'd for the shade.
>   This sacred shade, and solitude, what is it?
> 'Tis the felt presence of the Deity.[99]

Much earlier than Young, David Mallet had sounded the note
of celestial intercourse in rural solitudes:

> Celestial intercourse! superior bliss,
> Which vice ne'er knew! health of th' enliven'd soul,
> And heaven on earth begun! Thus ever fix'd,
> In solitude, may I, obscurely safe,
> Deceive mankind, and steal thro life along . . .[100]

Save for Wesley, Young, and Mallet the poets were quite willing
to settle for a calmly contented retirement removed alike from
the bustle of the worldly and the raptures of the mystic.

> *This is what I prayed for!—a piece of land not so very
> large, where there would be a garden, and near the
> house a spring of ever flowing water, and up above
> these a bit of woodland. . . . O rural home! when shall
> I behold you! When shall I be able, now with books of
> the ancients, now with sleep and idle hours, to quaff
> sweet forgetfulness of life's cares!* [101]
>   —*Horace*, Satires, *II, 6*

Many an eighteenth-century poet echoed Horace's prayer, but
many an eighteenth-century poet hoped, unlike Horace, that his
prayer would not be granted. Their classical model had lived and

loved the rural life, but these neo-classicists were in fact inseparable from the dear, delightful town. In theory they might follow tradition in their avowed ambition to retreat to a secluded country spot, but in practice they clung closely to London,—fog, smoke, smells and all.

They were most conscientious about their classical imitations. Verse after verse described their desired rural estates complete with classical woodland, valley, garden, and spring. But the poets' hearts were not in the theme. A dispute over manners or morals might spur them to satire, the latest theories of philosophy or of science might inspire them to epics, but rural retirement was not the stuff of which neo-classical poets were made. At most it was a safe and correct subject which they pursued with pedestrian faithfulness in the impeccable train of Horace or of Virgil.

It is difficult to draw a hard and fast line between rural retirement for virtue and rural retirement in the Horatian tradition. Both are of classical origin and of literary inspiration. Both are examples of soft cultural primitivism. The Horatian tradition, however, claims verses which seek primarily comfort in rural seclusion, or which clearly bear the Horatian stamp in themes or in details borrowed from the Sabine bard.

The poets followed the general outline of their classical models with monotonous faithfulness; their occasional deviations were in the nature of added practical details. Pope and Swift, imitating the Horatian "o rus . . . ," illustrated respectively the general and the practical manner of interpreting the Latin lyrist. There was first the statement of the theme:

> O could I see my country seat!
> There leaning near a gentle brook,
> Sleep, or peruse some ancient book,
> And there, in sweet oblivion drown
> Those cares that haunt the court and town.[102]

But there was also the practical expression of the wishful thinking, the vulgar details of pounds and pence:

> I often wish'd that I had clear,
> For life, six hundred pounds a year;

A handsome house to lodge a friend,
A river at my garden's end;
A terras walk, and half a rood
Of land, set out to plant a wood.[103]

That Swift spent thirty years of exile pining for London had nothing to do with the case. Horace had written in a certain fashion: it was fitting that an eighteenth-century versifier should imitate his sentiments. And imitation was all that the poets of rural retirement managed to accomplish. They added a few modern touches, but for the most part their desires followed Virgil's well-worn pattern:

A country cottage near a crystal flood,
A winding valley, and a lofty wood.[104]

Some of them went to the country for inspiration as well as for comfort. Echoing Horace's devotion to the muse-haunted groves, they sallied forth (on paper) to rest by cool streams, wander through woodland glades, seek the Muses in their forest homes, and generally find for themselves the truth of the motto "happy the man who to these shades retires! Happy who here enjoys the sacred Muse!" [105] Akenside, who joined to his own skill in poetry a real enthusiasm for the classics, elaborated the theme most gracefully:

On yonder verdant hillock laid,
Where oaks and elms, a friendly shade,
  O'erlook the falling stream,
O master of the Latin lyre,
A while with thee will I retire
  From summer's noontide beam.[106]

Not satisfied to wander in conventional English groves, he would travel, in imagination at least, to classic shores, hallowed by memories of the golden days of Greece and Rome:

Guide my way
Through fair Lyceum's walk, the green retreats
Of Academus, and the thymy vale,

Where oft inchanted with Socratic sounds,
Ilissus pure devolv'd his tuneful stream
In gentler murmurs.[107]

But the poets' aesthetic appreciation of the woodlands as the abode of the muses was far overshadowed by their practical approval of the country as a refuge from the discomforts of town life. They had not, most of them, an intimate knowledge of the country life they praised, but they had a varied and lengthy acquaintance with the urban inconveniences they bewailed.[108] Town quarrels, scandals, smells, dirty streets, "the roar of coaches and the belch of oaths," hurry, strife, dust, smoke, and, again and again, noise, set them piling up praises of "peaceful shade and rural charms."

Now and then a more vehement voice broke the even tenor of their praises. There was the poet who pleaded, "lift me, some God! from this tumultuous town!" [109] There was the distracted bard who vainly tried to write, "immers'd in smoke, stun'd with perpetual noise"; [110] there was the bored author caught in town during vacation who assured his country friend that the city was most dull, "we dine, we dawdle, we get drunk and sleep." [111] There was even a woman's view of the matter, pitched in a wistful tone:

From the court to the cottage convey me away,
For I'm weary of grandeur and what they call gay. . . .
Far remote and retir'd from the noise of the town,
I'll exchange my brocade for a plain russet gown.
    My friends should be few,
    But well chosen and true,
And sweet recreation our evening shall crown.[112]

A rather late piece (1749) by the Scotch poet William Hamilton of Bangour added some vivid details of natural scenery to its praises of country life:

    the flowers appear
Earth's smiling offspring, and the beauteous meads
Are cloath'd in pleasant green; now fruitful trees
Put forth their tender buds that soon shall swell

> With rich nectareous juice, and woo thy hand
> To pluck their ripen'd sweets. Forsake a while
> The noise of cities, and with me retire
> To rural solitude. . . .[113]

Here the details of natural beauty have wandered out of classic groves into Scottish meadows. A like wedding of local color to traditional themes enlivened Thomson's country walk:

> Now from the town,
> Buried in smoke and sleep and noisome damps,
> Oft let me wander o'er the dewy fields
> Where freshness breathes, and dash the trembling drops
> From the bent bush, as through the verdant maze
> Of sweet-briar hedges I pursue my walk. . . .[114]

Thomson's dewdrops sparkled in no ancient groves—they clung to the edges of an English roadside.

It was less the beauty of the countryside than its comfort that attracted the poets. They recounted over and over their specifications for convenient rural retirement. Their demands differed mainly in the amount per annum necessary to keep them in the style to which Horace was accustomed. Five thousand pounds would keep a man in "racy cider, amber ale, fresh fish" and a pleasant Norfolk home.[115] A hundred pounds a year might finance a small house, a hill, trees, and (something not found in Horace) a sum left over for charitable purposes.[116] Two hundred yearly purchased "a farm some twenty miles from town Small, tight, salubrious, and my own." [117] Eight hundred pounds a year, the desire of a more ambitious poet, could stretch to take care of a "new built house," a good wife, two or three children and the neighbouring poor.[118]

In more general terms, "a calm retreat" was the most popular wish, although the desired estate might also be described as "innocent," "little," quiet, or "cool." [119]

The poets had generous lists of comforts necessary to render their country seat agreeable. For the most part their demands were reasonable. "A little freehold tenement" of medium size, large enough to entertain "some friends . . . goodnatur'd, rational and true," would meet one man's desire.[120] Another would have "a little cottage on a lonely mead."[121] The poetess of Bath, Mary Chandler, desired rugged surroundings:

> Securely seated on a rock,
>   Whence silver streams descend,
> From cliffs, the ruins of old Time,
>   And murmur as they bend.[122]

She desired, not the pleasant groves of classical tradition, but wild scenes capable of inspiring poetic raptures:

> Romantic views these prospects yield,
>   That feed poetic fire;
> Each broken rock, and cave, and field,
>   And hill and vale, inspire.[123]

The Bath poetess might rhapsodize Nature's inspiration, but her masculine colleagues were more interested in real food for themselves than in figurative food for their muses. If vegetarians, they dined on the fruits and herbs and produce of their gardens.[124] If undeterred by humanitarian scruples, they feasted on nut-brown ale and sturdy joints,[125] or promised themselves still more luxurious banquets, "the daintiest meats our humble board should grace."[126] One poet, making sure that the cheering cup should circle his board, requested "good barley-land to make good beer."[127] An anonymous verse summarizing the pleasures of life in a country villa did full justice to the good fare to be enjoyed there:

> With wholesome fare our villa's stor'd.
> Our lands the best of corn afford.
> Nor Hartford wheat, or Derby rye,
> Or Ipswich peas, can ours out-vye;
> Let Irish wights no longer boast
> The fam'd potatoes of their coast;
> Potatoes now are Plaistow's pride,
> Whole markets are from hence supply'd.

The largest Ox, that England bred,
Was in our grassy pastures fed;
Nor finer mutton can you spend,
Than what our fatt'ning marshes send.[128]

By now the reader has realized that all the poets have accomplished has been to state and restate with little variation the time-worn sentiments of the classical retirement theme. Except for a few native touches, such as the barley-land for good beer, Mary Chandler's romantic landscape, and John Winstanley's demand for "rational" visitors, the persistent strain of Horatian retirement in the early eighteenth-century poets is conventionally classical in inspiration and expression. More—it is neo-classical: the warm glow of Horace's hospitality has grown chill in the practical light of eighteenth-century common sense, and the whole-hearted delight of the Latin poet in his sun-warmed hills, his fragrant grass, his ruddy plums and lofty poplars has hardened into the conventional patter of poets who would not have been caught an hour away from town, unless a patron's invitation to his country estate made that absence politic, or a creditor's dunning made it imperative.

Melancholy is a kind of demon that haunts our island, and often conveys itself to us in an easterly wind. A celebrated French novelist, in opposition to those who begin their romances with the flowery season of the year, enters on his story thus: 'In the gloomy month of November, when the people of England hang and drown themselves . . .' [129]

—Spectator, *No. 387*

The great prestige of Milton, the hallowed tradition of scholarly seclusion, the native strain of melancholy which has haunted English literature from the *Wanderer* on, made it inevitable that eighteenth-century poets should retire to Miltonic shades as well as to Horatian groves. "Melancholy is a kind of demon that haunts our island," Addison had lamented. The generation of poets which followed him had their full share of the gloomy spirit. Not only the mild pensiveness of the sage, endeared to them by Milton's *Il Penseroso*, but even the black melancholy of the morbid, if not quite the mad, appears stubbornly and consistently in their poetry right up to the mid-century. After that date the strain deepens in its terror-filled aspects as it approaches the period of "Gothic" glooms, and the still later era of romantic terror.[130]

In this earlier portion of the century, however, the poets give comparatively little place to the black moods that drive men to "hang and drown themselves." Their preoccupation is with the more pleasant and dignified type of gentle sadness peculiar to the retired scholar, and to the philosophic man of the world.

In many ways the theme of classical retirement shades imperceptibly into that of Miltonic derivation, for the classical theme of weariness of life had often been associated with retirement from the useless cares of the world. Both themes are in the tradition of soft primitivism. (Even when eighteenth-century poets, departing from classical and from Miltonic precedent, pursue their musings into wild and terrible scenes, the wildness is no incentive to hardihood,—it is no more than a backdrop from their gloomy speculations.) But the pseudo-Miltonic rather than the classical stamp is plain upon the poets who pursued quiet and contemplation from groves to gardens, from Richmond Park to the ruins of Stamford, hopeful that their diligent plodding after *Il Penseroso* would lead them to wisdom, to peace, and to literary inspiration.

The ordinary Miltonic imitations are perfectly obvious treatments of the popular themes of contemplation, solitude, melancholy, pleasing glooms and studious groves. The anonymous poet who took as his text "solitude sometimes is best Society" covered most of the conventional aspects of the subject:

> Hail rural Prospects, lovely silvan scenes!
> Hail happiest safest life! Ye verdant plains
> Receive, receive me to your blest abodes
> Dear solitary groves. May I reside
> Here, whilst the soothing scenery around

Charms ev'ry sense: her raptur'd votary
May wisdom thro' the mazy lab'rinth guide
Of science, may deep-musing contemplation lead
To the delightful mansions of the muse.[131]

His fellow poets would have accompanied him gladly to those solitary groves rich in the traditional blessings of sage retirement, wise contemplation and poetic inspiration. Vales and groves, gentle glooms and soft retreats constituted a made-to-order landscape for all the musing poets. The scenes were so like that one writer might be set down in his colleague's poem and scarcely notice the difference. The adjectives might vary sedately with the different verse-makers, but the pensive atmosphere remained constant.[132] Solitude was sweet, sacred, venerable, pleasing, learned: a guide to truth in life and a final consolation "when life's gay hours are past." Dusky groves inspired to holy contemplation, "learned solitudes" offered the "charms of philosophic life." An anonymous poet might welcome poverty as a guide to meditation,[133] and Richard Savage, restless even in a conventional theme, might pray for solitude in a distant clime,[134] but the rest of the poets were glad to stay home and think—in comfort.

Such devotion to "wholesome solitude the nurse of sense" [135] naturally inspired spirited denunciations of the maddening distractions of city life. The wickedness of the town's follies as contrasted with the "pleasures of the secret shade" [136] provoked a host of conventional complaints. A trace of intellectual snobbishness crept into the occasional suggestion that cultured retirement was for the few,[137] a touch of pathos (mostly inherent in the title) distinguished an "ode by a young gentleman of fifteen, since dead," [138] but on the whole verses in praise of Miltonic retirement hailed country living much as did their classic parallels: they simply added to the ancient theme groves and glooms and a more deliberate mood of meditation.[139]

Memories of the Sibylline cave, of Spenser's Cave of Sleep, consciousness of the popular mania for grotto building and of the equally popular pastime of speculating about caves and mines and all such evidences of earth's irregularity as being the ruins of the

antediluvian world, all these lay back of the poets' use of grottoes
as a background for conventional moralizings on retirement.[140]
Sometimes their grottoes were natural caves "scoop'd by Nature's
salvage [sic] hands," [141] a "green grott, or mossy cell" [142] that
offered the wanderer refuge from grief or invitation to study.
Among the many retreats that Thomson chose as his retired
haunts, he numbered:

> weeping grottoes, and prophetic glooms;
> Where angel forms athwart the solemn dusk,
> Tremendous, sweep, or seem to sweep along;
> And voices more than human, through the void
> Deep-sounding, seize the enthusiastic ear.[143]

Often the verses on retired grottoes reflected the fashionable
pursuit of constructing a cave wherever Nature refused to produce one. Despite the scorn with which a later generation met the
fad of hermitages and grottoes which took gentleman's estates by
storm during the early and mid-eighteenth century,[144] the land-
owners who built the artificial caves did so with self-conscious enjoyment. Miscellany verses "written by a Hermit" paid tribute
to the "peaceful grot, remov'd from guilty strife." [145] Panegyric
poems praised various estate owners for the "green retreat" [146]
or for the hermitages which they had constructed as fit haunts
of meditation. The subjects of that meditation had a pleasantly
eighteenth-century tone of nature and benevolence as a poet bade
"the Rev. Mr. R——" seek out his hermitage and:

> Here nature meditate, from her
> Learn what to shun, and what prefer:
> While tepid suns and vernal show'rs
> Impregnate trees, and plants, and flow'rs;
> And earth teems forth her kind supply,
> Meant to bless all beneath the sky.
> So let benevolence o'er flow,
> And think it godlike to bestow.[147]

The famous cave of Pope was a "solemn place" [148] where lesser
men might venerate the chosen solitude of a departed genius. Most

fashionable of grottoes, Queen Caroline's Hermitage at Richmond
Park (lampooned at a later date as a piece of most unaesthetic royal
meddling with architecture), inspired at this period fervent tributes as the "Muses sacred seat," a blest place where:

> at chosen hours,
> The Royal Hermit takes her lonely way,
> Indulging thoughts which lift the raptur'd soul
> Above mortality: her solemn busts
> Of sages (greater than proud Greece can boast,
> Or antient Rome, or those of modern date
> Innumerable, that blindly follow these)
> Sublimest themes suggest . . . The wondrous force
> Of human knowledge from the birth of thought,
> Working by slow gradations to the height
> Of mathematick certainty . . . The rules
> Of universal moral duty, taught
> By nature's book immutable . . . The light
> Of revelation that dispels the mists,
> Th' infectious mists, which sin and folly breath . . .[149]

Her majesty's grotto decked with the busts of Newton and Locke
offered eighteenth-century minds ample inspiration to meditate
"the wond'rous force Of human knowledge from the birth of
thought, Working by slow gradations to the height Of mathe-
matick certainty."

Nor were grottoes the only scene fit for meditation on that
favorite eighteenth-century theme, the wonders of science. The
shades sacred to contemplation were hospitable to intellectual
interests borrowed from contemporary themes as well as from
traditional sources. Eighteenth-century men were enormously
proud of the modern sage who had charted the tangled pathways
of the heavens. It is no wonder, then, but merely a sign of the
times that poets added to Miltonic glooms a thoroughly eighteenth-century eagerness about natural phenomena and the cosmic
order, and that the charm of Newtonian science eclipsed occasionally the ethereal graces of midnight scenes and poetic visions.

One poetic devotee of science would live "free from dependence, and the toils of trade." [150] Safe in his green walks and shady oaks he might confidently declare, "on Newton's wing I'd dare sublimer flight, from star to star direct my trembling sight." [151]

In the pursuit of cosmic knowledge Locke and Newton were man's guides to "the seats of thought," guides who direct him to

> turn the leaves of nature's volume o'er:
> Of each effect discern the latent spring,
> Or sail from world to world on fancy's wing.
> Coy science in her labyrinths pursue.
> Eye the vast whole; and look all nature thro' . . .[152]

Even an imaginative poet who sought out "the unfrequented green" [153] to watch the dark woods and shadowy hills, to count the stars that sparkle in heaven and to fancy

> the fairy elves
> Dance o'er their magick circles . . .[154]

cut short his imaginative holiday with the prayer:

> But chiefly Newton let me soar with thee . . .[155]

The day was coming when a truly imaginative poet would heap scorn on Newton for unweaving the rainbow, but that day was not yet. This was 1733: physics still had more charm than phantoms, and science was yet a "lovely star" to direct the way of the writer.[156]

A poetic invitation to "sweet solitudes" that combined the intense interest of eighteenth-century men in their science-illumined world with the traditional theme of retirement promised:

> Here, we a thousand secrets shall explore,
> That slept conceal'd in Nature's womb, before.
> Soon as the sun flames thro' the aethereal way,
> And breaks triumphant thro' the gates of day;
> Through every scene of nature will we run,
> And all the vast creation is our own.
> But when his golden globe with faded light,
> Yields to the solemn empire of the night;

And in her cloudy majesty, the moon,
With milder glories, mounts her silver throne,
Amidst ten thousand orbs with splendors crown'd,
That pour their tributary beams around;
Thro' the long levell'd tube, our stretching sight,
Shall make distinct the spangles of the night:
From world to world shall rove the boundless eye,
And dart from star to star, from sky to sky.
  The buzzing insect families appear,
When suns unbend the rigours of the year;
In the cool evening air they frisk and play,
Hosts of the hour! and nations of a day!
With pleasing wonder will we see them pass,
Stretcht out in bulk, within the polish'd glass;
Thro' whose small convex a new world we spy,
Ne'er seen before, but by a seraph's eye.
So long in darkness, shut from human-kind,
Lay half God's wonder, to a point confin'd:
But in one peopled drop we now survey,
In pride of pow'r, some little monster play;
O'er tribes invisible, he reigns alone,
And struts, the tyrant of a world his own.[157]

The ancient worthies had had no telescope to span the stars, or microscope to compass the insect race. And *Il Penseroso*, though he had the discoveries of Galileo to charm him, lacked the further incentive of Newtonian physics to lure him from country walks to the observatory. The introduction of details of contemporary science into the subject of rural retirement is a real addition on the part of early eighteenth-century verse writers. Their science-inspired "spangles of the night" are far more appealing than their routine invocations of sweet solitude and heavenly contemplation.

    Like contemplation, solitude, and retirement, melancholy inspired the poets to thoroughly traditional musings.

There is a kindly mood of melancholy
That wings the soul, and points her to the skies . . .[158]

Such a pleasing melancholy, "heavenly," "soothing," "philosophic," "sacred," reduced the writers' souls to a sage pensiveness.[159]
Melancholy itself seemed:

> That aged venerable seer,
> With sorrowing pale, with watchings spare,
> Of pleasing yet dejected air . . .[160]

His spirit loved the lonely grove, the glooms of night, "the time-
shook tow'r," "the pale sad influence" of faint stars.[161] His quiet
sadness was of more worth than "the dull pride of tasteless splen-
dor and magnificence." [162]

"Where all is melancholy, all is sweet" [163]—the poets followed
that bitter-sweet pensiveness in the true spirit of Milton's "studious
cloisters pale." The younger Thomas Warton paid eloquent tribute to

> Ye fretted pinnacles, ye fanes sublime,
> Ye towers that wear the mossy vest of time;
> Ye massy piles of old munificence,
> At once the pride of learning and defence;
> Ye cloisters pale, that lengthening to the sight,
> To contemplation, step by step, invite;
> Ye high-arch'd walks, where oft the whispers clear
> Of harps unseen have swept the poet's ear . . .[164]

And James Thomson was equally fervent in his welcome:

> He comes! he comes! in every breeze the Power
> Of Philosophic Melancholy comes!
> His near approach the sudden-starting tear,
> The glowing cheek, the mild dejected air,
> The softened feature, and the beating heart,
> Pierced deep with many a virtuous pang, declare.
> O'er all the soul his sacred influence breathes;
> Inflames imagination; through the breast

Infuses every tenderness; and far
Beyond dim earth exalts the swelling thought.
Ten thousand thousand fleet ideas, such
As never mingled with the vulgar dream.[165]

Melancholy solitudes inspired the muses: as Richard Savage explained:

Nature to rural scenes invites the muse;
She flies all public care, all venal strife,
To try the still, compar'd with active life;
To prove, by these the sons of men may owe
The fruits of bliss to bursting clouds of woe;
That e'en calamity, by thought refin'd,
Inspirits and adorns the thinking mind.
   Come, Contemplation, whose unbounded gaze,
Swift in a glance, the course of things surveys.[166]

In search of literary inspiration poetic muses docilely haunted such conventional glades as Richmond Park and the Royal Gardens [167] as well as the more general atmosphere of "sacred solitude and blest retreat." [168] The earliest of the poets to find the *furor poeticus* in the shades was Mary Masters. She described tamely enough her acceptance of an invitation "to breathe the fragrance of the country air," but the sight of rural beauties aroused in her a violent reaction of poetic fervor:

For while I view the products of the spring,
I find a God in the minutest thing,
I grow inspir'd, and hardly can restrain
The struggling muse, that would begin again . . .[169]

Fifteen years passed before that note of poetic frenzy sounded again. When it made itself heard in '48 and '49, close to the half-century mark, it added to praises of retirement the pre-romantic concept of the divinely inspired poet. Tributes to divine fury found in solitary groves a "wonted frenzy" [170] of poetry and a soul "of purer fire." [171] The best of them, an inscription by a nameless poet, mingled Miltonic groves with Platonic frenzy and with echoes of classical mythology:

Who by retirement to these sacred groves
Impregnate fancy, and on thought divine
Build harmony— If sudden glow your breast
With inspiration, and the rapt'rous song
Bursts from a mind unconscious whence it sprang:
    Know that the sisters of these hallow'd haunts,
Dryad or Hamadryad, though no more
From Jove to man prophetic truths they sing,
Are still attendant on the lonely bard,
Who step by step the silent woods among
Wanders contemplative, lifting the soul
From lower cares, by every whisp'ring breeze
Tun'd to poetic mood . . .[172]

With or without invocations to the Muse the poets continued to seek traditional groves. Sometimes their time-honored solitudes bloomed with fresh details of natural scenery as they pursued their thoughtful ways by murmuring waters, trembling shades and fragrant meadows.[173] Thomson who found contemplation by "dim grottoes, gleaming lakes and fountains clear" [174] painted the ideal retirement scene:

Thrice happy he, who on the sunless side
Of a romantic mountain, forest-crowned,
Beneath the whole collected shade reclines;
Or in the gelid caverns, woodbine-wrought
And fresh bedewed with ever-spouting streams,
Sits cooly calm; while all the world without,
Unsatisfied and sick, tosses in noon.[175]

An anonymous description of evening offered its reader the homely detail of smoke curling from the village huts as the evening gales died in the quivering trees.[176] An apostrophe to woodland shades bloomed with spring flowers:

Ye blooming groves, where zephyrs softly breath!—
Ye beds of primroses, which shine beneath!
Ye banks of violets! cowslips on the plain!

Roses in hedges! King-cups on the green!
Birds in the woods! and larks upon the skies! [177]

Even more charming than primroses and zephyrs were the light
and shade effects of David Mallet's evening solitude:

Distinction fails: and in the darkening west,
The last light, quivering, dimly dies away.
And not th' illusive flame, oft seen at eve,
Upborne and blazing on the light-wing'd gale,
Glides o'er the lawn, betokening night's approach:
Arising awful o'er the eastern sky,
Onward she comes with silent step and slow,
In her brown mantle wrapt, and brings along
The still, the mild, the melancholy hour,
And meditation, with his eye on heaven.[178]

Such scattered manifestations of interest in the scenic details of
solitude reach a climax in the five years before 1750. Then it was
that Gray mused beneath the "oak's thick branches" [179] and the
"rude and moss-grown beech," [180] that the Squire of Dames rested
in a grove redolent of Spenser and of English song-birds, that
minor poets wrote of "craggy hills" [181] and the "dew enamell'd
mead," [182] that at least one brave versifier, breaking loose from
formal heroic couplets and pseudo-Miltonic blank verse, hailed
his retreat in Sapphic strophe:

Nor less the rapture when cool evening rises
Girt in her dewy robe: And blithe invites us
To quaff the flowing bowl, and grateful praise the
Bounteous Creator.
But chiefly thee, mild queen of solemn midnight,
Thee thy bard hails: and jocund to thine honour,
New-strings the lyre, and swells the lofty theme to
Worthiest attention.[183]

It was at this time also that the younger Thomas Warton found
pleasing the dreary morn, when "deepest sadness wraps the face

of things," and saw the "Mother of Musings, contemplation sage" on the height of Teneriffe, "remote from man conversing with the spheres." [184]

Amid these hints of poetic things to come the best fore-shadowing of the growing spirit of romance is Collins' *Ode to Evening*, which adds to the old retirement theme a magic that looks back less to Milton and to the classics, than forward to the lyric scenes of the nineteenth century: his country of retirement is a far cry from the vine-crowned hills of the ancients, or from Milton's "meadows trim":

> Then lead, calm vot'ress, where some sheety lake,
> Cheers the lone heath, or some time-hallow'd pile,
>> Or up-land fallows grey
>> Reflects its last cool gleam.
> But when chill blust'ring winds, or driving rain,
> Forbid my willing feet, be mine the hut,
>> That from the mountain's side,
>> Views wilds, and swelling floods,
> And hamlets brown, and dim-discover'd spires,
> And hears their simple bell, and marks o'er all
>> Thy dewy fingers draw
>> The gradual dusky veil.[185]

The reader who reviews the poets' passages of Miltonic contemplation becomes gradually aware that the orderly thoughtfulness of traditional meditation is sometimes replaced by wilful indulgence in emotion, by outbursts of sorrow, of gloom, sometimes of despair. Melancholy leads the sage not to pastoral solitudes, but to graveyards and to ruins: it fills his visions with ghosts and black magic: it drives him to morbid speculations, to a fascinated preoccupation with death.

The gap between white melancholy and black, between the sage's pensive meditations and the distracted poet's haunted visions is partly bridged by those poems which link solitary retirement with excessive grief. In their tear-filled laments the reader begins to catch a glimpse of the deliberate delight in emotion which eventually dragged mild Miltonic contemplation to the weird watches of the charnel house.

By "mournful willows," or under the "baleful yew" and in the "solemn gloom" the poets took up their complaints.[186] To "weep in some sequester'd shade" [187] was the height of their desire for retirement. "The heart-felt harmony of woe" [188] was the greatest boon that solitude could grant them. They retired to the grove not to ponder intellectual problems, but to pour out their over-wrought emotions:

> For solitude's the truest nurse of woe:
> In silent shades sad melancholy reigns,
> But too indulgent to the mourner's pains . . .[189]

Most violent of all, a grief-maddened bard hailed the "sick twilight" of a winter's day as a fit match for the savage sadness of his thoughts:

> In this moss-cover'd cavern, hopeless laid,
> On the cold cliff I'll lean my aking head,
> And, pleas'd with winter's waste, unpitying, see
> All nature in an agony with me!
> Rough, rugged rocks, wet marshes, ruin'd tow'rs,
> Bare trees, brown brakes, bleak heaths, and rushy moors;
> Dead floods, huge cataracts, to my pleased eyes
> (Now I can smile!) in wild disorder rise:
> And now, the various dreadfulness combin'd,
> Black melancholy comes to doze my mind.[190]

In that explosion of sentiment the surrounding solitudes are as wild as the poet's grief, and the traditional mood of meditation has vanished in a violent fit of black melancholy. As the poet continued his sombre strain, his theme made the easy transition from pleasing glooms to pleasing horrors:

> See! night's wish'd shades rise, spreading through the air,
> And the lone, hollow gloom, for me prepare!

Hail! solitary ruler of the grave!
Parent of terrors! from thy dreary cave!
Let thy dumb silence midnight all the ground,
And spread a welcome horror all around.
But hark!—a sudden howl invades my ear!
The phantoms of the dreadful hour are near.
Shadows, from each dark cavern, now combine
And walk around, and mix their yells with mine.
Stop, flying time! repose thy restless wing;
Fix here—nor hasten to restore the spring . . .[191]

The step from welcome gloom to welcome horror was a short one, and once horrors delighted the poets they had no qualms about endowing quiet shades with the eerie atmosphere of a danse macabre. The "gloomy throng" of midnight visions, the pale spectre of Despair, "the lonely horror of the night" were suited to their melancholy meditations.[192] Joseph Warton's Solitude, a gloomy creature, cypress-crowned, arrayed in flowing black, walked in the pale moonlight or meditated in a wind-swept cavern.[193] Warton's lesser contemporaries were no less sombre in their imaginings. They loved melancholy scenes "awful as Death," [194] retired to the shade of rustling oaks that "with sacred sound and awful horror please," [195] and admired

> A gloomy grove, whose awful shade
> By rocks impervious, and thick branches made,
> A mixture of delight and horror had.[196]

(In their insistence on the delight and horror which gloomy scenes raise within the onlooker, the poets were carrying over into the theme of retirement a tendency that was growing steadily at this period in poetic appreciations of external Nature, namely the tendency to rejoice in scenes of fearful and awful grandeur.)

Sometimes it was the poets' own imaginings rather than the impressive grimness of their surroundings that rendered their meditations pleasingly sombre. Night, "sister of Ebon-scepter'd Hecat," [197] was fit time for musings on the outrageous crimes "that wake Heaven's vengeance." [198] How easily Miltonic meditations might lead to the realm of the supernatural was plain in one anonymous writer's account of his wanderings:

> Silently musing on the Ills of Life,
>   With equal Caution, weighing Love and Strife;
> O'er come with Heat, the open Plain I flew,
> And to a lonely Thicket's Side withdrew;
> Where not the Hyacinch [sic] or Violet blows,
> But baleful Hemlock, with wild Henbane grows;
> Whose spreading Briers, with prickly Thorns unite,
> Where solitary dwells the Bird of Night;
> Where hoary Witches Midnight Meetings make,
> And grizly Ghosts their nightly Wand'rings take. [199]

If the solitude he sought were wild enough, *Il Penseroso* might find himself at a witches' Sabbath.

Another theme of the darkly melancholy passages which increased in number and in gloom in the decade between 1740–1750 is the theme of meditation on death. [200] Death, like ruins and the gloom-filled scenes of Nature, was a subject calculated to raise wonder and terror in him who wrote of it and in him who read. Edward Young made clear that the gloom of the groves, the shade of ruins, the *memento mori* all struck the soul with the same welcome awe:

> Yet am I struck; as struck the soul, beneath
> Aerial groves' impenetrable gloom;
> Or, in some mighty ruin's solemn shade;
> Or, gazing by pale lamps on high-born dust,
> In vaults; thin courts of poor unflatter'd kings;
> Or, at the midnight altar's hallow'd flame. [201]

The period's supreme expression of quiet contemplation of the grave, Gray's *Elegy*, was quietly restrained in its setting:

> Beneath those rugged elms, that yew-tree's shades,
> Where heaves the turf in many a mould'ring heap,

Each in his narrow cell forever laid,
The rude forefathers of the hamlet sleep.[202]

But lesser poets who desired to "range the gloomy isles" [203] of the
dead sought their meditations in "gloomy vaults," [204] "hoary
cells," [205] "cloyster'd domes in ruin great." [206] A meditative sage
mused at midnight in the churchyard and watched "the graves give
up their dead." [207] Silence and Melancholy led the willing poet to
"search the gloomy world below":

> The gloomy horrors all around,
> The baleful yew, the hollow ground,
> The graves where many are at rest,
> Well sooth the melancholy breast.[208]

No longer did the poet seek the solitude of pleasant country retreats: he urged instead:

> Let us with retirement go
> To charnels and the house of woe . . .[209]

A melancholy bard, having made that journey, delighted in the
grim reflection:

> Thro' yon dark grove of mournful yews,
> With solitary steps I muse,
>   By thy direction led;
> Here, cold to pleasure's airy forms,
> Consociate with my sister worms,
>   And mingle with the dead.[210]

His attempt was horrible enough, but for a full effect of retirement, gloom, gothic atmosphere and graves, the reader must follow Thomas Warton to his rendezvous with ruins:

> Where through some western window the pale moon
> Pours her long-levell'd rule of streaming light;
> While sullen sacred silence reigns around,
> Save the lone screech-owl's note, who builds his bow'r
> Amid the mould'ring caverns, dark and damp,

Or the calm breeze, that rustles in the leaves
Of flaunting ivy, that with mantle green
Invests some wasted tow'r. Or let me tread
Its neigh'ring walk of pines, where mus'd of old
The cloyster'd brother: through the gloomy void
That far extends beneath their ample arch
As on I pace, religious horror wraps
My soul in dread repose. But when the world
Is clad in midnight's raven-colour'd robe,
'Mid hollow charnels let me watch the flame
Of taper dim, shedding a livid glare
O'er the wan heaps; while airy voices talk
Along the glimm'ring walls: or ghostly shape
At distance seen, invites with beck'ning hand
My lonesome steps, through the far-winding valuts.[211]

With that melancholy vigil, the variations on the theme of Miltonic
retirement reach their climax.

Within the framework of neo-classical tradition, retirement
after the manner of *Il Penseroso* linked itself easily with that thoroughly neo-classical interest—Newtonian science. Outside of that
framework the traditional solitudes lent themselves willingly to the
pre-romantic themes of love of external Nature, of poetic fire, of
violent emotion, and finally of ruins and the macabre. The second
strain, made eloquent by Collins, Akenside, Gray, Thomson and
the Wartons, is the stronger and the more significant. Ever-increas-
ing toward the approach of the mid-century it serves as still another signpost on the road to romanticism. Literary conventions
die hard, however, and side by side with these forecasts of the
future are scores of correctly dull little verses that plod along the
conventional road to Miltonic solitudes, threatening to overwhelm,
by sheer force of numbers, the few original treatments which link
the old theme with the trend of things to come.

V

*When a man looks about him, and with regard to riches
and poverty, beholds some drawn in pomp and equip-
age, and they, and their very servants, with an air of
scorn and triumph, overlooking the multitude that pass
by them; and in the same street, a creature of the same
make, crying out in the name of all that is good and
sacred to behold his misery, and give him some supply
against hunger and nakedness; who would believe these
two beings were of the same species?* [212]

Spectator, *No. 494*

Country gentlemen and retired sages led relatively unpretentious
lives, but for a real model of day-to-day simplicity the poets turned
to their fellow-citizens—the poor. Poverty (at least in theory)
seemed admirable in its freedom from inordinate desires, while
wealth (again in theory) seemed a burden, a heavy load of complex affairs and overweening ambitions. While verse writers had
made their ideal of rural retirement pleasantly comfortable, they
made room in their praise of the poor for both pastoral bliss and
everyday hardihood. Their admiration, however, usually stopped
short of praise for the beggared and destitute. Rich man was bad,
poor man was good, but beggar man was unfortunate.

Much that was conventional went into the poets' tributes to the
underprivileged classes of their day. Memories of Virgil's happy
husbandman, of Juvenal's outbursts against luxury, of Seneca's
counsel of moderation, of Milton's "low but loyal cottage," and of
a hundred other classical, medieval, Renaissance, and traditionally
English denunciations of the evils of wealth furnished a long conventional background for their verses. Somewhere along the centuries the poetic fury which had kindled at social injustice had
become dampened: the eighteenth-century versifiers of the theme
could not thunder at contemporary weakness, they could only rail
against it.

But the poets were preaching poverty to a generation that worshipped prosperity and enterprise. While English poets celebrated the joys of the homely hearth, English merchants were scouring the seas in search of trade, and were blessing Sir Robert Walpole for the low rate of interest which encouraged commercial enterprise. A generation of verses decried power and conquest, while a generation of shipbuilders added a hundred thousand tons of shipping to the might of the Royal Navy.

The poet's happy poor had no counterpart in eighteenth-century reality. The underprivileged of that day were working long, hard, and despairingly, bowed under the first blows of the approaching industrial revolution.[213] The second half of the century was to make the lot of the poor completely miserable, but the first fifty years saw them already unhappy enough—a public charge, poorly cared for under the provisions of the Workhouse Act of 1723, and badly neglected despite the increasing appropriations for poor relief which rose by three hundred thousand pounds during the course of the half century.[214]

At its best the lot of the country worker was one of long, unceasing toil, and few and simple pleasures. In the northern counties, where the new methods of farming and the enclosure system penetrated slowly and the old pattern of rural life continued to give the small farmer security and a place in a traditional social scheme, even there the poor agricultural laborer lived a life of Spartan simplicity and of steady, unremitting toil. For a while increased agricultural wages and lowered corn prices gave him a semblance of prosperity, but his increase in ready money was too often accompanied by loss of independence, as more and more small farm holders sold out to large land owners and became workers on the farms of others, or drifted to the manufacturing centers to become part of Britain's growing industrial machine.

The urban poor were no better off than their country fellows. Herded into overcrowded manufacturing districts of cities, they barely subsisted on wages from monotonous, mechanized factory jobs. Close to the display of luxury flaunted by the court and by the great trading families, the urban poor turned, in their prosperous moments to extravagance, and in their impoverished moments to thievery.

Both rural and urban poor, but especially the latter, felt the effect of the formidable rise in the consumption of hard liquor during the second quarter of the century.[215] French wines were barred by the government's trade policy, and the port which replaced them was for the tables of the gout-ridden rich, but so long as gin flowed plentifully, even the poorest might be "drunk for a penny."

The briefest glimpse of the condition of the English poor in the early eighteenth century is enough to convince the reader that the poets' idyllic pictures of the poor man's lot have no resemblance, real or imagined, to the conditions of contemporary society.

Poetic outbursts against luxury, on the other hand, have a literal as well as a literary significance. They have their source, not only in traditional denunciations of wealth, but in the actual misgivings of a generation that watched national prosperity skyrocket, and feared the day when the rocket would burn out. Sometimes to poetic distrust of luxury was added the poet's interest in politics, and versified attacks on wealth became another variation of Opposition propaganda. For forty years no collection of anti-luxury verses was complete without a goodly representation of pieces linking wealth with Walpole, and heartily damning both.

Sometimes the poets linked want of wealth with want of wickedness: sometimes they denounced national luxury, sometimes they wept over the suffering lowly and reassured the downtrodden that "a man's man for a' that." But whether they stormed or whether they sympathized, the writers kept their verses within the bounds of calm tradition. Praise of poverty with them was a convention rather than a cause.

> Shep: I can conduct you Lady to a low
> But loyal cottage, where you may be safe
> Till further quest!
>
> La.:   Shepherd, I take thy word,
> And trust thy honest offer'd courtesie,
> Which oft is sooner found in lowly sheds
> With smoaky rafters, than in tapstry Halls

And Courts of Princes, where it first was nam'd
And yet is most pretended. . . .[216]

—*Milton,* Comus

If the poets were to be believed, all virtuous poor folk were to be found in the country.[217] Except for the comparative lowliness of their station, there was little to distinguish them from gentlemen in rural retirement. They were peaceful and innocent—their virtues were a lesson to the pride, ambition and double dealing of city people:

> There decency shines forth in home-spun vest,
> There innocence with ever cheerful smiles,
> And health with all her fragrant roses drest,
> Uncertain physic's greedy art beguiles;
> Whilst lavish plenty, with her joyous train,
> Sings thro' th' extended vale, and laughs along
>   the plain . . .[218]

The "purple state" and "wanton luxury" of the great were small things compared with the happiness of the "contented swain." [219] Nor were the swain's spiritual excellences without material rewards. His temperance assured him of health, and his clear conscience was the guarantee of a good night's sleep. His diligent labor sweetened his plain fare, and softened his rushy pillow.[220] Shepherds, "lovely emblems of primaeval bliss," were "exempt from all the nameless num'rous round Of plaguing ills, which higher ranks confound." [221]

Impressed with the healthful temperance of country life, Dr. John Armstrong heartily sanctioned the routine of rural labour:

> Behold, the labourer of the glebe, who toils
> In dust, in rain, in cold and sultry skies. . . .
> He knows no laws by Esculapius given;
> He studies none. Yet him nor midnight fogs
> Infest, nor those envenom'd shafts that fly
> When rapid Sirius fires the autumnal noon.
> His habit pure with plain and temperate meals,

Robust with labour, and by custom steel'd,
To every casualty of varied life;
Serene he bears the peevish eastern blast,
And uninfected breathes the mortal south.
　　Such the reward of rude and sober life;
Of labor such. By health the peasant's toil
Is well repaid . . .[222]

More rollicking than the good doctor, John Winstanley remarked cheerfully:

> Then how pleasant and contented,
> 　Lives the lowly country clown
> In the valley unfrequented
> 　By the knaves who crowd the town.
> With the early lark awaking,
> 　He enjoys the chearful day;
> Labour ev'ry hour partaking
> Whistling thought and care away.[223]

This was soft primitivism, as Dr. Armstrong's had been primitivism of the hard variety. Soft also was the atmosphere of Thomson's story of Lavinia and Palemon.[224]

Allan Ramsay enlivened a dialogue between "He" and "She" with scraps of vivid detail about the vanities of town and the pleasures of the country.[225] His characters, off to the rural delights of oxen and apple trees, of corn and turkeys, of home-spun wool and linen, were glad for such joys to forego beaux and belles, dicers and knights, taverns and parks, and all the varied train of town wits and wickedness. "He" had the last word:

> Stockjobbers and swobbers,
> And packers and tackers,
> For ever adieu, and for ever:
> We know what you're doing,
> And home we are going;
> And so you may ring your bells.[226]

Ramsay managed a distinctively gay note, but most of the poets, even the celebrated ones, had only run-of-the-mill verses on the theme.

Edward Young reminded his readers that innocence sports on the green, while

> In wealthy towns
> Proud labour frowns,
> And painted sorrow smiles in courts.[227]

Samuel Johnson contributed a stately description of lowly content:

> When statutes glean the refuse of the sword,
> How much more safe the vassal than the lord,
> Low sculks the hind beneath the rage of pow'r,
> And leaves the wealthy traytor in the Tow'r,
> Untouch'd his cottage, and his slumbers sound,
> Tho' confiscation's vultures hover round.[228]

Joseph Warton slightly cracked the traditional mould by adorning his conventional moral with a hint of Nature's beauties:

> O falsely fond of what seems great,
> Of purple pomp, and robes of state,
>   And all life's tinsel glare!
> Rather with humble violets bind,
> Or give to wanton in the wind,
>   Your length of sable hair.[229]

To most of the poets the poor man was a traditional symbol—to a few of them he was a rollicking reality. A small group of verses, most of them by Allan Ramsay and Henry Carey, were not ashamed to celebrate a happy-go-lucky collection of lowly folk that ranged in respectability, or lack of it, from the "true tarr" to the queen of the beggars.

Such humble poor were perfectly complacent. The "true tarr" [230] prized his content above the diamonds of a dishonest knave. The miller had a steady satisfaction in life:

> He eats when he's hungry, and drinks when he's dry,
> And down when he's weary contented does ly,

Then rises up chearful to work and to sing:
If so happy a miller, then who'd be a king? [231]

The happy shepherd boasted his pleasant dreams above the restless
slumbers of city folk.[232] The cobbler's sole worry was his wife—
"and her he can strap if she vex him." [233] The surly peasant stood
stolidly for his rights:

A fig for your sir or your madam;
Our origin all is from Adam;
Then why should I buckle,
Palaver or truckle
To any pragmatical chuckle? [234]

At one end of the scale, one of the most mannerly of the poor folk,
Shenstone's schoolmistress, had a dignified simplicity:

A russet stole was o'er her shoulders thrown;
A russet kirtle fenc'd the nipping air;
'Twas her own country bred the flok so fair!
'Twas her own labour did the fleece prepare;
And, sooth to say, her pupils, rang'd around
Through pious awe, did term it passing rare;
For they in gaping wonderment abound,
And think, no doubt, she been the greatest wight on ground.[235]

At the opposite extreme, the happy beggars, forerunners perhaps
of Burns' vagabond crew, were brazen in the boast:

We know no shame or scandal,
The beggars law befriends us;
We all agree in liberty,
And poverty defends us.[236]

With such lighthearted models, no wonder a poet could vow
"and therefore a beggar, a beggar I'll be, For there's none leads a
life more jocund than he." [237]

Of all types of praiseworthy poor, the country girl easily won
the palm for popularity.[238] Sometimes she adorned the verse as
Chloe or Phyllis, tricked out in the dainty manners of a Dresden

shepherdess: more often she was Lizzie or Sally or Kitty, complete with milk pail or butter churn. Whatever her name, she was a diligent beauty, "superior to the shining toys of looser maidens, indolent with ease." [239] She spun, refrained from cards and scandal, and loved sincerely without mercenary motives. [240] She was quite capable of flinging down the gage to her urban rivals:

> Altho' I be but a country-lass,
> Yet a lofty mind I bear—O,
> And think mysell as good as those
> That rich apparel wear—O.
> Altho' my gown be hame-spun grey,
> My skin it is as saft—O
> As them that sattin weeds do wear,
> And carry their heads aloft—O. [241]

What wonder that such spirited and industrious lasses were recommended to bachelors as excellent matches. [242]

There is a strain of hard primitivism among the rural belles. They were practical, thrifty, prudent. Faced with the difficulties of life on a limited budget they could declare with confidence:

> I value no dainties a button,
> Coarse food will our stomachs allay;
> If we cannot get veal, beef, and mutton,
> A chine and a pudding we may.

> A fig for your richest brocadings;
> In lindsey there's nothing that's base;
> Your finery soon sets a fading,
> My dowlass will last beyond lace. [243]

Here and there heroines appeared by name. Lavinia, before she fell victim to the town's corrupting influence, "claim'd every charm that recommends a wife; Chearful, not airy, clean but never fine, Meek, humble, bashful, and a good divine." Kitty, the "good-humour'd highland lassie," blushing Fanny, "thrice happy Lizzie," Flora and Galatea, Chloe and Phyllis queened it over the poets' hearts. [244] Most original of the artless beauties was "Sally at the

Chop-house, at the Lamb behind the Royal-Exchange," to whom
a grateful customer penned the novel tribute:

> Dear Sally, emblem of the chop-house ware,
>   As broth reviving, and as white bread fair;
> As small beer grateful, and as pepper strong;
> As beef-stake tender, as fresh pot herbs young;
> As sharp as knife, and piercing as a fork,
> Soft as new butter, white as fairest pork;
> Sweet as young mutton, brisk as bottl'd beer;
> Smooth as is oil, juicy as cucumber,
> And bright as cruet void of vinegar.[245]

Sally might have an urban setting, but she was kin in charm to
the rural beauties.

All in all, the country belle of the poets with her fore-shadowing of Burns' Highland Mary, and her echoes of Swift and Gay's
Molly Mog, is very like the simple lass who carried off as husband
"the gay, the loud, the vain Will Honeycomb." [246] Will's prose re-
port of her charms may stand as a summary of her sisters in poetry:

> She is born of honest parents, and though she has no portion,
> she has a great deal of virtue. The natural sweetness and inno-
> cence of her behavior, the freshness of her complexion, the un-
> affected turn of her shape and person, shot me through and
> through every time I saw her, and did more execution upon
> me in grogram, than the greatest beauty in town or court had
> ever done in brocade.[247]

A touch of homespun reality, an affectionate air of kinship with
the poor adds charm even to the least skilled of the poems that celebrate specific members of the poorer classes. Neither the pen por-
traits nor their authors are particularly distinguished, but they do
possess a breath of life which the reader hails with welcome relief
after a series of moralizings borrowed from Juvenal and Seneca.

Unhappy restless man, who first disdain'd these peace-
ful labours, gentle rural tasks, perform'd with such de-
light! What pride or what ambition bred this scorn?
Hence all those fatal evils of your race. . . . Not satis-
fy'd to turn and manure for their use the wholesome
and beneficial mould of this their earth, they dig yet
deeper, and seeking out imaginary wealth, they search
its very entrails . . .[248]

—*Shaftesbury*, Moralists, *3*

The poets who celebrated the poor man's lot would have agreed
with Shaftesbury. Their repeated praises of the country poor and
their almost total disregard of the urban laborer and the miner,
were kin in spirit to his contempt for those who disdained "gentle
rural tasks" to follow the call of pride and ambition. Their varied
denunciations of luxury were close to the philosopher's terse criticism—"hence all those fatal evils of your race."

Wealth to these writers was the force which visited on England
a complex series of evils:

> Can wealth give happiness? look round, and see
> What gay distress! what splendid misery! [249]

So Edward Young stated the case: his fellow poets would have
echoed him to a man. The luxury they all feared was real enough.
Shipping was booming, land prices were on the rise, money was
plentiful. In twenty-five years, the average annual exports of England had increased five million pounds.[250] As early as 1725 Daniel
Defoe was complaining about the spirit of luxury that was demoral-
izing the tradesmen of the metropolis:

> there was never a time when luxury and extravagance were
> at so great a height. The apprentices now-a-days, in dress and
> appearance far outgo what their masters did formerly; and
> many young beginners rather ape the gaieties of the court than
> appear like what the grave and sober citizens of the last cen-
> tury were willing to be thought and to appear to be . . .[251]

The prosperity which had alarmed Defoe continued to grow up to and past the half-century mark. In 1748 John Chamberlayne might praise trade as the mainstay of that prosperity:

> But that which makes us so considerable in the eyes of the world is the wonderful greatness of our maritime trade; for upon the three articles of exportation, transportation or re-exportation, and importation, no kingdom or state in the world can any ways match us.[252]

But three years after Chamberlayne's expression of pride in the greatness of English commercial enterprise, Fielding was blaming that rise in trade for the spread of vice among the lower classes of Englishmen:

> But nothing hath wrought such an alteration in this order of people, as the introduction of trade. This hath indeed given a new face to the whole nation, hath in a great measure sub-verted the former state of affairs, and hath almost totally changed the manners, customs, and habits of the people, more especially of the lower sort. The narrowness of their fortune is changed into wealth; the simplicity of their manners into craft; their frugality into luxury; their humility into pride, and their subjection into equality.[253]

Although, as Fielding noted, politicians will praise trade, and de-cry luxury, the two are really inseparable, and if one be sought, the second must follow. Britain had gained in trade, she had gained in luxury; hence of necessity she had gained in crime:

> First then, I think, that the vast torrent of luxury which of late years hath poured itself into this nation, hath greatly con-tributed to produce, among many others, the mischief I here complain of. . . . it reaches the very dregs of the people, who aspiring still to a degree beyond that which belongs to them, and not being able by the fruits of honest labour to support the state which they affect, they disdain the wages to which their industry would entitle them; and abandoning themselves to idleness, the more simple and poor-spirited betake themselves

to a state of starving and beggary, while those of more art and courage become thieves, sharpers, and robbers.[254]

Finding the traditional theme of the evils of wealth amply justified by contemporary conditions, the poets were loud in their protests. Loudest of all were Thomson, Young and Pope. The first part of Thomson's *Castle of Indolence* abounded in expositions of the vanities of man's quest for power and wealth,[255] the city's "giddy rout," "the puzzling sons of party," "the nations all on fire, In cruel broils engaged, and deadly strife." His commentary on the evil had a gently persuasive tone:

> O grievous folly! to heap up estate,
> Losing the days you see beneath the sun;
> When, sudden, comes blind unrelenting fate,
> And gives the untasted portion you have won
> With ruthless toil, and many a wretch undone,
> To those who mock you gone to Pluto's reign,
> There with sad ghosts to pine, and shadows dun . . .[256]

In other words, Thomson protested, not the uselessness of luxury to the individual, but its degrading influence upon the state. In *Liberty* he censured "luxury rapacious, cruel, mean, Mother of vice," [257] and in *Britannia*, even in the midst of his paean to England's power he prayed that his country might be spared the dire consequences of increasing wealth:

> Oh, let not the soft penetrating plague
> Creep on the freeborn mind and working there,
> With the sharp tooth of many a new-formed want,
> Endless, and idle all, eat out the heart
> Of liberty; the high conception blast;
> The noble sentiment, the impatient scorn
> Of base subjection, and the swelling wish
> For general good, erasing from the mind.[258]

The same theme of the corruption of a state by riches fired the third of Pope's *Moral Epistles*. His attack on wealth was sharper and more biting than Thomson's. The sad career of "a plain good man, and Balaam was his name," [259] who began as a poor respectable citizen and ended a traitor on the gallows, served to point the moral of the evils of luxury. "The Devil and the King divide the prize, And sad Sir Balaam curses God and dies." [260]

Pope gave the old tale of political evil a new twist in his lament that modern paper credit had made bribery so simple and so convenient:

> Blest paper credit! last and best supply!
> That lends corruption lighter wings to fly!
> Gold imp'd by thee, can compass hardest things,
> Can pocket states, can fetch and carry kings;
> A single leaf shall waft an army o'er,
> Or ship off senates to some distant shore. . . .
> Pregnant with thousands flits the scrap unseen,
> And silent sells a King or buys a Queen.[261]

While Pope protested the political evils of wealth, Edward Young, both in his early satire the *Love of Fame* and in his later *Night Thoughts,* decried luxury as the bane of the individual soul. Warning that "gold glitters most, where virtue shines no more," [262] he depicted with grim seriousness the insatiable quality of man's passion for wealth:

> Dost court abundance for the sake of peace?
> Learn, and lament thy self-defeated scheme:
> Riches enable to be richer still;
> And richer still, what mortal can resist?
> Thus wealth (a cruel taskmaster!) enjoins
> New toils, succeeding toils, an endless train!
> And murders peace, which taught it first to shine.
> The poor are half as wretched as the rich;
> Whose proud and painful privilege it is
> At once, to bear a double load of woe;
> To feel the stings of envy, and of want,
> Outrageous want! both Indies cannot cure.[263]

Love of gold, "the meanest of amours," [264] cheated its victim with its ultimate uselessness:

> Can gold calm passion, or make reason shine?
> Can we dig peace, or wisdom, from the mine?
> Wisdom to gold prefer; for 'tis much less
> To make our fortune, than our happiness.[265]

Gold penalized its followers by leading them into vice:

> For sordid lucre plunge we in the mire?
> Drudge, sweat, through every shame, for every gain,
> For vile contaminating trash; throw up
> Our hope in heaven, our dignity with man?
> And deify the dirt, matured to gold? [266]

Such condemnations of luxury by the major poets make it easy for the reader to examine in proper perspective the sympathy which they offered to the victims of that luxury—the poor.

> *The sufferings of the poor are indeed less observed than their misdeeds; not from any want of compassion, but because they are less known. . . . But if we were to make a progress through the outskirts of this town, and look into the habitations of the poor, we should there behold such pictures of human misery as must move the compassion of every heart that deserves the name of human.*[267]

—*Fielding*, Proposals . . . Poor

What to do with ever growing numbers of indigent citizens puzzled the eighteenth century, as it has continued to puzzle the nineteenth and the twentieth. Then as now the opposing schools of public and private charity offered solutions to the problem of poor relief. In the persons of Sir Roger de Coverley and Sir Andrew Freeport [268] the *Spectator* papers furnished classic examples of both opinions. Sir Roger would give liberally to beggars, and go his complacent way, haloed with prayers and blessings. Sir Andrew would put his faith in state-administered charity, circumscribed by rule and law:

Besides I see no occasion for this charity to common beggars, since every beggar is an inhabitant of a parish, and every parish is taxed to the maintenance of their own poor. For my own part, I cannot be mightily pleased with the laws which have done this, which have provided better to feed than employ the poor.[269]

If concern with poor law legislation is any indication of popular interest the good merchant's countrymen seem to have been of his opinion. The Workhouse Act, and the constantly rising poor rates had made eighteenth-century England "a country where the poor are, beyond all comparison, more liberally provided for than in any other part of the habitable globe": [270] but alas for the hopes of those who expected state aid to vanquish poverty,—despite repeated poor law statutes, England remained a nation in which "there should be found more beggars, more distrest and miserable objects than are to be seen throughout all the states of Europe." [271]

Conscious perhaps of the weightiness of the problem, the poets did not attempt to solve the question of poor relief; they remained content to commiserate poverty without seeking to cure it. They were quick to sympathize with the sufferings by which the poor counterbalanced the extravagances of the rich. Lofty columns and "the united arts of Greece and Rome" [272] could not cover the infamy of the lord who kept a hundred servants to insure his comfort and that of his hangers-on:

> These sons of sloth who by profusion thrive,
> His pride inveigled from the public hive:
> And numbers pine in solitary woe,
> Who furnish'd out this phantasy of show.[273]

The haughty lord need not admire his proud forests and gilded turrets:

> While guilt's black train each conscious walk invade,
> And cries of orphans haunt him in the shade.
> Mistaken man! by crimes to hope for fame!
> Thy imag'd glory leads to real shame . . .[274]

"The gay licentious proud" should remember their precarious hold on life and pause in their pleasure-mad course to pity those who, at every moment, perish in the flood, languish in prison, and "shrink into the sordid hut Of cheerless poverty." [275] The wealthy man of kindly heart did not heap up greater riches "to leave a race more exquisitely poor," [276] but scattered his gold to help the needy. The just country gentleman gave up London pleasures to remain with his people, insuring their loyalty to himself and to their country, as his forefathers had insur'd it, "by succor, faithful counsel, courteous cheer." [277]

Few must have heeded the poets' advice, for the admonitions in verse endlessly recounted the hardships of the poor. The rich cheated them of their birthright. Sometimes the elements themselves seemed to conspire against them. Scarcely a reader of eighteenth-century poetry has failed to mourn Thomson's snow-trapped swain,[278] or to pay the tribute of a sigh to his sympathetic description of the unfortunate peasant who sees flocks, farm and home swept away in the Autumn floods:

> . . . all that the wind had spared
> In one wild moment ruined, the big hopes
> And well-earned treasures of the painful year. . . .
> Yes, masters, then
> Be mindful of the rough laborious hand
> That sinks you soft in elegance and ease;
> Be mindful of those limbs in russet clad
> Whose toil to yours is warmth and graceful pride;
> And oh, be mindful of that sparing board
> Which covers yours with luxury profuse,
> Makes your glass sparkle, and your sense rejoice;
> Nor cruelly demand what the deep rains
> And all-involving winds have swept away! [279]

Thomson's injunction to masters was in keeping with his native spirit of benevolence: that such reminders were sorely needed, is clear from the lines of later poets who pictured the poor man ground down by driving overseers:

The poor man labours for his bread in vain,
Whilst the stern master, heedless of his pain,
Keeps back the wages of his weekly task,
And frowns and threatens, if he's bold to ask:
The weary slave goes home with wat'ry eyes,
And languishes for Nature's due supplies.
The Mother and her babes together mourn,
Finding no kind relief at his return;
They all are pinch'd, all want the dear earn'd stock
That should suffice himself and little flock.[280]

Public-spirited poets might assure their fellowmen that "man by nature free, by nature made" [281] had inalienable rights to a share in Nature's produce, but for too many of the poor those rights to a livelihood remained idle theories:

Satan, the world, and sin too long
    Have robb'd the children of their bread,
Poor labouring souls they suffer'd wrong,
    Nor saw their legal toil succeed.[282]

Want sought relief in vain.[283] Hunger and pain and winter cold might be the poor man's lot, but it got him little compassion from his prosperous neighbors: "the meagre visage, and the garment rent, Furnish out subjects for their sawcy cruel merriment." [284]

Under the circumstances it was scarcely surprising that poverty-harried Londoners tried to drown their troubles:

Oft here I've seen the lees of mortal race,
Whom want and hunger, dread companions, ey'd
With ghastly grin askance, quaff the rich juice,
Till the strong fumes intoxicate their brain.[285]

They might drink their troubles out of mind, but they could be assured of unnumbered lecturings and punishments for their misdeeds when they were sober enough to be conscious of them. Expediency dictated that horrible examples for moralizing purposes should be taken from the ranks of the poor. As Dick Steele had observed with quiet irony,[286] "it is not, it seems, within the rules

of good breeding to tax the vices of people of quality, and the com-
mandments were made for the vulgar."

Certainly the poor had need enough of poetic sympathy. Sometimes the poet's sentiments were sharpened by a note of personal
suffering.[287] Johnson's complaint, "slow rises worth, by poverty
depress'd," [288] might have served as motto for the host of starving
eighteenth-century writers who attempted to keep alive by literary endeavor. The bitterness of personal experience backed Johnson's charge:

> All crimes are safe, but hated poverty.
> This, only this, provokes the snarling muse,
> This, only this the rigid law pursues.[289]

Such first-hand resentment of the hardships of poverty was a
far cry from Gray's gentle expressions of sympathy for the underprivileged:

> Let not ambition mock their useful toil,
> Their homely joys, and destiny obscure;
> Nor Grandeur hear with a disdainful smile,
> The short and simple annals of the poor.[290]

In contrast to Johnson's vigorous lines, the milder bard's sentiments seem faintly condescending.

Smollett, who, like Johnson, had known the grinding bitterness
of poverty, exploded in verse which was the antithesis of that rose-
colored tradition which persisted in finding the poor man's lot a
happy one:

> Enough, enough; all this we knew before;
> 'Tis infamous, I grant it, to be poor:
> And who so much to sense and glory lost,
> Will hug the curse that not one joy can boast!
> From the pale hag, O! could I once break loose;
> Divorc'd, all hell shall not re-tie the noose! [291]

Despite Smollett's violence and Johnson's grimness, the poems
which broke through the pretty tradition of the happy poor were
in the minority. Idyllic pictures of poverty carried the day—evi-

dence once more of the triumph of literary convention in the face of harsh reality.

Though you deck your hall from end to end with an-
cient waxen images, virtue is the one and only true no-
bility.[292]

—*Juvenal,* Satires, *8*

Even the urbane aristocracy of eighteenth-century London was not proof against the venerable tradition of the nobility of the poor but honest man. Steele had reproved his generation: "It is to me a very great meanness, and something much below a philosopher, which is what I mean by a gentleman, to rank a man among the vulgar for the condition of life he is in, and not according to his behavior, his thoughts and sentiments, in that condition." [293] More than a quarter of a century after Steele, Samuel Johnson was expressing, in his dignified periods, much the same opinion of the relationship of wealth and merit: [294] "wealth cannot confer greatness, for nothing can make that great, which the decree of nature has ordained to be little."

And in the years between the gentle didacticism of the *Tatler* and the formal moralizing of the *Rambler,* the poets had been busy reminding Englishmen that some humble hearts for merit might claim a crown, that a peasant's soul was equal to a monarch's, that wealth and pride of name were as nothing compared to lowly virtue, that in the end "an honest man's the noblest work of God." [295]

The country clown's honest heart made up for his lack of the courtier's grace, "the supple knee, and promisory [sic] face." [296] Highborn ladies must remember that "nature makes no distinction, Between the high blood and low." [297] "Birth, honours, or the empty name of great," could not of themselves purchase happiness: industry alone gave value to titles.[298]

The emptiness of high position was a favorite subject with the writers.[299] A democratic poet challenged the aristocracy:

Say, what's nobility, ye gilded train!
Does nature give it, or can guilt sustain. . . .

What! though a long patrician line ye claim,
Are noble souls entail'd upon a name?

The fame of a low-born genius would outlive those "gilded titles, empty things." Virtue, the true nobility, outshone a beau's ribbons, or a minister's titles. The poor might boast, "we'll shine with more substantial honours, And to be noble, we'll be good."
    Pope's telling couplets summed up every phase of the subject. Pride of birth was a delusion:

What can ennoble sots, or slaves, or cowards?
Alas! not all the blood of all the Howards.[300]

Kings were slaves in comparison to humble men of merit.[301] Titles fell by the wayside, but the dignity of lowly virtue endured.[302] Again Pope gave the decisive statement of the case:

Worth makes the man, and want of it, the fellow;
The rest is all but leather or prunella.[303]

Only one of Pope's contemporaries was not wholly represented by the terse couplets of the supreme neo-classicist. Here as elsewhere Edward Young deviated from the common path. Like his fellows he admitted that [304] "merit in a low estate" outranked [305] "vice, though descended from the conqueror," and that an honest man was in worth superior to a king.[306] But he justified the essential democracy of mankind on a slightly different basis. Not content with emphasizing the levelling power of virtue, he explained the relations between men on the grounds of their spiritual kinship:

The monarch and his slave;—'A deathless soul,
Unbounded prospect, and immortal kin,
A father God, and brothers in the skies';
Elder, indeed, in time, but less remote
In excellence, perhaps, than thought by man;
Why greater what can fall, than what can rise? [307]

As usual, Young's approach was spiritual where the approach of his contemporaries was philosophical or ethical. Allowing for Edward Young's ultimate explanation of human brotherhood, the most representative statement of early eighteenth-century poets' concept of the poor man's worth was Pope's restatement of an axiom old as the world itself:

> A Wit's a feather, and a Chief a rod;
> An Honest Man's the noblest work of God.[308]

PART TWO

Vivere Secundum Naturam

The history of primitivism is in great part a phase of a larger historical tendency . . . the use of the term "nature" to express the standard of human values, the identity of good with that which is "natural" or "according to nature."
—*Lovejoy*, Documentary Evidence

Philosophical Aspects

NEVER had the ambiguous injunction *Vivere Secundum Naturam* held more complex and more contradictory meanings than it did for the eighteenth century. Man had long looked to Nature for a model, but the new astronomy and the discoveries of micro-biology had given him as pattern a universe that encompassed at once the realms of infinite space and the design of the microscopic atom.[1] "Worlds within worlds of infinite minuteness"[2] springing to life under his microscope taught man the lesson of universal variety. "Those wild fields of ether, that reach in height as far as from Saturn to the fixed stars, and run abroad almost to an infinitude,"[3] overwhelmed him with a realization of cosmic immensity.

In the faint of heart the grandeur of the universe awakened Pascal's despairing question, "what is man in the Infinite?"[4] and the millions of creatures crowding creation evoked feelings of bewilderment and fear. But braver souls watched the cosmic show with eagerness and enthusiasm. With Shaftesbury they hailed the marvels of the world:

> All nature's wonders serve to excite and perfect this idea of their author. . . . Whence we are naturally taught the immensity of that being, who thro these immense spaces has dispos'd such an infinitude of bodys, belonging each as we may well presume to systems as compleat as our own world: since even the smallest spark of this bright galaxy may vie with this our sun; which shining now full out, gives us new life, exalts our spirits, and makes us feel divinity more present.[5]

Whether they quailed or whether they exulted, eighteenth-century gentlemen were fascinated by the spectacle of creation. Deeply impressed by the successful efforts which men of their generation had made to explain the structure of the universe, they took heart at the thought that, in time, man, "that little insignificant figure" in the universe, might yet understand the great system around him. They studied on, believing that "the more extended our reason is, and the more able to grapple with immense objects, the greater still are those discoveries which it makes of wisdom and providence in the works of creation." [6] Their quest for knowledge was lighted by the master genius of their time. Thanks to the achievements of Newton, men might find the cosmic heavens a comfortable country, vast indeed, but conveniently charted for human exploring. Well might the eighteenth century repeat with added emphasis the pleasant boast of Richard Cumberland in the preceding age:

> We congratulate, indeed the happy genius of this learned age, that the intellectual part of the world has been much illustrated by that great accession of light which former proofs of the Being of God, and the Immortality of the Soul have receiv'd from the daily increasing knowledge of the inferior part of matter. We also congratulate, both the present age and posterity, that, now at length, the material part of the universe begins to be explain'd by introducing Mathematicks into the study of nature.[7]

While the physics of Newton assured them of the order of creation, and the discoveries of the micro-biologists illustrated for them its variety, the favorite concepts of eighteenth-century philosophy served further to strengthen men's belief that all things under the sun had at last been rendered comprehensible. The principle of plenitude (that popular eighteenth-century version of the Platonic *plenum formarum*) justified the teeming variety of the universe: the chain of being (given impetus at the close of the preceding century in the discussions of Locke) ordered the endless varieties of existence into a regular scale.[8]

To any who felt that the discoveries of science had reduced man to an insignificant speck in a tremendous system, Locke's chain brought the comforting reassurance that *homo sapiens* was a necessary part of the scheme of things. No gap was possible in the chain of being: midway between nothing and the Infinite, the link marked "man" helped hold the creation together:

> In this system of being, there is no creature so wonderful in its nature, and which so much deserves our particular attention, as man, who fills up the middle space between the animal and intellectual nature, the visible and invisible world, and is that link in the chain of beings which has been often termed the *nexus utriusque mundi*.[9]

As man in his midway link contemplated the creation of which he was a part, he felt with renewed perplexity the fundamental problem posed by the doctrine of *vivere secundum naturam*. Should he try to duplicate in his works the wild variety of a superabundant, riotous creation? Should he imitate the regularity of an essentially ordered world? In aesthetics the dual concept of Nature forced on him a choice between lawless genius and rule-bound artistry, in morals, a decision between the life of feeling and the life of reason.

The problem was as acute for early eighteenth-century poets as it was for all men of their generation. In their more or less philosophical speculations they reacted to the vision of the universe according to their temperaments; some were awed, some inspired, a few were depressed. Most of them loved the new worlds of the vast and the minute, and accepted the current conviction that the world had been explained as the best world possible. In aesthetic discussions they continued the old feud between genius and the rules, and fought out a lively skirmish between divergent concepts of external Nature. On moral questions they turned either to reason or to passion as principles of life: extremists among them backed stoic contempt of feeling or the naturalistic life of instinct.

As we follow them from philosophy to literature, from literature to life, we are conscious of the changing concepts of Nature which influenced their views on the universe about them, the landscapes before them, the authors they read, the lives they lived (or rather the principles by which they professed to live). Whether they criticized the structure of the creation or the design of a garden, the practise of a dramatist or the manners of a belle, behind all their speculations lay the Sphinx-like mystery of Nature,

—a term that meant many things to many men—especially to men of the eighteenth century.

The Chain of Being

The whole chasm of nature, from a plant to a man, is filled up with diverse kinds of creatures, rising one over another, by such gentle and easy ascent, that the little transitions and deviations from one species to another are almost insensible. This intermediate space is so well husbanded and managed, that there is scarce a degree of perception which does not appear in some one part of the world of life. . . . If the scale of being rises by such a regular progress so high as man, we may, by a parity of reason, suppose that it still proceeds gradually through those beings which are of a superior nature to him.[10]

—Spectator *No. 519*

The energy with which poets pursued the theme of the chain of being was charged with a vivid satisfaction in the scientific advances of their times, a pride in their own era which had pushed the frontiers of knowledge to the edge of cosmic horizons. They never forgot that thanks to the discoveries of Newton their generation was liberated from the hazy doubts of the past and set free to spread its intellectual wings in an enlightened universe. "The system never was from errors free, Till Newton rose and said, Let darkness flee." [11] More than a half century after the *Principia* men were still exulting:

But here, we're brought to banquet with the gods!
To know great nature's laws and secret springs!
Th' eternal order of the works divine!
And truths conceal'd from all the ages past.[12]

Newton had put his age and race above all times and nations. He had outdone the ancient worthies, "at thy Newton all their laurels fade"; [13] he had eclipsed the moderns. "Hugenus, Tycho, Kepler, high in fame, Bow to the honours of an English name." [14] For his countrymen, and for all men Newton had untwisted the "golden threads of light," unmasked the harmony of the universe, laid bare the "Soul of Nature" and marked the Almighty in the rolling spheres.[15] "The lamp of science through the jealous maze Of nature guides," [16] and while Newton held high that lamp the poets could watch at will

> where wedded worlds far distant worlds embrace
> With mutual bands, yet keep their destin'd space;
> Roll endless measures through th' etherial plain,
> Link'd by the social, strong, attractive chain.[17]

"The strong attractive chain" which held the planets in their courses was a fit emblem of that interdependent system of creation which bound together all beings in existence. "From lowly reptiles to the pride of man," [18] and thence to the power of the Almighty, the immense design of the chain of being ranked every creature in orderly gradation:

> from the seraph's intellectual ray,
> To reason's spark, that gilds our sensual clay;
> To life (scarce conscious) in th' instinctive brute;
> To reptile, plant, and vegetating root;
> The features in conspicuous semblance shine,
> And speak, through all, One Parent all Divine.[19]

While they admired the structure of the "long chain of miracles," [20] the poets were quick to mark its essential democracy. Pope might gently chide ambitious man, "all are but parts of one stupendous whole," [21] but Henry Brooke had a sharper reminder for human pride:

> Alas! what's man, thus insolent and vain?
> One single link of nature's mighty chain.
> Each hated toad, each crawling worm we see,
> Is needful to the whole as well as he.

> Like some grand building is the universe,
> Where ev'ry part is useful in its place;
> As well the pins, which all together hold,
> As the rich carvings, or the glowing gold.[22]

Wherever man looked for poetic counsel he found the same note of warning. He was but a link in an infinite series, he must rest content, "plac'd on this isthmus of a middle state, A Being darkly wise, and rudely great."[23] Like Gulliver in Lilliput he might retain some shreds of pride by reflecting on the infinite series of beings beneath him, but like Gulliver in Brobdingnag, his pride must turn to dust at the recollection of the legions of superior beings above him: "since there is an infinitely greater space and room for different degrees of perfection, between the Supreme Being and man, than between man and the most despicable insect."[24] Higher than man in the scale were creatures so wonderful that

> Superior beings, when of late they saw
> A mortal man unfold all Nature's law,
> Admir'd such wisdom in an earthly shape,
> And shew'd a NEWTON as we shew an ape.[25]

To a generation that all but deified Newton the simile had a special force. Overawed by the poetic clamor reminding him of his limited sphere,[26] man might yet find a crumb of comfort in Edward Young's insistence that man was needed to hold together the material and immaterial halves of creation:

> Connexion exquisite of distant worlds!
> Distinguish'd link in being's endless chain!
> Midway from nothing to the Deity![27]

Through all the poets' expressions of admiration for the architecture of the chain of being, through all their descriptions of man's status in the whole, the reader can sense their lively satisfaction in the order of creation. The poets who revel in the gradations of the chain, in its uniformity and its regularity, marvel at Nature as at a great machine, complex in its numberless parts, but ordered in its complexity:

Nature, bright effulence of the One Supreme!
O how connected is thy wondrous frame!
Thy grand machine, through many a wanton maze,
Steer'd where it winds, and strait'ning where it strays,
There most direct where seeming most inflex'd,
As though perfection on disorder hung,
And perfect order from incaution sprung.[28]

This was the reasonable, orderly way of looking at the universe.
But there were many poets who admired less the neat order of the
chain of being than the infinite variety involved in the principle
of plenitude. Dazzled by the vision of the science-illumined universe, they gazed in rapture at the mighty plan wherein infinite
order was matched with infinite variety:

How well this orb, where fate has fix'd thy lot:
Seest thou one useless or one empty spot?
Observe, the air, the waters, and the earth,
Each moment give ten thousand creatures birth.
Here, ev'ry place, so far from lying waste,
With life is crouded, and with beauty grac'd:
Nor can those other worlds, unknown by thee,
Less stor'd with creatures, or with beauty, be.
For God is uniform in all his Ways,
And every where his boundless pow'r displays:
His Goodness fills immensurable space,
Restrain'd by time nor limited to place . . .[29]

The endless diversity of creation convinced them that "infinite
goodness is of so communicative a nature that it seems to delight in
the conferring of existence upon every degree of perceptive being." [30] They rejoiced that

Nature delights in variety; every element abounds with species
of a different kind. A thousand, and ten thousand sorts of
birds wing the regions of the air. The waters produce as great
a number of different kinds of finny inhabitants.—The earth
of reptiles, insects, and beasts; and even men, when born in

different climates, differ in colour, shape, and manners from each other.[31]

They saw God less as the Infinite Designer, than as the Infinite Creator, the "Godhead streaming through a thousand worlds," [32] "whose blessings all without distinction share." [33] He was the endlessly creating Power, pouring Himself throughout the universe:

> Profusely—wide the boundless blessings flow,
> Which heav'n enrich, and gladden worlds below!
> Which are no less, when properly defin'd,
> Than emanations of th' Eternal Mind.[34]

All manner of things received their being from His Hands:

> Yet endless how, from One! each varying essence flows;
> Each vegetable set in beds of bliss,
> Their sap exhaling from the Prime Abyss.[35]

Akenside described that outpouring of Divine Bounty:

> Know then, the Sovereign Spirit of the world,
> Though, self-collected from eternal time . . .
> Yet by immense benignity inclined
> To spread around him that primeval joy
> Which fill'd himself, he raised his plastic arm,
> And sounded through the hollow depths of space
> The strong, creative mandate. Straight arose
> Those heavenly orbs, the glad abodes of life,
> Effusive kindled by his breath divine
> Through endless forms of being . . .[36]

Those "endless forms of being" enchanted the poets. "How eager is the prying busy mind, The heights and depths of nature's works to find." [37] The telescope had shown them "new worlds on high," the microscope revealed "new scenes of wonders here." [38] The marvels of the starry heavens represented one kind of variety: the miracles of microscopic phenomena another: poets welcomed both:

> Hence let me to immensity wide-stretch
> Imagination, lab'ring to conceive

Planets, and stars, and firmaments, and suns,
And worlds, sunk in unfathomable depths
Of aether, till weak fancy's narrowness
In Nature's multiplicity is lost.
     Then let me in profoundest thought again
Work downwards thro' the gradual descents
Of magnitude, from vastness of the sun
To pygmy bulk of man, again from thence
To viewless mites, by steps insensible
Decreasing;—Thence pursue a particle
Of matter thro' th' untold varieties
Of infinite divisibility.
—Then fancy (if 'tis possible for men
To fancy) how each infinite division,
Fashion'd and molded by Omnipotence,
New quantities of matter may produce,
New suns, new worlds, another universe.[39]

Dearly as the poets loved "planets, and stars, and firmaments, and suns," and all the grand phenomena of Nature, they had as lively a curiosity about the minutiae of creation:

The train of beings, all the gradual scale
Descending, sumless orders and degrees;
Th' unfounded depth, which mortals dare not try.[40]

Not a few of them dared that "unfounded depth" with the help of that fashionable toy, the microscope. Most willingly they heeded the admonition, "extend thy narrow sight: consult with Art: And gladly use what helps it can impart." [41] Doubtless they hoped, as did the "Female Spectator," that

A little time, therefore, given to consideration of these, which are by a vulgar eye looked upon as the most insignificant works of nature, could not fail leading us to contemplation of a more elevated kind, and be one great step towards rendering our ideas sublime, refined, and pure, and fit to travel through the immense wonders of those starry heavens, which we behold with so much admiration.[42]

Give them a miscroscope and a summer evening and they were free to watch with delight "the buzzing insect families appear":

> Stretch'd out in bulk, within the polish'd glass;
> Thro' whose small convex, a new world we spy,
> Ne'er seen before, but by a seraph's eye.
> So long in darkness, shut from human-kind,
> Lay half God's wonders, to a point confined;
> But in one peopled drop we now survey,
> In pride of pow'r, some little monster play;
> O'er tribes invisible, he reigns alone,
> And struts, the tyrant of a world his own.[43]

Even the internal as well as the external structure of the infinitely tiny creatures stirred their speculations:

> Their smallness hides them from the naked eye;
>   But Fancy their construction could perceive
> And wand'ring thro' the veins could plainly spy
>   The wond'rous animation they receive.
> By circling blood convey'd, I travers'd o'er,
>   The microcosm's slender fabrick view'd,
> Saw things, at least conceal'd from sight before.[44]

A generous bard, having paid due tribute to the wonders of telescopic discoveries, bade his friend "close awhile thy astronomick wing, Leave Jove's Satellites and old Saturn's wing," and discover what wonders the microscope could make known. He accompanied his admonition with a present of that instrument:

> The gift I send, (tho' small the present seems)
> Shall find thee, nearer yet, as wond'rous themes.
> New species this, alert with life, expands
> Num'rous as dew-drops, or as ocean's sands.
> There's scarce a leaf that trembles in the air
> Whose hills and valleys do not millions bear;
> Who range at large and plenteous herbage find,
> And drink at streams which thro' their meadows wind.
> A single drop of water can embrace
> Ten thousand creatures of aquatick race:
> The space which scarce a grain of sand contains,

Infolds more lives than fell on Blenheim's plains. . . .
Such curious views the microscope bestows,
Such food for thought, such useful knowledge flows.[45]

Momentarily a writer might feel, as did James Thomson, a sense of horror of the minute. Thomson's lines beginning "full Nature swarms with life" have been cited again and again as evidence of his interest in and his repulsion for the swarming microcosms of the universe. But Thomson stood alone in his uneasiness amid earth's myriad creatures. His fellow poets liked a crowded world where "fulness bounds, and all are fill'd with bliss." [46] Their interest in the principle of plenitude, their examination of minute creatures by means of the inventions of science, their enthusiasm for man's ever-growing knowledge of the structure of the material world, typified the spirit of their generation. Their poetic speculations were practical applications of the theory:

> This is the highest pitch of human reason, to follow all the links of the chain, till all their secrets are open to our minds, and their works advanc'd, or imitated by our hands. . . . This is truly to command the world; to rank all the varieties and degrees of things, so orderly one upon another, that standing on top of them, we may perfectly behold all that are below, and make them serviceable to the quiet, and peace, and plenty of man's life.[47]

The Book of Nature

> *All nature's wonders serve to excite and perfect this idea of their author. 'Tis here he suffers us to see, and even converse with him, in a manner suitable to our frailty. How glorious is it to contemplate him, in this the noblest of his works apparent to us, the system of the bigger world!* [48]
>
> —*Shaftesbury*, Moralists

A full yet ordered world was not the limit of an eighteenth-century man's blessings. His joys included the conviction, fostered

by Locke, and after him by the deists, that the truths necessary
to man were clearly written out for him in the book of Nature.
No longer need man puzzle over the mysteries of Scriptural revela-
tion, no longer weary his ears with the clamor of the two and
seventy jarring sects, no more strain the eyes of his spirit towards
the dim horizons of the supernatural. All truths necessary for him
were plainly imprinted on the external universe, and he might
read them out with ease and assurance.

The workings of the theory left something to be desired. Men
had a habit of reading their own prejudices, opinions, and interests
into the universe, and of reading them out again and calling the
result the message of Nature. The hypothesis, designed to call men
back to a few simple objective truths, was to lead by degrees to
extreme individualism, but at this early period the end of the trail
was not in sight. Men still believed that

> In nature's book the weakest brain may speed,
> Th' untaught may learn it, and th' unletter'd read;
> Nor need of pedant, or a pedant's rod,
> The book of nature is the book of God.[49]

What the poets read in the "world's harmonious volume" was a
lesson of restraint and conformity. Their enthusiasm for diversity
was confined to the material sphere: locked up with their tele-
scopes and microscopes it remained an innocuous hobby. The time
had not yet come when enthusiasm for variety would carry over
into the moral realm and would cause a shift from objective to
subjective standards in matters of human conduct.

The first lesson they showed man lay in the world around him.
Memories of the seventeenth-century controversies over the decay of Nature still lingered in men's minds: poets pointed to the
"ruined" face of Nature and chided man as the cause of her dis-
figurement. Sixty years after Bishop Burnet's explanation of the
"ruins of the broken world" which had attributed the wilder aspects of earth to the deluge, and ultimately to the sins of men
which had drawn down the floods from heaven in punishment,

a poet looking at dreary plains and torrid mountains saw the wild scene as the vast ruins "of desert nature." [50]

The poets were sensitive to the irregularities that evidenced earth's ruin. One writer, sharing Shaftesbury's horror of those rash men who "explore earth's bosom, and her entrails tear," described mines, as terrible and ugly places

> Where horror ever holds her dark domain,
> And Shade and Erebus eternal reign:
> Cold damps arise from subterranean cells,
> And sulph'rous vapours fill the gloomy space,
> Arch'd caverns yawn, and tapers faintly blaze:
> Here nature's face a frightful image wears,
> And threat'ning death in sundry shapes appears: [51]

Others did not search such gloomy depths for signs of Nature's irregularity. They saw around them ruin enough. The world itself seemed in great part "a waste, rocks, deserts, frozen seas, and burning sands." [52] Even the man-made ruins of Queen Caroline's Hermitage seemed "the relict of a thousand years," and the old hedges without the building appeared the "spoils of antient time, as if reduc'd from some once glorious prime." [53] The whole earth was in decay, and its decay was progressive:

> This huge rotundity we tread grows old;
> And all the worlds that roll around the sun,
> The sun himself, shall die; and ancient Night
> Again involve the desolate abyss. [54]

Man was left to survey that broken world and to reflect that it was human sin that had caused the Almighty to "deform the World, and change its antient plan, And fit the climates to the state of man." [55] Major poet and minor told the same story of earth's pristine perfection and subsequent decay. James Thomson had the tale of deluge and "streaming clouds" and "fractured earth," [56] so did the nameless bard who reminded his readers:

Some think ere this [i. e., the Fall] nor sea nor hill was found,
But a smooth surface cloath'd our planet round,
Till torn by earthquakes its convexive shell,
Sapp'd by th' unbosom'd waters, inward fell;
When strait th' unbroken fountains pour'd their stores,
With wide confusion, and o'er topp'd the shores:
Hence seas and mountains their formation owe,
Relicts of ruin and deforming woe.[57]

For a poet of more cheerful temper there was still beauty in the ruined earth:

The shatter'd rocks and strata seem to say,
  'Nature is old, and tends to her decay';
Yet, lovely in decay, and green in age,
Her beauty lasts her to her latest stage.[58]

If man were not sufficiently humbled by the sight of the disorders which he had brought on the world about him, Nature had for him a further lesson in humility. In the universe itself man seemed something of a misfit. The order and precision which the mathematicians and astronomers of the sixteenth and seventeenth centuries had discovered in the universe threw into sharp and unflattering relief the disorder and inefficiency of the creature man.[59] He was the disturbing element in the calm realm of mathematical truths, the monkey wrench in the universal machine. Sadly rose the complaint:

O Nature whom the song aspires to scan!
O Beauty, trod by proud insulting man,
This boasted tyrant of thy wondrous ball,
This mighty, haughty, little lord of all;
This king o'er reason, but this slave to sense,
Towards Thee, incurious, ignorant, profane!
But of his own, dear, strange, productions vain! [60]

Small wonder then that the poets were quick to read to man a lesson of order and regularity from the book of Nature. They

marked how greatly he needed such a lesson. "Man, only man,
. . . starts back from nature's rule." [61] Only he wasted his time
and talents.[62] All other creatures followed their appointed courses;
man, obstinate and headstrong, went where he would.[63] "Ah, Nature! thou hadst 'scaped thy only blot, Could man but cease to
be—or hitherto were not." [64]

Now that Nature's book had taught him remorse and humility,
man could go further and learn from it wisdom and peace. He
need not go so far as the learned lady:

> To convince her of God the good dean did indeavour,
> But still in her heart she held Nature more clever,[65]

but he might send his soul questing through Nature for the Supreme
Truth:

> Among aetherial worlds, with large survey
> Contemplating the mighty maker's works:
> Unnumber'd systems, in unmeasur'd space
> Rolling, the motions of their orbs impos'd
> By wisdom infinite: the seats perhaps
> Thro' which the transmigrating soul shall pass
> To vision beatifick . . .[66]

Study of Nature showed man the duties assigned to each creature
and convinced him of the intimate presence of God and the wisdom of "the great Creative Will." [67] Contemplation of Nature's
works surpassed in value the learning of the schools, the follies
of the proud, the empty retirement of the idle.[68] It was the source
unequalled of wisdom:

> O slighted Nature—in whose changing face,
> Wisdom and truth immutable we trace,
> How just thy laws,—How regular they shine,
> Thy views how sweet,—thy seasons how benign.[69]

The most eloquent readers of the book of Nature were James
Thomson and Edward Young. Thomson's ideal was that of the retired sage who goes apart and

> To Nature's voice attends from month to month,
> And day to day, through the revolving year—
> Admiring, sees her in her every shape;
> Feels all her sweet emotions at his heart;
> Takes what she liberal gives, nor thinks of more.[70]

Eagerly he pleaded:

> O Nature! all sufficient! over all
> Enrich me with the knowledge of thy works;
> Snatch me to heaven; thy rolling wonders there,
> World beyond world, in infinite extent
> Profusely scattered o'er the blue immense,
> Show me; their motions, periods, and their laws
> Give me to scan; through the disclosing deep
> Light my blind way; the mineral strata there;
> Thrust blooming thence the vegetable world;
> O'er that the rising system, more complex,
> Of animals; and, higher still, the mind,
> The varied scene of quick-compounded thought,
> And where the mixing passions endless shift;
> There ever open to my ravished eye—
> A search, the flight of time can ne'er exhaust! [71]

Thomson was a terrestrial tourist leisurely admiring the beauties of earth; Young, a cosmic adventurer setting off with rare enthusiasm to span the boundless halls of space:

> Come, my Prometheus, from thy pointed rock
> Of false ambition; if unchain'd, we'll mount;
> We'll, innocently, steal celestial fire,
> And kindle our devotion at the stars;
> A theft, that shall not chain, but set us free.[72]

Nature to Young connoted the glories of the infinite heavens, the grandeur of the star-spangled firmament. The heavens proclaimed the glory of God to him never more grandly than in terms of the universe of the new astronomy, but it was a religious rather than a scientific inspiration which the skies exercised upon his poetry. To Young, Nature was the "proud sceptic's foe," the oracle of God, the standard of good.[73] The stars, "arrang'd, and disciplined, and clothed in gold" offered a guide to unbelieving man:

> Stars teach, as well as shine. At Nature's birth,
> Thus their commission ran—'Be kind to Man.'
> Where art thou, poor benighted traveller?
> The stars will light thee, though the moon should fall.
> Where art thou, more benighted! more astray!
> In ways immoral? The stars will call thee back;
> And if obey'd their counsel, set thee right.[74]

For the human race Nature was the "elder Scripture," "Scripture authentic, uncorrupt by man":

> Divine Instructor! Thy first volume, this,
> For man's perusal; all in capitals!
> In moon, and stars (heaven's golden alphabet!)
> Emblazed to seize the sight; who runs, may read;
> Who reads, can understand. 'Tis unconfined
> To Christian land, or Jewry; fairly writ,
> In language, lofty to the learn'd: yet plain
> To those that feed the flock, or guide the plough,
> Or, from his husk, strike out the bounding grain.
> A language, worthy the Great Mind, that speaks!
> Preface, and comment, to the sacred page!
> Which oft refers its reader to the skies,
> As presupposing his first lesson there,
> And Scripture self a fragment, that unread.[75]

Had Young gone from the premise that Scripture was but a fragment of the scripture of Nature to the conclusion that the Scriptural fragment was an unnecessary addition to universal lore, Lorenzo might have enrolled the defender of orthodoxy among the disciples of the religion of Nature. Young did not go to the deistic extreme, but his glowing account of "Scripture authentic" showed that even a conservative thinker might be infected with the current enthusiasm for the book of Nature.

All in all man's lessons from Nature had in common an ideal of regularity. Whether abashed, man was led by the poets to contemplate the ruins of Nature, or whether heartened, he was exhorted to soar beyond the stars, in either case he had before him a Nature that gloried in order and conformity. In this connection at least, *vivere secundum naturam* meant regularity and order.

Optimism

> *How incomparably more beautiful is this structure, than if we suppos'd so many distinct volitions in the deity, producing every particular effect, and preventing some of the accidental evils which casually flow from the general law! . . . One would rather chuse to run the hazard of its casual evils, than part with that harmonious form which has been an unexhausted source of delight to the successive spectators in all ages.*[76]
> —*Hutcheson,* An Inquiry into the Original of our Ideas of Beauty and Virtue

Out of the chain of being and the principle of plenitude grew that most popular of eighteenth-century concepts—optimism, an optimism which had little but its name in common with that forward-looking hopefulness which sums up the modern meaning of the term.[77] It had nothing at all to do with shallow cheerfulness of the Pollyanna variety. The same generation that heard Pope proclaim, "whatever is, is right," lived to read Young's complaint, "but endless is the list of human ills, And sighs might sooner fail than cause to sigh." [78] Moreover it managed to combine those extremes of sentiment.

Having admitted that every link in the chain of being was where it had to be in order to fill a certain gap in creation, the eighteenth century accepted the consequence of those equally necessary links. All things pleasant and unpleasant must remain that being's series might be complete—one evil less and creation would collapse. The explanation served well enough for physical evils. Physical evil was, after all, an evil of limitation, and all degrees of limitation were needed to complete the chain of being. But the problem of moral evil remained, and continued to remain a source of infinite embarrassment to the optimist. Not daring to say that moral evil as well as physical was the work of the Creator, the hard-pressed thinker usually evaded the issue, contending that such evil seemed a flaw to human minds, because " 'tis but a part we see, and not the whole." [79]

The poets shared the confidence of their generation in the essential rightness of things as they were. A few of them, optimists in the modern sense, voiced cheerful pride in national achievement. The rule of the first two Georges was conducive to national complacency. Despite the mutterings of the Opposition press, the Walpole régime had given England an era of general prosperity.[80] Exports had soared, credit had improved; men might still say, as they had said in the reign of good Queen Anne: "but it is still more pleasing to an Englishman to see his own country give the chief influence to so illustrious an age, and stand in the strongest point of light amidst the diffused glory that surrounds it." [81] From 1737 to 1743 scattered poems expressed great satisfaction with the state of foreign and domestic affairs. Thomson, forgetting his displeasure with the Whig ministry, often assured England that

> On every hand
> Thy villas shine. Thy country teems with wealth;
> And Property assures it to the swain,
> Pleased and unwearied in his guarded toil.[82]

Colley Cibber, diligently earning his laureate's pension, boasted:

> Your antient annals, Britain, read,
>   And mark the reign you most admire;
> The present shall the past exceed,
>   And yield enjoyment to desire.[83]

Others besides Thomson and Cibber paused to congratulate England that peace brightened her isle while war darkened the continent, that trade and wealth were the property of her citizens, that contentment ruled within her borders.[84] A verse which would have driven an Opposition poet to despair explained happily:

> In Britain's beauteous, ever-charming isle,
> Warm is the sun, and fruitful is the soil,
> And, thanks to Walpole's care, success attends their toil.[85]

A generation had passed since Addison had celebrated the glories of the Royal Exchange and Defoe had praised commerce as an international blessing, but Colley Cibber did not hesitate to put into poor verse the same enthusiasm for trade that the essayists had expressed in elegant prose:

> What land, or what nation, tho' nearer the sun,
> Throughout in its station had Britain outdone?
> Whate'er in high measure our climate denies,
> For use or for pleasure, the ocean supplies;
> If gold or gems glaring we fetch from the mine;
> We're not in the wearing burnt under the line,
> Nor tho' our occasions far northward may roll,
> Are starv'd like the nations froze under the pole.[86]

And a decade after Cibber an anonymous magazine poet could ask with pride, "in such blest state what nation round us lies, At home so merry, and abroad so wise?" [87]

That natural and perennial optimism which arises from satisfaction at good times at home and peace abroad may be found in any century and in any generation which experiences an era of good feeling. It is not the optimism peculiarly associated with eighteenth-century thinking. To find that phenomenon the reader must turn from the surface cheerfulness of complacent nationalists, and must consider the poetry which not only admitted the existence of evils in England and in the world, but also attempted to convince men that such evils were ultimately for the benefit of the whole creation.

Edward Young's catalogue of human ills might have served eighteenth-century optimists as a terrible reminder of the evils they were bound to explain away:

War, famine, pest, volcano, storm, and fire
Intestine broils, oppression, with her heart
Wrapt up in triple brass, besiege mankind. . . . .
There, beings deathless as their haughty lord,
Are hammer'd to the galling oar for life;
And plough the winter's wave, and reap despair.
Some, for hard masters, broken under arms,
In battle lopp'd away, with half their limbs,
Beg bitter bread through realms their valour saved,
If so the tyrant, or his minion, doom.
Want and incurable disease (fell pair!)
On hopeless multitudes remorseless seize
At once; and make a refuge of the grave.[88]

To all the plaints the optimist had a stubborn answer:

'Tis hard vice triumphs, and that virtue grieves;
Yet oft affliction purifies the mind,
Kind benefits oft flow from means unkind.
Were the whole known, that we uncouth suppose,
Doubtless, would beauteous symmetry disclose.[89]

That was to be man's consolation for every hardship, his sustaining thought in every tragedy. The flaws in the world seemed imperfections only because of man's limited vision; in the sight of the Supreme Designer, they were essential parts of the universal pattern. Repeatedly the poets reminded man of the narrow scope of human knowledge:

But of this frame, the bearings and the ties,
The strong connections, nice dependencies,
Gradations just, has thy pervading soul
Look'd thro'; or can a part contain the whole?
Is the great chain that draws all to agree,
And drawn supports, upheld by God—or thee? [90]

The moral concisely stated by Pope was drawn and redrawn by others. Mark Akenside's reproof to human pride followed the usual course of optimistic opinion:

> O let thy soul
> Remember, what the will of heaven ordains
> Is ever good for all; and if for all,
> Then good for thee.[91]

Like Pope and Akenside, Thomson added his word of chiding:

> Let no presuming impious railer tax
> Creative Wisdom, as if aught was formed
> In vain, or not for admirable ends.
> Shall little haughty Ignorance pronounce
> His works unwise, of which the smallest part
> Exceeds the narrow vision of her mind? [92]

Major writers and minor were agreed that "man's imperfect views" could not rightly judge the laws of Nature.[93] "But 'cause we cannot see must God be blind?" [94] Let man be content to believe "that the providence of Heaven Has some peculiar blessing given To each allotted state below." [95] God alone "surveys the nice barrier of wrong and right." [96] Man might as well give up the struggle to understand, and confess, as did an anonymous poet:

> Whence the deep shades of sin and sorrow came,
> And evil mingled with the gen'ral frame;
> Why spread the dark dominions of the grave,
> Or why I wish more virtue than I have.
> These secret things to none but Thee are known,
> O! let my soul be still content to know,
> Thy love, thy wisdom rules the world below.[97]

The poets not only bade man recognize his limitations, they bade him rejoice in them. Man possessed as did every other creature just those powers which best suited his place in life. " 'Tis murmur, discontent, distrust, That makes you wretched, God is just." [98] Actually addressed to a poor man who complained of his position in society, the reproach might have been leveled at mankind itself. For man, "to reason right is to submit," and, as Pope pointed out most eloquently, submission was not necessarily a dreary thing, human limitations had their conveniences:

> Each want of happiness by Hope supply'd,
> And each vacuity of sense by Pride . . .
> One prospect lost, another still we gain;
> And not a vanity is giv'n in vain.[99]

While most of the poets read man lectures on resignation, Edward Young had a somewhat different message for humanity. He argued that human ills were not a necessary end in themselves, but rather were a means by which man could reach a higher state of happiness:

> Affliction is the good man's shining scene;
> Prosperity conceals his brightest ray;
> As night to stars, woe lustre gives to man.
> Heroes in battle, pilots in the storm,
> And virtue in calamities, admire.
> The crown of manhood is a winter-joy;
> An evergreen, that stands the northern blast.[100]

To Young pain was no ontological evil to be endured for the good of the universe: it was a direct gift of Heaven to be borne well for the personal good of the individual soul:

> Those we call wretched are a chosen band,
> Compell'd to refuge in the right, for peace.
> Amid my list of blessings infinite,
> Stands this the foremost, 'That my heart has bled.'
> 'Tis Heaven's last effort of good-will to man;
> When Pain can't bless, Heaven quits us in despair.[101]

The poets did their best to justify worldly ills: it was scarcely their fault that the haunting spectre of moral evil was not wholly exorcised with optimistic formulae. Hard as the writers tried to inter the inconvenient phantom in the grave of things-not-for-human-comprehension, occasionally in minor verse it rose up to disconcert them:

> And thus the mystery is understood,
> By granting ill with man, with God is good.
> Is vice and virtue then but nominal?

What! no rewards or punishments at all?
Be not so mercenary, or severe;
Heav'n in due time perhaps the point will clear.[102]

The lame conclusion did little to lay the ghost. An anonymous
magazine verse, "Of the Deist's Scheme of Fitness" brought up a
host of questions embarrassing to the philosophical optimist. On
the score of moral evil it demanded:

That fitness who can see, himself why man
Is born to so much misery and pain?
Why in such troubled scenes he draws that breath,
Which sighs in anguish, and expires in death?
On man why misery's entail'd at all?
Let those explain, who disbelieve his fall;
And let them shew us on their principle,
Whence springs each natural and moral ill.
And whence are they disorder'd but by sin,
The world without us, and the mind within.[103]

From the optimist's point of view the classic answer to that challenge was Pope's explanation:

All Nature is but Art, unknown to thee;
All chance, direction, which thou canst not see;
All discord, harmony not understood;
All partial evil, universal good:
And spite of Pride, in erring Reason's spite,
One truth is clear, *Whatever is, is right.*[104]

If that answer failed to satisfy the doubting, the optimist had
nothing more to say.

The optimistic poets did more than discuss the limitations of
man and the evils of the world. They poured out their pride and
joy in the excellent universe of which they were a part. Thomson,
famous for his paeans to the beautiful world and its immanent
Creator, saw Nature smiling for joy at God's goodness, praising
the Almighty when men were silent.[105] He loved the God of Seasons, "at once the head, the heart, the tongue of all." [106] An en-

thusiasm for Nature that merged with pantheism inspired his confident prayer

> I cannot go
> Where universal love not smiles around,
> Sustaining all yon orbs and all their suns;
> From seeming evil still educing good,
> And better thence again, and better still,
> In infinite progression . . .[107]

Thomson's fervor was peculiar to him. Other poets did not match his depth of feeling in celebrating Nature, nor did they share his sense of a Creator immanent in His Creation.

Not the least of the beauties of the universe as the optimist saw them was the mutual attraction that bound every being to its fellow in creation.[108] Mutual love held the planets in their courses.[109] Social love linked man with his neighbor and with the creatures below him.[110] Moved by that all-compelling harmony men calmed their passions, civilized their instincts, and drew close together in a loving "chain of converse." [111] In bonds of intercourse and love Earth's universal family "basked in the blessings of a benevolent world.[112] The Creator was Universal Love and Infinite Mercy.[113] His "vast benevolence" lighted every corner of the universe.[114] In a world where "all smiles benevolent and good to man" small wonder that the optimists rejoiced:

> Profusely wide the boundless blessings flow,
> Which heav'n enrich, and gladden worlds below!
> Which are no less, when properly defin'd,
> Than emanations of th' Eternal Mind! [115]

Now and then the optimist grew impatient with views opposed to his happy tenets: a periodical verse writer resentful of a creed which denied his concept of a completely merciful Deity upbraided Whitefield for preaching that a just God held punishment in store for his errant children:

> Hear, Whitefield, hear, and answer, if you can;
> Learn you from nature's wise, and perfect plan,
> That heav'n design'd ne'er-ending woe for man?

Behold this earth, with every beauty gay;
See, all-rejoicing, shine the god of day;
The feather'd songsters hear, in every grove,
Fearless of future woe, sweet warbling love;
The flow'ry mead, the wide-spread dawn survey,
Where grace the herds, and where the lambkins play;
And when ascends the peaceful queen of night,
Let the fair starry host attract thy sight:
From every view can ought be understood,
But one Creator, infinitely good?
Say, through all nature canst thou find one trace,
That pain eternal waits the human race?
Or learn'st thou this from kindness and from grace? [116]

That same poet and his fellow optimists would doubtless have resented the ironical "directions how to make and preach a sermon
that shall please":

Nor mention hell, 'twill make your hearers gaze
Sneer at your faith, and ridicule its blaze. . . .
Let not God's wrath then in your work abound,
But of His mercy take at least—a pound. [117]

They most certainly would have winced as Edward Young ac-
cused:

Not, thus, our infidels th' Eternal draw,
A God all o'er, consummate, absolute,
Full-orb'd, in his whole round of rays complete;
They set at odds Heaven's jarring attributes:
And, with one excellence, another wound;
Maim Heaven's perfection, break its equal beams,
Bid mercy triumph over—God himself,
Undeified by their opprobrious praise:
A God all mercy, is a God unjust. [118]

But despite the occasional voices of dissent, the majority of the
poets preferred, like Henry Baker, to believe that human life was

a state of felicity, and that man might confidently address his Creator:

> Almighty tho Thou art, thy Pow'r is shown
> By infinite Beneficence alone,
> And Mercy sits, triumphant, on thy Throne.[119]

[Such a concept of an all-merciful God was essential to the optimist's belief that evils were either apparent (i. e., non-existent) or necessary: in either case the nature of things absolved man from the possibility of moral guilt.]

In numerical strength the optimists had the best of it. Right up to the mid-century optimism remained the strongest and most persistent of the poets' philosophical interests. Whether regularity or diversity inspired their admiration of the universal scheme, their conclusion was the same:

> Here fix our basis, own the power divine;
> And one immense, wise, perfect, good design;
> Where all subsists that can, of happiness,
> And if there evil be, can be no less.[120]

2

Aesthetics

IN the second quarter of the eighteenth century the problem of "Nature" was painfully acute for gentlemen with aesthetic leanings. The nobleman replanning his ancestral acres and the critic pondering his next literary pronouncement struggled manfully with the dual concept of a Nature tame and methodized and a universe bountiful and overflowing. Lovers of regularity championed sculptured hedgerows and rule-bound literature: champions of diversity hailed wild landscapes and the outpourings of untrammeled genius. Both groups agreed on *vivere secundum naturam*—but *naturam* meant a radically different thing for each.

By the mid-century time was running out for the defenders of regularity. Slowly but steadily the formal garden surrendered to mazes, ruins, and Strawberry Hill: the elegant artistry of Pope gave way before the lyricism of Gray and the Wartons.

Art

> *The great master* [*William Kent*] . . . *truly the disciple of nature, imitated her in the agreeable wildness and beautiful irregularity of her plans.*[121]
> —The World, *No. 15*

Praise of William Kent's wildness and beautiful irregularity in landscaping symbolized a minor revolution in aesthetics that within fifty years had led English gardens from the formality of clipped yew trees to serpentining walks and pseudo-Gothicism. For centuries English gardens had followed foreign fashions. Formal Elizabethan gardens had copied the classical style of Italian

estates; Restoration landscaping had aped the mannered magnificence of Versailles; estates in the time of William the Third had
adopted the canal gardens of Holland. By the end of the seventeenth century, Englishmen with a taste for landscaping had cut
down century-old trees and leveled picturesque hills, all to achieve
the effect:

> Grove nods at grove, each alley has a brother,
> And half the platform just reflects the other.
> The suffering eye inverted Nature sees,
> Trees cut to statues, statues thick as trees.[122]

Even when Pope set down his satiric lines the formal garden he
ridiculed was already a little out of date. It became still more out-
moded during the following decades when such professional
gardeners as Batty Langley, Stephen Switzer, William Kent and
"Capability" Brown labored to landscape English acres into a pattern of pleasing wildness. By the mid-century "Nature abhors a
straight line" had become a popular principle in landscaping, and
English gardens turned and twisted, fashionably free.

The paths of eighteenth-century gardening-theorists were
strewn with dangers. It was easy enough to repeat that "God Almighty first planted a garden," [123] and that man should do likewise.
The century-old question yet remained—was it a regular or an
irregular garden that the Divine Horticulturist had fashioned?
Milton's description of Eden offered support to both sides of the
debate. Formalists cited the pruning practices of his Adam and Eve
in defence of regularizing Nature.[124] Progressive gardeners recalled his flowers "which not nice Art . . . but Nature boon
Poured forth profuse" in behalf of luxuriant landscapes.[125] Eighteenth-century gardeners anxious to break away from contemporary formality reminded men that Milton's bounteous garden of
Eden was superior in itself and in his description of it, to modern
efforts at gardening and writing:

> What a variety of natural thought is here found? as much
> beyond the trifling dimunitive beauties of some of our mod-
> ern gardens, as the poem is superior to the meanest ballad. In

those scenes 'tis hard to turn one's head any way without wonder and surprise; whilst in our modern gardens a few clipt plants and hedges is the utmost of our variety.[126]

Of course the gardener who was also a reading man was never at a loss for classic literary comment on gardens. Spenser's Garden of Adonis, "so faire a place as nature can devise," made vivid a bounteous and abundant Nature.[127] The ambiguous Shakespearean blessing "the art itself is nature" [128] dignified the practice of grafting, that much-discussed method of augmenting Nature's variety. The practice had drawn Cowley's approval also, but it had earned Marvell's angry censure as a crime against Nature's beautiful simplicity.[129] The gardener's dilemma persisted.

Seventeenth-century prose had offered interesting sidelights on the subject of landscaping. Sir Thomas Browne justified his discussion of gardens (he himself had none) on the grounds that "the earth is the garden of nature, and each fruitful country a paradise." [130] John Evelyn recorded carefully his admiration for the beautiful formal gardens of the continent.[131] Sir William Temple divided his tributes between the regular beauties of Moor Park and the irregular charms of far-off Chinese landscapes.[132] Prose writers of the early eighteenth century offered the gardener most eloquent pleas in defence of the unadorned beauty of Nature. Pope insisted:

> There is certainly something in the amiable simplicity of unadorned nature, that spreads over the mind a more noble sort of tranquillity, and a loftier sensation of pleasure than can be raised from the nicer scenes of art.
> This was the taste of the ancients in their gardens. . . .
> How contrary to this simplicity is the modern practice of gardening! We seem to make it our study to recede from nature, not only in the various tonsures of greens into the most regular and formal shapes, but even in monstrous attempts beyond the reach of art itself.[133]

Shaftesbury rhapsodized:

> I shall no longer resist the passions growing in me for things of a natural kind; where neither art, nor the conceit of man

has spoil'd their genuine order by breaking in upon that primitive state. Even the rude rocks, the mossy caverns, the irregular unwrought grotto's, and broken falls of waters, with all the horrid graces of the wilderness itself, as representing nature more, will be the more engaging, and appear with a magnificence beyond the formal mockery of princely gardens.[134]

Yet more impressively, Addison himself championed "the beautiful wildness of nature without the elegancies of art."[135] His critical doctrines paid tribute both to Nature and to art, but though he offered ammunition to both sides of the controversy, his approval of the "Pindaric manner" of gardening, his sanction of the appeal of the uncommon, above all, his discussions of natural genius constituted a particularly impressive support for the ideal of diverse Nature.[136] When Addison marveled at the infinite variety of the universe and bade men mirror Nature in their works, he was disapproving equally of the formal garden and the rule-bound writer—neither of them a reflection of Nature's infinite variety. Defenders of irregular Nature cannot claim Addison as wholly theirs, but they can to an important extent avail themselves of his support—a support at once respected and redoubtable.

However prose critics and fashionable gardeners decried regularity in landscapes, there were some poets who were reluctant to relinquish it. Stubbornly conservative, they continued to praise art's improvements on Nature's extravagance. Their conventional verses threw into vivid contrast those paeans to artless Nature, which gaining in volume through the seventeen-forties, foreshadowed the final triumph of the ideal of the irregular landscape.

Conservative poets reserved their mild affections for the scene "where art and nature in one landscape join, And with united beauties doubly shine."[137] Carefully they balanced the rival claimants. "The sov'reign part" was nature's; art, her handmaid, added the finishing touches. Art "rules o'er Nature, and to Nature yields." Both "mutual powers exert." "Art brightens Nature, Nature brightens Art." The complementary beauties pleased the fancy, charmed the sense and cheered the mind.[138]

Writers whose tepid fancies were further warmed by the charms of art, celebrated "beauteous nature . . . deck'd with each hand-maid art, each polish'd grace." They believed in regularizing the "barren mountain side" and correcting Nature's irregular wanderings.[139] One of their number undertook to renovate the landscape single-handed:

> On some lone wild, shou'd my large house be plac'd,
> Vastly surrounded by a healthful waste!
> Steril, and coarse, the untry'd soil shou'd be,
> Till forc'd to flourish, and subdu'd by me. . . .
> Where—e'er I walk'd, effects of my past pains,
> Shou'd plume the mountain tops, and paint the plains.[140]

But the majority were content with dignified gentleman farming:

> To raise the insipid nature of the ground:
> Or tame its savage genius to the grace
> Of careless sweet rusticity, that seems
> The amiable result of happy chance,
> Is to create; and gives the god-like joy,
> Which every year improves. Nor thou disdain
> To check the lawless riot of the trees,
> To plant the grove, or turn the barren mould.[141]

All the loveliness of art-mended Nature bloomed for them in formal gardens. The level walks and rising terraces of the earlier style, the mazes and labyrinths of later gardens pleased them as improvements on Nature. When parterres replaced Nature's "bushes, brakes, and briars," the poets were content.[142] If a famous estate were formally landscaped, they had the added pleasure of mingling admiration for aristocratic taste with admiration for regular design. Richmond Park and Stowe adorned many a mediocre verse. The royal park fired Stephen Duck to aesthetic and patriotic enthusiasm:

> thorny brakes the traveller repell'd
> And weeds and thistles overspread the field;

Til Royal George, and heav'nly Caroline,
Bid Nature in harmonious lustre shine;
The sacred fiat thro' the chaos rung,
And symmetry from wild disorder sprung.[143]

Stowe afforded Thomson a chance to assure Pitt that:

Not Persian Cyrus on Ionia's shore
E'er saw such sylvan scenes, such various art
By genius fired, such ardent genius tamed
By cool judicious art, that in the strife
All-beauteous Nature fears to be outdone.[144]

An anonymous "Epistle to Lord B." (probably the Earl of Burlington) having described his lordship's formal estate with its vistas, covered walks, canals, shaven turf and complex flower borders, complimented the nobleman "with studied art on nature you refine."[145] A minor panegyrist of Kensington Gardens was careful to note:

That hollow space, where now in living rows,
Line above line the yew's sad verdure grows,
Was, ere the planter's hand its beauty gave,
A common pit, a rude unfashion'd cave . . .[146]

Nature was not allowed to retain even her pride in her varied scene: John Winstanley, admiring the complexity of a labyrinth on a landscaped estate marveled:

So rude it seems, yet must by art be wrought:
Dame Nature, sure, ne'er deck'd a place like this,
So rich, so gay, so fraught with fragrant bliss.[147]

In the eyes of conservative versifiers art-mended Nature was the epitome of landscape beauty. Their stubborn devotion to formality reached a climax in a paean of praise to Versailles:

Let fame no more her Syrian Gardens boast,
Those eastern fables, here, in truth are lost,
Since earth was blighted, and by heav'n accurst,

This Eden only can approach the first;
A new creation seems in every part,
And vanquished nature is a slave to art.[148]

Although persistent expressions of admiration for regular Nature attested the die-hard quality of traditional standards, the praises themselves were neither loud nor eloquent: the reactionary chorus was in a decidedly minor key.

Nature

Poetic defence of the supreme artistry of Nature ranged in enthusiasm from a mild pleasure in "artless" flowers to wild delight in the black heath, the foamy stream and the pinetopt precipice.

Sometimes the poets' love for variety expressed itself in praise of Nature's lavish goodness.[149] "Luxuriant Nature" "pours around her sweets." "The earth profusely spreads her charms to view." "Pleasing, gay confusion" graced the fields. Indulgent, artless, Nature offered a "bounteous, blooming store" for all men's pleasure.

"Millions of beauteous landscapes" glowed with her bounty.[150] The Isle of Wight "laughs with the wealth of lavish nature grac'd." [151] In the fields "where nature wantons in a thousand dyes," the flowers in gay profusion "spring unbidden o'er the ground"; [152] nor were floral beauties confined to garden walls:

Nor to the garden sole . . .
                  does Nature boon
Indulge her gifts: but to each nameless field,
When the warm sun rejoicing in the year
Stirs up the latent juice, she scatters wide
Her rosy children: then innumerous births,
As from the womb spring up, and wide perfume
Their cradles with ambrosial sweets around.
Far as the eye can reach all nature smiles.[153]

Wherever man looked a bounteous world was spread out for his admiration:

When plastick nature moulds the wondrous clay,
When beams on man the animating ray;
Still fond in all her works divine, to see
A beauteous system of variety.[154]

The beauteous system included the "rich profusion" of the
enamelled meads, the red of the rose, the blue of the violet, and
all the colors glowing in "that wide-stretch'd coelestial bow" of
heaven.[155] Even fashionable gardens felt the charm of diverse Nature and with deliberate art pursued the ideal—variety:

Two neighb'ring domes on spiral columns rise,
With shells and pebbles spangled to the eyes.
Whence, still directed, by the winding stream,
Amus'd we to the three-arch'd building came.
Hence west the church adorns the opening height,
Eastward the spacious pond relieved the sight:
In which of form Chinese a structure lies,
Where all her wild grotesques display'd surprise;
Within Japan her glittering treasure yields,
And ships of amber sail on golden fields!
In radiant clouds are silver turrets found,
And mimic glories glitter all around. . . .
Such gay romantic prospects rise around,
With such profusion smiles the flow'ry ground!
So steals th' ambrosial pleasure on the mind,
We think 'tis heav'n—and leave the world behind.[156]

The scene is a good example of studied "wildness" in the gardens
of the seventeen-forties. How much better Nature herself
achieved that beautiful diversity is clear from Thomas Warton's
description of Spring fields in the morning sunshine: "fancy may
paint, but nature gives the joys":

Who swell'd the lilly with a pearly dew,
Who bad [sic] gay earth her radiant robe renew,
The stream in concert with the linnet run,
And the world smile beneath a warmer sun?
'Tis nature's pow'r!—Thy all-benignant hand

Spreads every joy, and blesses every land!
Grant, gentle goddess, no corroding care
In rankling chains our restless hearts ensnare.[157]

Poetic defence of Nature's self-sufficiency against the restraining practices of art made up in fervor what it lacked in skill. The verses, however halting, were staunch in their insistence on Nature's "empire o'er the works of art." [158] Most detailed and most unskilful of the pedestrian praises was a bit of magazine verse, "The Landskip," which mingled censure of formal gardens, joy in Nature's variety and admiration of natural grandeur into a serious but uninspired whole. Its flat treatment of the charms of irregular landscapes offers a good contrast to the poetic fire which other Nature-lovers, notably the Wartons, brought to the same theme:

In seasons mild
With nature wild
Conversing, far I rove;
I cannot find in gardens prim,
With all their pretty little trim,
The beauties of a grove.

No palace grand
The artist's hand
Can form my taste to please,
Like rocks and mountains, seas and hills,
Where native grandeur ever fills
And feeds the eye with ease.

Here unconfin'd
The thoughtful mind
Ten thousand charms surveys;
Here order in confusion lies,
Here great and small alike surprize,
And shine with blended rays.[159]

Fortunately the beauties of Nature fared better at other poets' hands. Thomson early voiced the challenge:

But who can paint
Like Nature? Can imagination boast,
Amid its gay creation, hues like hers? [160]

On occasion he might uphold the claims of art, but his real love
belonged to the wild heath and the flowery mead:

Full of fresh verdure and unnumbered flowers,
The negligence of nature wide and wild,
Where, undisguised by mimic art, she spreads
Unbounded beauty to the roving eye.[161]

He was alone in his poetic skill, but not in his sentiments. Minor
nameless writers praised the "beauteous stains" of the wild blossoms, the natural artistry of "each grain of sand, or humblest
weed." [162] Thomas Warton the elder celebrated the artless beauty
of the cowslips and the artless song of the lark and the nightingale.[163] William Hamilton of Bangour delighted in the skill of
Nature's pencil, that tinged the valley with green and spread the
"tulip's parted streaks." [164] But even praises like these paled before
Joseph Warton's romantic question:

Can Kent design like Nature? Mark where Thames
Plenty and pleasure pours through Lincoln's meads;
Can the great artist, though with taste supreme
Endu'd, one beauty to this Eden add?
Though he, by rules unfetter'd boldly scorns
Formality and method, round and square
Disdaining, plans irregularly great.
Creative Titian, can thy vivid strokes
Or thine, O graceful Raphael, dare to vie
With the rich tints that paint the breathing mead?
The thousand-colour'd tulip, violet's bell,
Snow-clad and meek, the vermil-tinctur'd rose,
And golden crocus? [165]

Praises of vari-colored wild flowers were but part of the growing delight in the irregularities of natural scenes. The flowers,
however varied, represented Nature in a mild and gentle mood. A

more radical admiration of irregularity found beauty in Nature's wild and terrible landscapes. Good critical justification for such admiration was not far for the poets to seek. Addison had analysed man's pleasure at the sight of "what is great, uncommon, or beautiful." [166] His "great" had included "the prospects of an open champaign country, a vast uncultivated desert of huge heaps of mountains, high rocks, and precipices." His three categories might compass any number of wild and irregular objects:

> There may be, indeed, something so terrible or offensive, that the horror or loathsomeness of an object may overbear the pleasure which results from its greatness, novelty, or beauty; but still there will be such a mixture of delight in the very disgust it gives us, as any of these three qualifications are most conspicuous and prevailing.[167]

Addison's views, received as authoritative criticism by a large and appreciative reading public, were valuable justification for writers who found beauty in the terrifying prospects of natural grandeur.

Many a poet felt that the "rude beauties" of Nature surpassed in charm the planned cascade and the regular grove, the weak effects of human art.[168] "Torturing regularity" turned streams from their appointed courses:

> From step to step with sullen sound
> The forc'd cascades indignant leap,
> 'Till pent they fill the bason's measur'd round,
> There in a dull stagnation doom'd to sleep.[169]

Tyrant art captured what Nature had meant as "wanton waters, volatile and free." [170] Not formal landscapes, but "the rudest prospects" of Nature's wilds served to fire the sensitive soul.[171] A poet could rejoice:

> A mountain fades into the sky;
> While winding round, diffus'd and deep,
> A river rowls with sounding sweep.
> Of human art no traces near,
> I seem alone with Nature here! [172]

To be alone with Nature was Joseph Warton's poetic dream. To him gilt alcoves, marble-mimic gods, parterres, obelisks, urns, were as nothing compared with the "thrush-haunted copse" and the venerable oak beneath whose boughs the bards of old had composed their songs. With one sweeping gesture he dismissed the old formalities and set his face towards scenes of untrammeled beauty:

> Rich in her weeping country's spoils, Versailles
> May boast a thousand fountains, that can cast
> The tortur'd water to the distant Heav'ns;
> Yet let me choose some pine-topt precipice
> Abrupt and shaggy, whence a foamy stream,
> Like Anio, tumbling roars; or some black heath,
> Where straggling stands the mournful juniper,
> Or yew-tree scath'd.[173]

Warton made vocal his preference for Nature's wild magnificence. Other poets not so explicit, implied the same emotion in their descriptions of awesome landscapes.[174] Thomson gloried in the stormy scenes of winter. From the moment "when from the pallid sky the sun descends, with many a spot," through billowing seas and mountain thunders to the climax when

> Huge uproar lords it wide. The clouds commixed
> With stars swift-gliding, sweep along the sky.
> All Nature reels . . .[175]

his verse shook with sound and fury, and signified a fervent interest in the wilder phenomena of Nature. His famous roll call of the mountains, if not an original tribute to the summits of the earth, was yet a sonorous recounting of their grandeur.[176] Thomson felt the connection between the wild greatness of Nature and the upsurge of poetic genius; his Muse soaring amid wintry clouds, sought

> To swell her note with all the rushing winds,
> To suit her sounding cadence to the floods;
> As is her theme, her numbers wildly great.[177]

Other poets who felt the force of Nature's terrible beauty could deliberately bid the Muse

> a while to wintry Horrors turn
> The Song of Night, be the sad sullen Gloom,
> Unsightly, ghastly Scene the dreadful Theme.[178]

Wintry or no the horrors were there. Shapeless rocks, "the raven's haunt," headlong torrents, a "horrid pile" of hills "with many a sable cliff and glittering stream," "Gorgonian horror" of "the middle woods, whose lofty shade darkens, with everlasting night the realms below," gathering tempests, the stormy Atlantic, loomed grimly in the poets' verses.[179] Vastness and variety were the chief charms of the scene that a minor bard spread before his hero's wondering gaze:

> In this moss-cover'd cavern, hopeless laid,
> On the cold cliff I'll lean my aching head,
> And, pleas'd with winter's waste, unpitying, see
> All nature in an agony with me!
> Rough, ragged rocks, wet marshes, ruin'd tow'rs,
> Bare trees, brown brakes, bleak heaths, and ruby moors,
> Dead floods, huge cataracts, to my pleased eyes
> (Now I can smile!) in wild disorder rise:
> And now, the various dreadfulness combin'd,
> Black melancholy comes to doze my mind.[180]

Here was no landscape politely scaled down to the whim of man, no planned regularity, no studied simplicity: this was Nature herself, varied in her magnificence and terrible in her grandeur: Nature that charmed with the clouds of evening and amazed with "rock pil'd on rock amazing up to heaven." [181] This was a match for Addison's vast uncultivated desert," [182] a prospect to enlarge the imagination, to terrify, but to delight it also.

The vast in Nature fired the poets' imaginations with sublime pictures, their emotions with sensations of awe. The tempest, the wintry wastes "awake to solemn thought." [183] The raging ocean inspired "wonder and delight." [184] The sable woods shading the mountain's brow commanded "religious awe." [185] "Stupendous

solitude" roused the soul to "noble horror." [186] Just as in Miltonic
contemplation the pursuit of awe and of emotion in solitudes
blended easily into the pursuit of the mysterious and the supernatural, so admiration for the grandeur of Nature, her terrible
glooms, and still more terrible magnificence tended to prepare the
mind for the enjoyment of other kinds of "delightful horror." [187]
Armstrong, for instance, gave to his description of rivers of the
East a vastness of outline and a solitary gloom calculated to prepare
the onlooker for supernatural visions:

> What solemn twilight! What stupendous shades
> Enwrap these infant floods! Through every nerve
> A sacred horror thrills, a pleasing fear
> Glides o'er my frame. The forest deepens round;
> And more gigantic still the impending trees
> Stretch their extravagant arms athwart the gloom.
> Are these the confines of some fairy world?
> A land of genii? Say, beyond these wilds
> What unknown nations? If indeed beyond
> Aught habitable lies.[188]

Freed from admiration for trim gardens and sculptured hedgerows, the poets could seek delight not only in irregular landscapes,
but in irregularity of a different kind, the irregularity of ruins.
Nature's wild scenes, the ruins of the world, offered one kind of
irregularity, the ruins of man-made structures offered another:
both could inspire beauty and terror.

Pride in national remains fostered by the London Society of
Antiquaries was one element in the interest in ruins. A growing
taste for the irregular was another. Critical praises of Shakespeare
and of Spenser in terms of Gothic architecture helped the cause.
Milton's "studious cloisters pale" had endeared Gothic fanes to
a generation of would-be Il Penserosos. Earlier writers' (e. g., Anthony à Wood's) praise of medieval architecture laid the seeds
of a later enthusiasm. By the seventeen-forties the fad for building in the Gothic style, and the growing conviction that "the best
Gothic buildings in Magnificence and Beauty greatly exceed all
that have been done by both Greeks and Romans" [189] further justi-

fied interest in the remains of English monuments and buildings of an earlier day.

The poets who evidenced such an interest made no pretense of being antiquarians. They did however reveal in their enthusiasm for ruins a preference for gloom, for irregularity, for impressive massiveness, and a ready willingness to feel wonder, delight and awe at the sight of the relics of the past. Pride in native ruins was natural to a generation that could hail the antiquary as "friend of the moss-grown spire and crumbling arch," [190] and rebuke those who sought abroad for "vestiga of antiquity," while

> here, methinks, on British ground
> I've ample scope to range around,
> And objects trace, strange, rare, antique,
> In Wales, the Highlands, or the peak; [191]

Among the strange objects which claimed their attention were the primitive remains of Sarum, and the later ruins of medieval architecture. The stones on Salisbury Plain, for centuries objects of antiquarian speculation, huge, mysterious, linked by Geoffrey of Monmouth with Merlin's magic, and by Stukeley with Druid sacrifices, charmed the poets with their rude grandeur. The vastness of the "rude enormous obelisks, that rise orb within orb, stupendous monuments of artless architecture," [192] roused the writers' amazement and exhausted their invention:

> Rude heaps of massy stones confus'dly stand,
> Their use unknown as whose the raising hand,
> Which oft the vain enquirer have amaz'd,
> And the deep-learn'd in various strife confus'd.
> Here the check'd muse, unable to pursue,
> Retires with the exhaustless theme in view.[193]

Primitive in their appeal, the stones of Sarum held the poets partly by their suggestion of earlier, long-forgotten peoples, and partly by their huge and massive greatness of outline.

Without the suggestion of the primitive, but with equal charms of grandeur and with the added charms of irregularity, Gothic architecture, preferably in ruins, captivated more poets than did

the remains of the Druids.[194] The buildings whose spires dared "to
rush into the skies," whose battlements even in ruin shone with
"wild magnificence," fired poetic imaginations.[195] Fountain Abbey, "stupendous act of antient piety," [196] loomed large in admiring descriptions:

> This venerable Pile with drooping Head,
> Abandon'd and forlorn, in Ruins laid,
> Mourns desolate . . .
> Up roofless Walls the clinging Ivy creep,
> Where num'rous Birds of Prey in Safety sleep,
> Or find in dreary Caves obscure Retreats . . .
> Long Isles are spread with craggy Ruins o'er
> And hollow Winds thro' empty Caverns roar, . . .[197]

The ruins of Bury St. Edmund's with its "broken walls in
craggy fragments" reminded the poets of vanished grandeur.[198]
Ancient towers, chapels, abbeys, castles, prisons, raised awe and
wonder in their hearts.[199] "A Pleasurable sadness" overcame them
in the shadow of Tintern Abbey, "majestic" in "sublime decay."
There was more than a hint of the romanticism to come in the admonition:

> Enter with reverence her hallow'd gate,
> And trace the glorious relics of her state;
> The meeting arches, pillar'd walks admire,
> Or musing hearken to the silenc'd choir.
> Encircling groves diffuse a solemn grace,
> And dimly fill th' historic window's place;
> While pitying shrubs on the bare summit try
> To give the roofless pile a canopy.[200]

The same mixture of awe, pleasure, and fear which had raised the
poets' emotions at the sight of Nature's grandeur, filled their souls
as they viewed the remains of old magnificence:

> On a huge Cliff, whose Summit tow'ring stands,
> Whose Floor impresses deep the Ocean Sands;
> A spacious Citadel in view appears,

Now quite dismantled and subdu'd by Years.
Its drooping Roofs afford an awful Sight,
And mix with Dread the Gazer's large Delight.[201]

It is easy to sense dimly the kindred feelings roused in more or less pre-romantic poets by grand natural scenes, by ruins, by the more emotional aspects of Miltonic contemplation. It is not so easy to illustrate concretely that shift of emotional stimulus from theme to theme. Especially welcome then to the "collector" is a magazine poem that links the topics in a single piece. "The Prospect" in the *Gentleman's Magazine* (1743) may leave the literary critic coldly disapproving, but it wakens to warm enthusiasm the student searching for evidence of early eighteenth-century poetical trends. In it the reader can almost see the author's mind gliding from one association to another, to natural grandeur, to Burnet, to awe, to poetic inspiration, to pleasing dread, to celestial visions—but let the bard speak for himself:

When plac'd on Grampian's lofty brow I stand,
What solemn prospects strike on ev'ry hand!
Here nature in majestic grandeur reigns,
While from her throne she views her wide domains.
Hills pil'd on hills, and rocks together hurl'd,
Sure, Burnet these the ruins of thy world!
Trembling, I ask, what mighty arm could raise
Those spiring summits from their rooted base?
Whose cloudless points as high in Aether glow,
As sink the caverns of the deep below;
What awe, what thoughts these pathless wilds impart?
They whisper omnipresence to the heart!
Here meditation broods—and sheds around
A pleasing stillness o'er the russet ground!
I wonder not the bards of old inspir'd,
Or prophets by celestial vision fir'd,
To unfrequented scenes like these retir'd;
On Sinai's top, possess'd with pious awe,
Moses receiv'd the heav'n-descended law;
In Carmel's shades perus'd by Abab's hate,

The good Elijah shun'd his threaten'd fate.
Here let me as these airy wilds I tread,
(Where ev'ry object prints a secret dread)
Here let me learn, as purer air I breathe,
To scorn the bustling world that lies beneath!
In wisdom's search the lonely walk improve,
And view the realms of bliss that shine above.
 See what romantic views surprize around;
Where'er I tread seems visionary ground! [202]

After such a summary what need to say more? By the mid-
century the drift of poetic interest was plain. The tide had turned
in favor of irregular grandeur, and the best poets of the period
were riding the crest of the wave. Gifted writers, the Wartons for
instance, might voice most gracefully the general admiration for
diversity, but their poems were but part of the general trend. By
the time they wrote, poets and prose writers alike had already set
foot upon the road that led from parterres to a pinetopt precipice,
from an eighteenth-century drawing-room to grim scenes

> Where broken walls in craggy fragments rise;
> An abbey's grandeur, and a prince's court
> O'ergrown with ivy, mould'ring into dirt.[203]

Shakespeare

Among the great geniuses those few draw the admira-
tion of all the world upon them, and stand up as the
prodigies of mankind, who by mere strength of natural
parts, and without any assistance of art or learning, have
produced works that were the delight of their own
times and the wonder of posterity. . . . There is an-
other kind of great genius that I shall place in second
place. . . .
 The genius in both these classes of writers may be

*equally great, but shows itself after a different manner.
In the first, it is like a rich soil in a happy climate, that
produces a whole wilderness of noble plants rising in a
thousand beautiful landscapes, without any certain
order or regularity. In the other, it is the same rich soil
under the same happy climate, that has been laid out in
walks and parterres, and cut into shape and beauty by
the skill of the gardener.*[204]

                        —Spectator, *No. 160*

As the aesthetic battleground shifted from landscapes to literature, "genius" and the "rules" became the watchwords of the opposing factions. The familiar conflict between regularity and irregularity that haunted the poets' discussions of groves and gardens
fired with equal vigor their disputes over literary genius. Since the
bitterest battles of the critics raged around Shakespeare's head, and
since defenders of literary freedom talked of his wildly irregular
genius in terms of the splendid profusion of Nature itself, poetic
tributes to the great Elizabethan offer a useful transition between
the two branches of the aesthetic argument.

In the early years of the eighteenth century the quarrel over
Shakespeare's boundless genius was already acute. At one extreme
of critical opinion, the formalist Charles Gildon declared "Shakespeare is great in nothing but what is according to the rules of
art." [205] At the opposite extreme the dramatist George Farquahar
made clear that, if the choice lay between Aristotle and Shakespeare, his allegiance belonged to his brother playwright: "But it
must be so, because Aristotle said it; now I say it must be otherwise because Shakespear said it, and I'm sure that Shakespear was
the greater poet of the two." [206] It was Shakespeare's irregularity
that stirred up the hornets' nest of criticism. Gildon and his fellow
formalists damned that irregularity on the grounds of lack of art,
Farquahar justified it on the grounds of dramatic expediency. Addison defended it by reference to like irregularities in the works
of the ancients: "I could give instances out of all the tragic writers
of antiquity who have shown their judgment in this particular;
and purposely receded from an established rule of the drama, when

it has made way for a much higher beauty than the observation of such a rule would have been." [207]

While prose critics wrangled, the poets who took up the dispute were content rather to rhapsodize Shakespeare's greatness than to analyse it. "Immortal Shakespeare! we thy claim admit; For, like thy Caesar, thou art mighty yet!" [208] Learning counted for nothing beside the natural insight of Stratford's bard. "Unschool'd," he knew

> More than all Egypt, Greece, or Asia taught.
> Not Homer's self such matchless honours won;
> The Greek has rivals, but thy Shakespear none. [209]

Many a critic of the preceding age had prized the careful artistry of Ben Jonson above the unbridled genius of Shakespeare, but there were eighteenth-century men who thought

> Too nicely Johnson [sic] knew the critic's part;
> Nature in him was almost lost in art. . . .
> But stronger Shakespear felt for man alone:
> Drawn by his pen, our ruder passions stand
> Th' unrival'd picture of his early hand. [210]

The tribute was Collins': he added to that tribute when he put the artless genius of Shakespeare above the rule-ridden artistry of Corneille and Racine. [211]

Sometimes poets imagined Shakespeare himself as challenging his critics:

> What though the footsteps of my devious Muse
> The measur'd walks of Grecian art refuse?
> Or though the frankness of my hardy style
> Mock the nice touches of the critic's file?
> Yet, what my age and climate held to view,
> Impartial I survey'd and fearless drew.
> And say, ye skillful in the human heart,
> Who know to prize a poet's noblest part,
> What age, what clime, could e'er an ampler field
> For lofty thought, for daring fancy, yield? [212]

They fancied he warned his admirers:

> Guard me, ye Britons, from the pedant's page;
> Let not the critick charm your tastes away
> To waste, on trifling words, the studious day:
> No, to the idly busy bookworm leave
> Himself with length of thinking to deceive,
> Let him the dross, and not the metal chuse,
> And my true genius in his language lose:
> Do you, the unimportant toil neglect,
> Pay to your poet's shade the due respect.[213]

Throughout all the poetic praises the keynote was admiration for Shakespeare's irregularity. The bard's most skilful defenders held to the same theme. Thomson challenged, "is not wild Shakespeare thine and nature's boast?" [214] Collins hailed the Elizabethan's poetic fury, his power over the passions, his genius for depicting the supernatural:

> There Shakespeare's self, with ev'ry garland crown'd,
>   In musing hour, his wayward sisters found,
> And with their terrors drest the magic scene,
> From them he sung, when mid his bold design,
>   Before the Scot afflicted and aghast,
> The shadowy kings of Banquo's fated line
>   Through the dark cave in gleamy pageant past.[215]

Akenside placed Shakespeare among those whose natural taste was for the wild and unconfined:

>   Different minds
> Incline to different objects; one pursues
> The vast alone, the wonderful, the wild;
> Another sighs for harmony, and grace,
> And gentlest beauty. Hence when lightning fires
> The arch of heaven and thunders rock the ground,
> When furious whirlwinds rend the howling air,
> And ocean, groaning from his lowest bed,
> Heaves his tempestuous billows to the sky;

Amid the mighty uproar, while below
The nations tremble, Shakespeare looks abroad
From some high cliff, superior, and enjoys
The elemental war.[216]

While to Akenside Shakespeare was the lover of Nature's wildness, and to Collins he was the master of the supernatural, to Joseph Warton, Shakespeare was the child of Nature, fancy-taught amid scenes of natural beauty:

Whom on the winding Avon's willow'd banks
Fair Fancy found, and bore the smiling babe
To a close cavern: (still the shepherds show
The sacred place, whence with religious awe
They hear, returning from the field at eve,
Strange whisp'rings of sweet music through the air)
Here, as with honey gather'd from the rock,
She fed the little prattler, and with songs
Oft soothed his wondering ears; with deep delight
On her soft lap he sat, and caught the sounds.[217]

Whether in the guise of a little prattler, or of an unsurpassed poet, Shakespeare appeared in the writers' verses as the free and unconfined genius disdainful of the rigors of art. Many said or implied that he was the child of Nature: Warton pictured him as fancy's foster-child surrounded by natural beauties: it remained for a nameless poet bluntly to explain Shakespeare's genius in terms of Nature itself:

Exalted Shakespeare, with a boundless mind,
Rang'd far and wide; a genius unconfin'd!
The passions sway'd, and captive led the heart,
Without the critick's rules or aid of art:
So some fair clime, by smiling Phoebus blest,
And in a thousand charms by nature drest,
Where limpid streams in wild meanders flow,
And on the mountains tow'ring forests grow . . .
No industry of man, no needless toil,
Can mend the rich uncultivated soil.[218]

From that rich uncultivated soil had sprung the choicest flowers of English poetry, and formal critics were at a loss to account for the blossoms. But praise of Shakespeare, ranged staunchly on the side of genius, was only part of the story: on the general question of genius and the rules the poets had more to say—on both sides.

Rules

Often it is asked whether a praiseworthy poem be due to Nature or to Art. For my part, I do not see of what avail is either study, when not enriched by Nature's vein; or native wit, if untrained; so truly does each claim the other's aid, and to make with it a friendly league.[219]

—*Horace,* Art of Poetry

Early eighteenth-century writers who listed labor and learning as essentials of poetic composition were only continuing the traditions of respect for the ancients and for reason which had already blended in the seventeenth-century decision that "the rules of Aristotle were nothing but nature and good sense reduc'd to a method," or, as the eighteenth century itself expressed it, "nature still but nature methodized." [220] To classicists the rules were hallowed by the practice of the ancients ("to study nature is to study them"); to rationalists the rules were confirmed by "reason and experience," but to none were those rules so sacred that he dared substitute them for natural genius.[221] Ben Jonson, for all his tirades against those who decried art in writing, admitted freely that "there is no doctrine will do good where nature is wanting." [222] Milton, himself indebted both to Nature and to art, granted: "Yet natural ability without art is thought to avail more than art without natural ability; but neither one can function adequately unless supplemented by practice." [223] The rigid eighteenth-century formalist Charles Gildon conceded that "the rules of poetry are necessary to the forming of all valuable poems, but they are not able to make a poet without genius and practice too." [224] On the questions of genius and the rules the poets for the most part fell into the usual liberal and conservative groups. Traditionalists emphasized rules, "vigilance and labor"; [225] liberals dwelt on genius and poetic fury. But each side admitted something to the other.

Conservative poets who continued the venerable tradition of the learned writer modestly deprecated their own lack of talent and generously praised their contemporaries' wisdom. They lauded Addison for his just and easy style, commended Cibber for his "wit and sense," and found the ideal fusion of philosophy and poetry in the works of Pope, "where Nature pours the genial strain, With the fair springs of learning fraught." [226] At once poet and critic, Pope remained

> Imperial in his art, prescribing laws
> Clear from the knitted brow, and squinted sneer;
> Learn'd without pedantry; correctly bold,
> And regularly easy. Gentle, now,
> As rising incense, or descending dews,
> The variegated echo of his theme,
> Now animated flame commands the soul
> To glow with sacred wonder.[227]

Occasionally reverence for regularity carried minor poets into indiscreet criticisms. The modern reader shudders at their pleasure in Pope's and Dryden's improvements of Chaucer's "style grown obsolete, his numbers rude," and despairs at their congratulations to Aaron Hill for his transmuting the copper of Shakespeare's works into gold.[228] Fortunately few went to such imprudent lengths: most poetic praise of the rules was soberly sensible. The rules of the ancients were the beginnings of poetic wisdom. Modern taste must learn to brook "the bondage of laborious art." "What Horace, what Quintillian thought, Join'd with a little mother wit," might do much to make a poet. The wise author must strive for lucid order and the "wondrous pow'r of art! That gives its proper grace to every part." [229] For the ambitious poet a magazine verse offered a bibliography of aesthetic instruction:

> To bound your thoughts, to form your judgment right,
> The wise improvers of poetick wit
> Can well direct; Stagyra's learned sage,
> That glory, pride, and wonder of his age,
> With studious care and diligence peruse;
> The Roman bard will next instruct your muse,
> With graceful elegance of taste to please,
> To write politely, and to write with ease:
> Vida, that sung in Leo's golden days,
> Demands alike your study and your praise.
> Where Vida, Horace, Aristotle fail,
> A Buckingham, or Pope may well prevail:
> From them you'll learn those skilful strokes of art,
> At once to sooth the ear, and touch the heart.[230]

Any tyro brave enough to tackle so formidable an array of authorities might find encouragement in the thought that

> this poetick turn of mind,
> With steady resolution join'd
> And application, may, in time
> Fill gilded streams with nervous rhime.[231]

But loyally as the conservatives defended "steady resolution" and "application," they numbered among their company no notable names. Except for a passing comment by Thomson, all the traditional pieces were the work of minor or anonymous poets who mildly repeated with neo-classical reasonableness the sentiment that Ben Jonson had once propounded with Elizabethan vigor—that a writer must study to be great:

> And not thinke hee can leape forth suddainly a poet by dreaming hee hath been in Parnassus, or having washt his lipps, as they say, in Helicon. There goes more to his making then so: for to nature, exercise, imitation, and studie, art must bee added to make all these perfect. And though these challenge to themselves much in the making up of our maker, it is art only can lead him to perfection, and leave him there in possession, as planted by her hand.[232]

Genius

All good poets, epic as well as lyric, compose their beau-
tiful poems not by art, but because they are inspired
and possessed. . . . For the poet is a light and winged
and holy thing, and there is no invention in him until he
has been inspired and is out of his senses.[233]

—*Plato,* Ion

Staunchly the minor poets stood by the old order, but their repe-
tition of timeworn formulae had a mechanical sound; the voice of
conviction had gone. The appeal to reason on the part of such late
seventeenth-century critics as Davenant and Hobbes had shaken
the strength of the rules as based on the authority of the ancients.
The growing tradition of taste, of the *je ne sais quoi* in estimates of
beauty fostered an attitude of subjective individualism that eventually refused the rules on any authority whatsoever. Dennis' insistence on the importance of feeling in poetry and Shaftesbury's and
Hutcheson's appeal to a sixth sense of beauty had encouraged rebellion against aesthetic regulations. Addison's claim that "there is
more beauty in the work of a great genius who is ignorant of all
the rules of art, than in the works of a little genius, who not only
knows, but scrupulously observes them," [234] encouraged men gradually but definitely to progress towards that critical code which
put the rules out of court for all poets great or little.

The poetic rebels against the rules prized inspiration, fancy, and
emotional appeal above elegance, art or polish, but their rebellion
varied in degree if not in kind. Mildest were the modest versifiers
who insisted that their panegyrics made up in sincerity what they
lacked in art.[235] Typical of such poetic alibis was Mallet's apology
to the Prince of Orange:

> Receive, Lov'd Prince, the tribute of our praise,
> This hasty welcome, in unfinish'd lays,
> At best the pomp of song, the paint of art,
> Display the genius, but not speak the heart.[236]

More interesting and more significant than such gentle protests
were outright denunciations of the tyranny of literary rules. One
bard relied on good country ale to free his Muse for the writing
of "homespun English verse." [237] Another, rapt in a poetic vision,
followed Plato—at an infinite distance:

> I'm incorrect, the Learned say,
> That I write well, but not their Way. . . .
> My freeborn Thoughts I'll not confine,
> Tho' all Parnassus could be mine.
> No, let my Genius have its way,
> My Genius I will still obey;
> Nor, with their stupid Rules, control
> The sacred Pulse that beats within my Soul. . . .
> With Transport I the Pen employ,
> And every Line reveals my joy:
> No Pangs of Thought I undergo . . .[238]

The modern reader agrees with the last line at least. Still a third
poetic liberal went to Nature itself for justification for the variety
in his writings:

> I answer you in verse, you see,
> And verse of great variety.
> If at elections you have been,
> All the electors you have seen
> Were not alike: You always find,
> They're of a multifarious kind;
> Humps, long-shanks, cripples, asses, owls, and apes,
> And nature in a thousand shapes.
> So reverend sir, you'll meet with here
> As many oddities as there:
> For all my verses, you will find,
> Are of a multifarious kind . . .
> Irregulars of every sort
> To make variety of sport.[239]

Some of the poets sounded a graver warning:

Lean not, sustain'd, a weight no muse allows!
Pilf'ring the faded bays, from classic brows
Nor creep, contented, in the modern way;
A dry, dull, soft, low, languid, tiresome lay!
But, strongly sacred, and sublimely warm,
Strike the aw'd soul, and the touch'd passions charm.[240]

If warning were not enough, the horrid example might impress:

> Thus some who feel Apollo's rage,
> Would teach their muse her dress and time,
> 'Till hamper'd so with rules of art,
> They smother quite the vital flame.

> They daily chime the same dull tone,
> Their muse no daring sallies grace,
> But stiffly held with bit and curb,
> Keeps heavy trot, tho' equal pace.[241]

Not the curb of the bit but the wings of Pegasus, not restraint but
freedom, not order but variety should be the portion of poetry.
Freedom in verse might rouse the pedant's ire, but poetic rebels
were beyond worrying about critical lashes. A nameless bard could
bid the doubting:

> Be not so scrupulously nice,
>   Methinks you rather ought to praise
>   The manly freedom of their phrase,
> Where luck the want of care supplies,
>   Rather with this illustrious band,
> Some trivial errors I'd commit,
>   Than with so scrupulous a hand
> Stand weighing every word that's writ.[242]

If the critics still proved adamant, the poet was free to appeal to
non-learned judges: Ramsay for instance brought his case to the
ladies:

> Fair judges to your censure I submit,
> If you allow this poem to have wit,

> I'll look with scorn upon these musty fools,
> Who only move by old worm-eaten rules.[243]

Both Ramsay and his anonymous colleague were appealing from old objective canons of criticism to newer subjective ones.

Impatience of rule and emphasis on the subjective led some poets from the beaten track of conventional opinion. Farther afield still wandered the bards who exalted the emotional content of poetry. To them sincerity of feeling was the test of poetic worth. Only a love-lorn muse could paint "the anguish of a heart that bleeds." "How diff'rent moves the fancy, or the heart, What streams from genius, and what drops from art." The prayers of simple devotion winged heavenwards, while the "labour'd phrase" remained below.[244] John Wesley described in detail his substitution of feeling for rhetoric:

> When first my feeble verse essay'd
> Of heavenly joys to sing. . . .
>
> With studied words each rising thought
> I deck'd with nicest art,
> And shining metaphors I sought
> To burnish every part.
>
> Meanwhile I whispering heard a Friend,
> "Why all this vain pretence?
> Love has a sweetness ready penn'd;
> Take that, and save expense." [245]

Not the learned versifier weighted with rules and regulations, but the artless genius blessed with feeling and freedom was the poetic ideal of "nature's simple plan." Stephen Duck was praised for his "untutor'd Muse," Mrs. Rowe for her contempt for art's borrowed grandeur.[246] Milton won acclaim as the hero who had rescued Albion's Muse from trite themes and cramping style:

> Unpractis'd themes, his lofty muse presum'd;
> Disdaining coupl'd sounds. In wondrous thought
> High-rais'd, and soaring with unclouded light,
> She boldly shook the cramping fetters off;

And sovereign, built a model unconfin'd,
Immortal as his name.[247]

Symbolic of the changing fashion was Thomas Warton's preference for the "wildly-warbled song" of Spenser to the Attic wit
of Pope:

> Thro' Pope's soft song tho' all the Graces breathe,
> And happiest art adorn his Attic page;
> Yet does my mind with sweeter transport glow,
> As at the root of mossy trunk reclin'd,
> In magic Spenser's wildly-warbled song
> I see deserted Una wander wide
> Thro' wasteful solitudes, and lurid heaths,
> Weary, forlorn; than when the fated fair
> Upon the bosom bright of silver Thames
> Launches in all the lustre of brocade,
> Amid the splendours of the laughing Sun.[248]

The extreme of such admiration for aesthetic freedom found
expression in the writings of poets who gave allegiance to the
Platonic tradition of poetic fury. Some there were who had never
forgotten that "he who, having no touch of the Muses' madness in
his soul, comes to the door and thinks that he will get into the
temple by the help of art—he, I say, and his poetry are not admitted; the same man disappears and is nowhere when he enters
into rivalry with the madman." [249] Faithful to that creed of divine
madness, they rhapsodized the poet's soaring imagination, his exalted vision, his headlong composition at the dictates of enthusiasm.
Inspired by celestial visions, their "ambitious Pegasus wou'd fly In
transport, wrapt above the sky." [250] They sought in the ancients,
not elegance but inspired frenzy:

> O could I catch one ray divine
> From thy intolerable blaze!
> To pour strong lustre on my line,
> And my aspiring tongue to raise.[251]

Nature wakened in them a strong romantic fervor:

> I felt a pow'r too strong to be supprest,
> Move with poetick rapture in my breast.
> Scenes all-transporting set my soul on fire,
> And fields and meads their wonted thoughts inspire.
> Each fruitful hedge inviting themes supplies,
> In ev'ry field harmonious numbers rise.[252]

Only the "sacred few" touched with the "strong, enthusiastic heat" [253] might

> Alone thro' darling fields pursue
> Th' aerial regions bright. . . .
> While art, with hard laborious pains,
> Creeps on unseen, nor much attains,
> By slow progressive toil.[254]

Loudly the voices of Collins, Akenside and Joseph Warton defended the cause of poetic fury. To Collins the poet was the lover of fancy, whose heart burning with a "wild enthusiast heat" poured out its passions "in numbers warmly pure, and sweetly strong." [255] Akenside scorned the rule-ridden genius of France "which fetters eloquence to scantiest bounds, And maims the cadence of poetic sounds." [256] Rules will not suffice for poetry:

> Nature's kindling breath
> Must fire the chosen genius; Nature's hand
> Must string his nerves, and imp his eagle-wings,
> Impatient of the painful steep, to soar
> High as the summit; there to breathe at large
> Aethereal air: with bards and sages old,
> Immortal sons of praise . . .[257]

Blessed with the "dread prophetic heat," the chosen genius wrote under the twin influences of judgment and poetic fury, with fury dominating:

> By degrees, the mind
> Feels her young nerves dilate: the plastic powers
> Labour for action: blind emotions heave

His bosom; and with loveliest frenzy caught,
From earth to heaven he rowls his daring eye,
From heaven to earth. Anon ten thousand shapes,
Like spectres trooping to the wisard's call,
Flit swift before him. From the womb of earth,
From ocean's bed they come: the eternal heavens
Disclose their splendors, and the dark abyss
Pours out her births unknown. With fixed gaze
He marks the rising phantoms. Now compares
Their different forms; now blends them, now divides,
Enlarges and attenuates by turns;
Opposes, ranges in fantastic bands,
And infinitely varies. Hither now,
Now thither fluctuates his inconstant aim,
With endless choice perplex'd. At length his plan
Begins to open. Lucid order dawns . . .[258]

Joseph Warton's tributes to the inspired poet resemble Akenside's in their essential details, but there is a distinctive touch of cultural primitivism in Warton's evocation of a Fancy half goddess, half noble savage:

O nymph with loosely-flowing hair,
With buskin'd leg, and bosom bare,
Thy waist with myrtle-girdle bound,
Thy brows with Indian feathers crown'd.[259]

Gilbert West's translation of Pindar gave Warton an opportunity to celebrate the fury of the Greek original. Pindar's odes, so widely and so woefully imitated by a myriad mediocre versifiers, had long symbolized the height of poetic frenzy. Pindar, like Shakespeare, was of that class of "nobly wild and extravagant" geniuses "who by mere strength of natural parts, and without any assistance of art or learning, have produced works that were the delight of their own times and the wonder of posterity." [260] For just such unbridled poetic strength Warton lauded the Greek lyrist:

The fearful, frigid lays of cold and creeping art,
Nor touch, nor can transport th' unfeeling heart;

Pindar, our inmost bosom piercing, warms
With glory's love, and eager thirst of arms.[261]

Among the early eighteenth-century poets both "cold and creeping art" and Pindaric transports had their defenders. If a representative of each faction were to sum up the case for his side, the
conservatives would best be represented, not by their own journey-
men verse, but by the vigorous prose of the seventeenth-century
classicist, Thomas Rymer:

> Fancy leaps and frisks, and away she's gone, whilst reason
> rattles the chains and follows after. Reason must consent and
> ratify whatever by fancy is attempted in its absence, or else 'tis
> all null and void in law. Those who object against reason are
> Fanaticks in Poetry, and are never to be sav'd by their good
> works.[262]

At the opposite extreme, the defiers of tradition had an eloquent
spokesman in the person of Joseph Warton whose invocation to
Fancy welded together praise of Shakespeare, contempt for art,
and love of poetic fury into an aesthetic ideal of boundless freedom
and feeling. He begged the "warm enthusiastic maid"

> O hear our prayer, O hither come
> From thy lamented Shakespeare's tomb,
> On which thou lov'st to sit at eve,
> Musing o'er thy darling's grave;
> O queen of numbers, once again
> Animate some chosen swain,
> Who, fill'd with unexhausted fire,
> May boldly smite the sounding lyre . . .
> Teach him to scorn with frigid art,
> Feebly to touch th' unraptur'd heart;
> Like lightning, let his mighty verse
> The bosom's inmost foldings pierce;
> With native beauties win applause
> Beyond cold critics' studied laws.[263]

As the mid-century approached that irregular ideal grew ever
stronger. Only minor, uninspired voices remained to support the

rules—the poets and the poetry were on the side of "the enthusiast or lover of nature."

Taste

For even rude nature itself, in its primitive simplicity is a better guide to judgment than improv'd sophistry, and pedantick learning.[264]
—*Shaftesbury*, Advice to an Author

The story of the decline of the rules during the early eighteenth century cannot be told without some mention of the doctrine of taste. Eighteenth-century "taste" had much in common with the "common sense" of the seventeenth century. Both were sure in judgment, accurate in criticism, capable of cultivation and improvement. In the seventeenth century Rymer had chosen the common sense criticism of untrained judges as preferable to the learned opinions of professional scholars.[265] The Royal Society, in its self-conscious program for a reform of prose style, preferred "the Language of Artizans, Countrymen, and Merchants, before that of Wits and Scholars." [266] In the early years of the next century Addison graciously praised a belle for that "natural sense which makes her a better judge than a thousand criticks." [267] But Addison made plain on occasion that taste, though innate, could and should be cultivated: "But notwithstanding this faculty must in some measure be born with us, there are several methods for cultivating and improving it, and without which it will be very uncertain and of little use to the person that possesses it." [268] Shaftesbury, himself something of a scholarly dilettante, put the taste of a cultivated gentleman above the booklore of the pedant, but like Addison, he carefully pointed out that "labour and pains are requir'd, and time to cultivate a natural genius." [269] Shaftesbury's disciple Hutcheson was inclined to stress the innate quality of man's sense of beauty more than the necessity of its cultivation; "thus education and custom may influence our internal sense . . . but all this presupposes our sense of beauty to be natural." [270]

In literature the doctrine of taste encouraged the concept of literary beauties that must be intuitively perceived. Leonard Welsted, for instance, condemned the hackneyed treatises of critics because "the soul of good writing is not to be come at thro' such mechanic laws . . . these beauties in a word, are rather to be felt than described." [271] Whether championed by critics or by philosophers the doctrine of taste tended in its aesthetic aspects to encourage feeling and individualism at the expense of reason and conformity.

Although by 1750 the doctrine of taste was playing a major part in undermining rigid standards of criticism, poetic references to the term were few. Collins, in passing, coupled taste with genius as a source of "divine excess" in poetry.[272] Dr. Armstrong admired taste's far-reaching influence:

> 'Tis chiefly taste, or blunt, or gross, or fine,
> Makes life insipid, bestial, or divine.
> Better be born with taste to little rent,
> Than the dull monarch of a continent.[273]

Akenside made clear the democratic quality of the gift. The untutored peasant, watching the sunset, responded to "the form of beauty smiling at his heart"; neither wealth nor position guaranteed to man that

> discerning sense
> Of decent and sublime, with quick disgust
> From things deform'd, or disarrang'd, or gross
> In species? This, nor gems, nor stores of gold,
> Nor purple state, nor culture can bestow;
> But God alone, when first his active hand
> Imprints the secret bias of the soul.[274]

Though the poets so seldom wrote directly on the doctrine of taste, one minor bard did come out bluntly against it. His attack, an ironic commentary on the "man of taste," made clear the connection between the idea of taste as an individual standard, and

the ideal of the poet as a law unto himself. The mock hero declared:

> So I was tragi-comically got.
> My infant tears a sort of measure kept,
> I squall'd in distichs, and in triplets wept.
> No youth did I in education waste,
> Happy in an heriditary taste. . . .
> Good parts are better than eight parts of speech;
> Since these declin'd, those undeclin'd they call,
> I thank my stars, that I declin'd them all.
> To Greek or Latin tongues without pretence,
> To trust to mother wit and father sense.
> Nature's my guide, all sciences I scorn,
> Pains I abhor, I was a poet born.[275]

He spoke the last line in jest—the era was approaching when poets
would speak it in earnest.

3

Ethics

Comus: *Wherefore did nature pour her bounties forth*
With such a full and unwithdrawing hand,
Covering the earth with odours, fruits, and
flocks,
Thronging the seas with spawn innumberable,
But all to please and sate the curious taste. . . .
Lady: *Impostor! do not charge most innocent Na-*
ture,
As if she would her children should be riotous
With her abundance. She, good Catress,
Means her provision only to the good,
That live according to her sober laws,
And holy dictate of spare Temperance.[276]
—*Milton,* Comus

WHEN the poets attempted to apply the doctrine of *vivere secundum naturam* to man's life itself, they entered into the age-old debate over reason and passion as guides to human life. Nor did they confine themselves to discussions of man's intelligence and emotions: their efforts to settle on "Nature" as a norm for human conduct led them into the allied problems of the relative merits of man and beast, the innate benevolence of mankind, and the need for humane treatment of all living creatures.

The fundamental quarrel underlying the debate of Comus and the Lady reached back at least to the ancient days of the Stoics and Epicureans. Eighteenth-century gentlemen interested in the time-honored conflict could ponder Milton's classic expression of the dispute: they could recall Shakespeare's Troilus with his scornful, "Nay, if we talk of reason, Let's shut our gates and sleep . . ."

and Hector with his reasonable reminder, "the heavens themselves, the planets and this centre Observe degree, priority, and place." [277] Even without literary reminders, men of the early eighteenth century had reason to be acutely conscious of the struggle. Their own generation saw the rule of reason, reinforced though it was by the philosophy of Locke and the physics of Newton, fighting a gradually losing battle with the philosophy of the moral sense which bade man follow not his head, but his heart.

As early eighteenth-century poets considered the rival roles of Nature and art in the drama of life, their opinions reflected the ancient debate over the ethical implications of "Nature." As usual, the term "Nature" had many meanings. To a few versifiers it meant ruleless but valid instinct, to others it connoted simplicity of manners, to still more it indicated a rude, unpolished state of primitive man, sorely in need of the refinements of law and custom.

Those writers (a small minority) who urged art in conduct advocated it as a means of mental discipline or of social advancement. A period which idolized the exquisite polish of a Chesterfield could scarcely omit some expressions of admiration for cultivated social graces. In defiance of current admonitions to the artless fair to remain artless, some realistic bards extolled the beauty "with native charms adorn'd, improv'd by art," admired the Princess of Orange for her polished wisdom, and approved the precocious beauty of fifteen who added "the choice embellishments of art" to her native graces.[278] The belle who just missed social success failed because she proved "with too much kindness and too little art Prone to indulge the dictates of her heart." [279] The wise fair knew the value of social subterfuge:

> But beauty, wit, and youth may sometimes fail,
> Nor always o'er the stubborn soul prevail;
> Then let the fair one have recourse to art,
> Who cannot storm, may undermine the heart,
> First form your artful looks with studious care,
> From mild to grave, from tender to severe . . .[280]

In the world of polite manners:

> Arts that embellish life none discommend,
> If duly check'd to no excess they tend:
> The peer should differ from gross, unbred swain,
> Gay, but not glittering; polite, but plain.[281]

Nor was the usefulness of art confined to the social sphere. Art inspired the prudent pursuit of happiness. It formed "the rude, unpolish'd mind." [282] Education won men to the "polish'd arts Each moral, generous sentiment imparts." [283] Feminine as well as masculine minds might profit by art's improvements. Ambrose Philips, with echoes of Locke, bade a girl's parents "figure on her waxen mind, Images of life refin'd." [284] "A Lady" urged Pope to persuade society to give the fair sex educational advantages, since "women, if taught, would be as bold and wise As haughty men, improv'd by art and rules." [285] James Thomson, often the exponent of man's innate goodness, apostrophized philosophy as the source of mankind's achievement:

> Without thee what were unenlightened man?
> A savage, roaming through the woods and wilds
> In quest of prey; and with the unfashioned fur
> Rough-clad; devoid of every finer art
> And elegance of life. . . .
>   but, taught by thee,
> Ours are the plans of policy and peace;
> To live like brothers, and, conjunctive all,
> Embellish life.[286]

Less elegant but more original than Thomson, an anonymous poet applied to the cultivation of man's social system all the prosaic detail of a farmer's cultivation of the soil:

> Pursue the glorious task, the pleasing toil,
> Forsake the fields, and till the nobler soil;
> Extend the farmer's care to human kind,
> Manure the heart, and cultivate the mind;
> There plant religion, reason, freedom, truth,
> And sow the seeds of virtue in our youth;
> Let no rank weeds corrupt, or brambles choak,

And shake the vermin from the British oak;
From northern blasts protect the vernal bloom,
And guard our pastures from the wolves of Rome.
On Britain's liberty ingraft thy name,
And reap the harvest of immortal fame! [287]

While the defenders of social graces advised deliberate pursuit
of polished charms, advocates of natural simplicity insisted that
pleasant, unaffected manners were better than elegant courtesies,
and that an honest heart more than compensated for a neglected
education. As the elegant beauties languished behind their fans,
the poets who defended "Nature" sharply censured elaborate dress
and makeup.[288] The ideal girl "shou'd not want the foreign aid Of
silk, embroid'ry or brocade." She best pleased by native graces:
to seek to mend natural beauties was to forfeit devotion: "if man
your slave you would desire, Let him your person, not your art
admire." The complaints of disillusioned poets were pointed. A
beauty was warned:

> Don't Caelia, strive that face to mend;
> Where nature plaid her part;
> That Venus gave mankind t' enslave.
> Art spoils the beauty nature gave,
> And nature spoils your art.[289]

Phyllis heard her saddened lover declare she had lost his admiration by her deception—in using rouge:

> How have I prais'd thy cheeks where roses blow!
> How dwell'd with wonder on thy sable brow!
> How have I well thou know'st, fatigu'd my eyes
> On thy dear lips where coral seem'd to rise!
> What sighs I gave thee at the parting look,
> And fond the work of art for nature took!
> The charm is ended: I my heart command,
> And when I praise thee next shall praise thy hand.[290]

Such fashionable coquettes were outshone by gentle heroines who
counted among their virtues simplicity, beauty, truth, lively sym-

pathy and artless wisdom.[291] Their "matchless virtues void of art"
were freely growing gifts of nature:

> Virtue in others the forc'd child of art,
> Is but the native temper of her heart;
> All charms, her sex so often court in vain,
> (Like Indian fruits which our cold earth disdain)
> In her grow wild, as in their native air,
> And she has all perfection without care.[292]

William Hamilton's favorite charmer was typical of all the natural
beauties:

> Whose soul with gen'rous friendship glows;
> Who feels the blessing she bestows;
> Gentle to all, but kind to me,
> Such be mine, if such there be.
>   Whose genuine thoughts devoid of art,
> Are all the natives of her heart;
> A simple train, from falsehood free,
> Such the maid that's made for me.[293]

"The Bachelor's choice," Delme of the artless voice, Miss Evans
of the unstudied charms, helped swell the roll of nature's belles.[294]
Doubtless the most winning of all the simple heroines was the "Lass
of Peattie's Mill":

> Without the help of art,
> Like flowers which grace the wild,
> She did her sweets impart,
> Whene'er she spoke or smil'd,
> Her looks they were so mild,
> Free from affected pride,
> She me to love beguil'd;
> I wish'd her for my bride.[295]

When guileless maids had such native graces, what wonder that
poets advised:

> Mothers, and guardian aunts, forbear
> Your impious pains to form the fair,

> Nor lay out so much cost and art,
> But to deflow'r the virgin heart;
> Of every folly-fost'ring bed
> By quick'ning heat of custom bred:
> Rather than by your culture spoil'd,
> Desist, and give us nature wild,
> Delighted with a hoyden soul,
> Which truth and innocence control.
> Coquets, leave off affected arts,
> Gay fowlers at a flock of hearts . . .
> In love the artless catch the game.[296]

No doubt the poets did their best, but one glance at the elaborate costumes and courtesies of eighteenth-century beauties is enough to convince the modern reader that the ladies never really believed that "in love the artless catch the game."

Although the fair received most of the poetic admonitions, men as well as women were urged to be artless in manners and dress. The admirable man was the plain, good citizen, wise without learning, simple, honest, loyal, benevolent, blessed with "a strict integrity, devoid of art."[297] "A noble grace, self-taught, beyond the reach of mimic art, Adorn'd him."[298] "Nature's plain light," "nor warp'd by wit, nor by proud science taught," guided him to useful living.[299]

While Nature showered blessings upon mankind, art's baleful influence ruined human happiness. The unspoiled innocence of man's first happy state had given way to flattery and folly and a social code wherein "vice sulks beneath each modish art."[300] The depths to which artifice in conduct had dragged the youth of the continent caused one poet to contend:

> And rather would I see my Britons roam
> Untutor'd savages, among the woods,
> As once they did, in naked innocence,
> Than polish'd like the vile degenerate race
> Of modern Italy's corrupted sons.[301]

Edward Young blamed art for those hypocrites "who stifle nature, and subsist on art; Who coin the face, and petrify the heart."[302]

He damned "brainless art" for blinding men to their serious destinies, "cursed art" for destroying man's sense of shame, and "painted art's depraved allurements" for tempting man from Nature's lawful charms.[303]

Though in themselves neither numerous nor significant, poetic discussions of the rival positions of elegant polish and unadorned Nature as moulders of human manners and morals are useful as an introduction to the wider and graver quarrel over reason and passion which ranged eighteenth-century poets and philosophers in opposing camps.

Reason

I see no harm in supposing "that men are naturally dispos'd to virtue, and not left merely indifferent, to be engag'd in actions only as they appear to tend to their own private good." [304]

—*Hutcheson*, An Inquiry into the Original
of our Ideas of Beauty and Virtue

Hutcheson's benevolent view of man's nature represents the concept with which eighteenth-century optimists combatted the Christian tradition of a weakened human nature, and the naturalist's belief in an essentially selfish human animal. The immediate antecedents of the eighteenth-century quarrel over benevolence and selfishness as dominating motives in man's nature lay in the seventeenth-century struggle whose chief protagonists had been Hobbes and the Cambridge Platonists. Hobbes' state of Nature "where every man is enemy to every man," [305] and in which the good was that which a man desired, was countered by the Cambridge Platonists with a concept of human nature naturally disposed to generosity, responsible to an objective standard of good, and endowed with an "inward sense," "the Boniform Faculty of the Soul," which enabled man to know good intuitively, and possessing it, to enjoy "the relish and delectation thereof." [306]

It was that theory of the Boniform Faculty which foreshadowed the teaching of such philosophers of the moral sense as Shaftesbury and Hutcheson, for in time the objective quality of the good itself, upon which the Cambridge Platonists had insisted, was lost: the inward sense, discussed so often by means of analogies to the bodily senses, became a confused concept that tended to lose its spiritual quality. Men's feeling towards objects or actions sufficed as testimony of the objects' goodness. In the end the Boniform Faculty gave way to an inner sense of virtue, and became a standard of values as subjective as Hobbes' with this difference, that Hobbes had predicated a motive of choice essentially selfish, while his eighteenth-century opponents insisted on one essentially benevolent. It was chiefly opposition to Hobbes' insistence on human selfishness that fostered the early eighteenth-century concept of man as a naturally benevolent being, a creature of feeling—of good feeling.

Against such a concept of human nature were ranged the deists under the banner of Locke. The English philosopher had limited the scope of human reason even within the narrow sphere of the "paucity and imperfections of the ideas we have, and which we employ it about," [307] but within the bounds he set, he had given his generation a complete trust in the accuracy of reason and in its power to lead men to the millennium. Reason might outlaw enthusiasm, marvel, and miracle, but it would make men secure in the circumscribed universe which it then claimed to comprehend.

Nor were Locke and the deists the only supporters of reason's claim. The old Stoic admiration for reason as a rule of life, the traditional Stoic doctrine of the value of moderation and of the uselessness of passion, remained as active concepts in an age which liberally sprinkled its pages with maxims from Seneca and Cicero. A more powerful force than Locke or Seneca was on the side of reason. Christian tradition had tirelessly insisted that man, weakened in intellect and will by the Fall, must discipline his passions and submit to the rule of intellect if he was to lead a virtuous life. While feeling and reason had both been impaired by the Fall, reason was still the faculty more worthy of trust.

As the poets discussed the claims of reason and passion traces of all these strains appeared in their verses. Some of them trusted man's inner sense of good. Some, moralizing man's fallen state, warned humanity to submit heart and head to guidance from a Power above. Others confident of the power of reason reaffirmed the Stoic doctrine of peace through the suppression of passion. A few gloomy spirits repeated Hobbes' or Mandeville's belief that man's strongest passions were essentially evil.

On the whole reason had the best of the ethical quarrel. Philosophic and aesthetic discussions had paid ample compliments to irregularity and diversity, but in the moral sphere the traditional ideal of ordered restraint held fast. The writers who echoed the trust of their generation in the essential goodness of the human heart, who agreed with Shaftesbury that men's passions if left to themselves would establish a benevolent and prosperous society, were easily out-talked by grimmer poets who, looking out on a world torn by passionate conflict, cried warning that reason alone might restore the rule of order, which is peace.

Poetic defenders of reason outnumbered two to one the defenders of instinct and grew ever more numerous and more eloquent during the second quarter of the century. Noting their stubborn defense of regularity, the critic is forced to give over his hopes of a sweeping general statement of change and to rest with the tame reflection that the poets' respect for reason serves as another example of the strength of traditional ideals.

The writers' confidence in human judgment usually went hand in hand with a lack of confidence in human emotions. "The Christian Hero" feared to trust Nature alone as a guard against evil. "Corrupted Nature" needed the healing influence of books that please and instruct. The runaway passions must have the curb of reason strengthened by divine aid. Man's weak feelings led him to folly: wit and sense were his only protection.[308] Naturally Wesley contributed the grimmest descriptions of human corruption. He saw "rebel Nature" as a force opposing the Divine Will, a chain binding man to earth when his soul should be striving towards heaven.[309] Only constant prayer for Divine help could vanquish the rebel within man; "for ah! my Lord, if Thou depart, Straight

rebel Nature mounts Thy throne." [310] For Wesley, reason as well
as passion had been marred by original sin, and the way of salvation was not, as in the stoic creed, through the discipline of reason
and will, but through the intervention of Divine help.

Occasional poetic references to man's fallen nature prepare the
reader for the great number of poems which decried the evil effects of human passions. If the poets were right, the mortal poison
of the passions had indelibly stained the universal pattern:

> Not all the streams of an eternal flood,
> Can wash from poison Adam's tainted blood.
> Infectious streams swell ev'ry heaving vein,
> Thence nature draws an universal stain.
> From the black fountain the dire torrent flows
> And leaves the mortal poison as it goes
> From limb to limb; then circling to the heart,
> Plays the foul tide, and leaves a deathful smart. [311]

Fear and dishonesty followed in passion's train. " 'Tis good we
seek; but pride and prejudice Direct to evil in its gay disguise." [312]
Ambition and avarice ruined man's communal life." "Enthusiastic
rage" marred his spiritual devotion. [313] "Vain Passions" tore apart
his peace:

> O Heav'n! by what vain passions man is sway'd,
> Proud of his reason, by his will betray'd,
> Blindly he wanders in pursuit of vice,
> And hates confinement, tho' in Paradise;
> Doom'd when enlarg'd, instead of Eden's Bow'rs,
> To rove in wilds, and gather thorns for flow'rs;
> Between th' extremes, direct he sees the way
> Yet wilful swerves, perversely fond to stray! [314]

Even Pope, usually content to balance reason and passion as complementary forces in human affairs, conceded: "what Reason
weaves, by Passion is undone."

Edward Young's strictures on the passions seemed to compass
all the charges against them. "Gusts of passion" drove men to
"mutual hurt." "The dark labyrinth of human hearts" was

thronged with the basest motives.[315] A "momentary madness called delight" ruined human peace.[316] Disgust and satiety were the end of passion's road: what use, asked the poet

> To tread our former footsteps? pace the round
> Eternal? to climb life's worn, heavy wheel,
> Which draws up nothing new? to beat, and beat
> The beaten track? to bid each wretched day
> The former mock? to surfeit on the same,
> And yawn our joys? to thank a misery
> For change, though sad? to see what we have seen?
> Hear, till unheard, the same old slabber'd tale?
> To taste the tasted, and at each return
> Less tasteful? o'er our palates to decant
> Another vintage? strain a flatter year,
> Through loaded vessels, and a laxer tone?
> Crazy machines to grind earth's wasted fruits!
> Ill-ground, and worse concocted! load, not life!
> The rational foul kennels of excess!
> Still-streaming thoroughfares of dull debauch!
> Trembling each gulp, lest death should snatch the bowl.[317]

As a guard against the ravages of feeling the poets offered man the protection of reason. In a Stoic strain they reproved excessive grief as a weakness caused by "Nature." Reason, "mild returning, wisely does impart Sterner dictates to the tortur'd heart." Reason and conscious virtue solaces the grieving mind.[318] Reasonable reflection capable of checking sorrow might be inspired by external Nature, by history, by the classic Muse, or by the grim reminder:

> All those dismal looks and fretting
>   Cannot Damon's life restore;
> Long ago the worms have eat him,
>   You can never see him more.[319]

The ideal of the golden mean urged men to fly not grief alone, but all feeling, to live simply, reasonably, to govern life with "ripen'd thought," and "reason born to reign." To those who accepted its rule reason assured content, virtue, cheerfulness in life, and peace in death.[320]

The regularity of the science-explained universe served to re-inforce the classical stoicism of the golden mean:

> Fly all extremes, and keep the golden mean;
> The golden mean, where with an equal sway
> Reason presides, and appetites obey. . . .
> Great Nature thus thro' all her various ways
> Preserves the balance, and the means displays;
> See, earth and air, and ocean's liquid plain
> Within the bounds assign'd themselves contain;
> By each that universal law's obey'd,
> Thus far thou shalt proceed, and here be stay'd.[321]

The wise hero of the poets' verses would have delighted the hearts of Seneca and Cicero.[322] He had conquered fear and risen above ambition. His "measur'd passions" bowed to the yoke of reason. Contented with a mean estate he looked on the evil world and concluded "true fortitude assumes the patient mind." Pope summarized his exact balance of life," he knows to live who keeps the middle state, And neither leans on this side nor on that." [323] An anonymous versifier's compliment to a friend contained a good sketch of the ideally reasonable man

> Whose breast no tyrant passions ever seize,
> And whom too busy sense ne'er led astray.
> Not that you joys with moderation shun;
> You taste all pleasures, but indulge in none.[324]

That pride and intellectual exclusiveness often associated with the Stoic ideal occasionally moved the poets to scorn the "stupid race, whom culture can't exalt, nor science grace," the "vulgar wretches" who understood neither their own wants nor their country's needs.[325] One cold-hearted bard went so far as to claim:

> When pale disease some vulgar form invades,
> And adds the vile Plebian to the shades;
> Few are the tears that grace th' sunheeded urn,
> The obvious stroke forbids us long to mourn.[326]

In general, poetic approval of pride in knowledge admitted that "just education forms the man" but it restricted such education

to the "chosen wise," the "philosophic few." [327] In their moments
of intellectual snobbishness the poets believed:

> The vulgar, friend, are foes to thought,
>   Dull, servile, insolent, and proud:
> Shall we despise them, as we ought,
> And live above this various crowd?
>
>   Tis Meditation's friendly way,
>   A road that vulgar never trod.
>   There, unmolested may'st thou stray,
>   And mount thro' Nature up to God. [328]

More frequent than expressions of intellectual pride were poetic
outpourings of delight in reason. [329] Pope, moderate as ever, found
man a "chaos of thought and passion all confus'd," and called on
reason to restrain but not to overthrow the force of passion. Lesser
and less temperate writers made reason the root of true love, the
arbiter of pleasure, the chart to happiness. "Reason tempers passion's fire" and showed man the "strater [sic] path." It constituted
the essence of the "well-govern'd life," the source of decorum, of
wisdom, of morality. "The world's a state of discipline; a school,
Where we must learn our appetites to rule." To youthful heat,
to statesman's ambition, to unrequited love, to all the ills of passion, reason was the unfailing antidote. The path to virtue was
steep and rugged; the way to merit lay in the conscious pursuit
of goodness:

>   Hence knowledge proves the only test of truth,
>   And truth of knowledge: virtue the result
> Of both: mere innocence may be th' effect
> Of instinct; merit never: men must know
> And reason to deserve. . . . [330]

Reason, unmasking falsehood, showed man clearly the rightful
road:

>   Come then aspiring reason! Come with all
>   Thy rally'd pow'rs! Conception sharp and clear,
> Reflection slow, but sure; sage memory,

Quick recollection, penetrating wit,
Judgment profound and grey experience wise
Is the result of all! Come! Join to trace
This subtile Daemon! Wind her dubious maze
Of serpent cunning! Break her fences down
Of magisterial ignorance, and proud
Authorities! Disperse the empty train
Of phantoms grinning round, and purge away
The long establish'd gloom that shadows o'er
The real horrors of her tyrant-reign! [331]

After a series of earnest but unoriginal defences of reason, the
reader is pleasantly diverted by William Hamilton's "Soliloquy in
Imitation of Hamlet," in which the melancholy Dane unpacks his
heart with the calm detachment of a philosophe:

Life! death! dread objects of mankind's debate;
Whether superior to the shocks of fate,
To beat its fiercest ills with steadfast mind,
To Nature's order piously resign'd,
Or, with magnanimous and brave disdain,
Return her back th' injurious gift again. . . .
Then, Hamlet, cease; thy rash resolves forego;
God, Nature, Reason, all will have it so.[332]

Thomson and Young loomed large among the crowd of lesser
writers who took up cudgels in defence of reason. Thomson, ever
willing to admire the ancients, honored Socrates' obedience to
"calm reason's holy law" and revered the stern calm of Solon and
Lycurgus, who "bowed beneath the force Of strictest discipline,
severely wise, All human passions." [333]

Edward Young could, on occasion, be as conventional as his
fellow poets. He admitted that "few without long discipline are
sage": he revered "reason's golden chain" as the sure bond for
man's passions.[334] He counseled

'a rational repast;
Exertion, vigilance, a mind in arms,
A military discipline of thought,

To foil temptation in the doubtful field;
And ever-waking ardour for the right.'
'Tis these, first give, then guard, a cheerful heart.[335]

Yet as usual Young transcended convention: he attributed to reason the power not merely of keeping men from evil, but of raising them to heights of goodness. Reason not only bound man's baser self to subjection, it gave him wings to soar towards the infinite:

These Reason, with an energy divine,
O'erleaps; and claims the future and unseen;
The vast unseen! The future fathomless!
When the great soul buoys up to this high point,
Leaving gross nature's sediments below;
Then, and then only, Adam's offspring quits
The sage and hero of the fields and woods,
Asserts his rank, and rises into man.[336]

On the whole poetic defense of reason remained on a conventional level. Pope was neo-classically moderate: Thomson evidenced a proper respect for the intellectual discipline of the ancients and for the scientific acuteness of modern intellectuals. Wesley darkened his picture of human weakness to that vision of corruption which he dedicated his life to reforming. Young, always apart from his contemporaries, gave the theme a transcendent twist: his winged reason soared far beyond the timid concepts of his contemporaries.

Passion

Motivated by distrust of human reason or by trust in man's innate goodness (or by both) the poetic defenders of passion insisted vigorously that instinct alone was guide enough to happiness in life. Contempt for human reason was a reaction perhaps as old as man himself. It was the scorn of the Epicurean for the Stoic, of the dilettante for the pedant,—a scorn that echoed and reechoed wherever men used their reason to deny reason itself.

If the negative expression of admiration for the passions sprang
from distrust of reason, its positive support stemmed from faith
in the goodness of the human heart. The comfortable conviction,
inherited through Shaftesbury from the Cambridge Platønists, that
man is innately a kindly being, served eighteenth-century men as
useful ammunition against the cynical view of human nature willed
them by Hobbes and restated by Mandeville. The ideal of a benevolent mankind also fitted conveniently into the favorite
eighteenth-century concept of a chain of being which in its inter-
dependencies was a chain of love.

On the whole the poets were fairly moderate in their praises
of human passion. They declaimed conventionally against reason,
explained the good effects of certain emotions, bade man look
within for the law of God, and advocated the "silent worship of
the moral heart." Although now and then some reckless bard approved wild and lawless pursuit of desire, the writers in general
were discreetly restrained.

The extreme poetic advocates of instinct were informal versifiers who declared that men's passions were beyond reason or rebuke (hence beyond moral responsibility), that love was above
all bounds, that the "fair libertine" "free as the winds, and un-
controul'd as day," was but following "nature's noblest dictates." [337] A bitter personal note sharpened Richard Savage's ironic
commendation of his "mother's" contempt for "all the dry devoirs
of blood and line," [338] but most of the small group of radical verses
were gaily hedonistic:

> Foolish Creature,
> Follow Nature,
> Waste not thus your prime;
> Youth's a treasure,
> Love's a pleasure,
> Both destroyed by time.[339]

More conservative poets simply doubted the efficiency of reason
in finding a solution to human problems; "heaven's paths are found
by Nature more than Art, The Schoolman's Head misleads the
Layman's Heart." [340] Reason was a source of human arrogance,

an "encumber'd" faculty needing help to find its way.[341] "Virtue did, more than knowledge, grace the mind." [342] Too much thought made life "too soft decay," and wasted man's soul in pursuit of empty visions.[343] Custom, an outgrowth of man's pursuit of reason, spread vices and folly through human society, betraying into evil the native mould of good into which human nature had been originally cast.[344] Day-dreams and castles in Spain afforded man more happiness than wise reflections:

> Whatever wild chimera of the brain
> Lifts our conceits above the sense of pain,
> Suspends our cares, our hearts with gladness fills
> And gives us pow'r to dream away our ills;
> Whate'er you call this sort of reverie,
> 'Tis the best wisdom and philosophy.[345]

That "best wisdom and philosophy" of guileless reverie blessed the earliest days of human life: to recapture such early joys man must

> bid the morn of youth
> Rise to new light, and beam afresh the days
> Of innocence, simplicity, and truth,
> To cares estranged, and manhood's thorny ways,
> What transport to retrace our boyish plays,
> Our easy bliss, when each thing joy supplied—
> The woods, the mountains, and the warbling maze
> Of the wild brooks! [346]

The sentiment easily foreshadows Wordsworth.

Some of the poets were controversialists rather than dreamers: one magazine writer, for instance, defended passion by attacking the freethinkers:

> Against what parsons teach, with sneering spite,
> The bold Freethinker sets up reason's light:
> More than all ages past presumes to know,
> And levels all the fathers at a blow.
> Sure then, so prompt, so eloquent his tongue,
> Much he has toil'd to gain, and studied long;

The num'rous authors he confutes has read,
And treasur'd stores of learning in his head.
Alas! such formal aids as these how vain!
Fit for the plodding academick train:
To talk is all, to read is out of season;
'Tis ignorance denotes the man of reason.[347]

Edward Young, also disdainful of the "men of reason," reproached
the rationalists as

Men, that act to Reason's golden rule,
All weakness of affection quite subdu'd. . . .
See, the steel'd files of season'd veterans,
Train'd to the world, in burnish'd falsehood bright;
Deep in the fatal stratagems of peace;
All soft sensation, in the throng rubb'd off;
All their keen purpose, in politeness, sheath'd;
His friends eternal—during interest;
His foes implacable—when worth their while;
At war with every welfare, but their own;
As wise as Lucifer; and half as good;
And by whom none, but Lucifer, can gain.[348]

Not directly opposed to freethinkers, but opposed certainly to
their belief in the infallibility of reason, were the many poetic
warnings of man's intellectual limitations. "Reason, blind leader
of the blind," was circumscribed in its sphere. "Degen'rate reason
ever wants a guide." [349] Man could not solve the mysteries of the
universe:

Of reason's self design the just extent;
Nor let her aim beyond what nature meant;
External laws have fix'd her bounded sway,
Nor can she from her stated limits stray.[350]

Reason might be uncertain, but the passions were sure guides. Love
refined the individual and society: it cemented friendships and
commonwealths.[351] Without its grace the scholar was a boor:

> For what is life, its best enjoyments lost
> In the dull mazes of insipid schools?
> Love must refine what Science scarce began,
> And mould the letter'd savage into man.[352]

Grief as well as love had power over man. Sorrow was stronger than reason: in vain Stoics might urge the intellect to quell the rising tide of woe:

> misfortunes, like a flood,
> Rush in impetuous, grief o'erwhelms the soul,
> And in such periods, reason's power is lost,
> To calm the tumult of the troubled mind.[353]

Such indulgence in feeling at the expense of reason had a hint of romantic individualism: the hint became an outright declaration of joy in grief when a magazine poet vowed:

> I will court my grief, and in an heaving bosom
> Cherish the gen'rous melancholy, and mourn
> A soul so close endear'd; a loss unequall'd! [354]

As Edward Young outstripped his contemporaries in his views on reason, so he soared beyond them in his exaltation of man's feelings. Where others simply found feeling good, Young hailed it as a teacher of spiritual lessons; "grief! more proficients in thy school are made, Than genius, or proud learning, e'er could boast." [355] Man's instinct of shame raised him above the brutes.[356] His passions, unsatisfied by this world and the kingdoms thereof, attested his transcendent destiny, "our passions like our reason are divine":

> "Passions, which all on earth but more inflames?
> Fierce passions, so mismeasured to this scene,
> Stretch'd out, like eagles' wings, beyond our nest,
> Far, far beyond the world of all below,
> For earth too large, presage a nobler flight,
> And evidence our title to the skies." [357]

Young's belief in sorrow as a purifier of the spirit was in the orthodox Christian tradition as was his use of the unsatisfied desires of man as a proof of his immortality. But Young departed even from the tradition he defended in his belief that even in this life the passions, corrupted by the Fall, might through the influence of reason, be restored here on earth to their original power and purity:

Think not our passions from Corruption sprung,
Though to Corruption now they lend their wings;
That is their mistress, not their mother; All
(And justly) Reason deem divine: I see,
I feel a grandeur in the passions too,
Which speaks their high descent, and glorious end;
Which speaks them rays of an eternal fire.
In Paradise itself they burn'd as strong,
Ere Adam fell; though wiser in their aim. . . .
Yet still, through their disgrace, no feeble ray
Of greatness shines, and tells us whence they fell:
But these (like that fallen monarch when reclaim'd),
When Reason moderates the rein aright,
Shall reascend, remount their former sphere,
Where once they soar'd illustrious; ere seduced
By wanton Eve's debauch, to stroll on earth,
And set sublunary world on fire.[358]

Young's delight in passions "stretched out like eagles' wings" and Pope's calm satisfaction, "passions are the elements of life" belonged to different worlds—the latter to a neat neo-classical world of moderate goals and temperate desires, the former to a boundless romantic universe where the searching spirit strains ever in pursuit of the unattainable. Most of Young's colleagues however did not share his unbounded enthusiasm: they were content to let him strike out alone along untrodden ways, while they promenaded the well-frequented highways of poetic opinion.

One of those poetic highways had as its journey's end the chaste deistic temple inscribed "the worship of the heart." Poets who trusted man's moral heart either ignored or denied the doctrine of the Fall. In their eyes man retained his original perfection; he had only to follow the message of his heart rather than the corrupt-

ing dictates of custom. The voice of Nature offered a ready answer
to the seeker after spiritual truths; a poet might well confess:

> Here! I have set me down beneath this oak,
> This sacred shade,—to contemplate religion,
> The voice of nature tells me what it is;
> 'Tis to adore one being omnipotent,
> Eternal, infinite, and Lord of all.[359]

Creeds, churches, clerics served only to confuse the truths of religion; "each conscious bosom will our duty show, For pure religion there alone must flow." [360] The moral law which Nature had
implanted in man spoke even to the lowliest in the language of the
heart.[361] Let man but try "each doubtful proposition" by the truths
printed on his soul, and he might draw certainty from "the moral
Charm's superior pow'r." [362]

All the poets counseled men to recognize the importance of
feeling in affairs of the soul, but the religious experiences which
they depicted were of widely different types. At one extreme of
opinion deism had taught "the things we must believe are few and
plain." [363] In time the recognition of those truths came to be considered less a reasoned than an intuitive process. Intuitive knowledge was a felt knowledge, hence deism, which began as a hymn
to reason, ended as a prayer for the teachings of the heart. Pope
voiced the "deist's prayer" when he asked:

> If I am right, thy grace impart,
> Still in the right to stay;
> If I am wrong, O teach my heart
> To find the better way.[364]

Such praise of the "moral heart" was good deistic doctrine, but
terms are misleading, and when Wesley reminded man that " 'tis
from the heart you draw The living lustre, and unerring law,"
however closely his words resembled the deist's message, his meaning was its violent opposite. Deism held man to be naturally good
and sought to outlaw formal religion. Methodism believed man's
heart naturally corrupt and sought to awaken in cold religious

conventions an intense and burning zeal which would draw down from heaven the light that saved and sanctified the soul. Wesley asked repeatedly for childlike simplicity, for the "meekly loving heart," for the feeling that he belonged to God.[365] The just were "the simple men of heart sincere." [366] "Mystic powers of love" sustained the soul through spiritual tempests.[367] The followers of Christ felt His Presence at every moment:

> Thee through Thyself we understand,
> When Thou in us Thyself hast shown,
> We see Thy all-creating hand,
> We feel a God through faith alone.[368]

Understanding alone was not enough:

> O, give me, Saviour, give me more!
> Thy mercies to my soul reveal:
> Alas! I see their endless store,
> Yet, O! I cannot, cannot feel! [369]

An anonymous piece by a Methodist (or a Methodist sympathizer) made clear the special supernatural quality of those "inward feelings, or the happy experiences of devout souls":

> In vain to you th' experienc'd would reveal
> That peace the virtuous taste, those joys they feel.
> To you the joys of the regen'rate mind
> Are sounds to deafness, colours to the blind.
> What bliss, to theirs superior, reason tastes;
> So you, who only sensual pleasures know,
> Can ne'er conceive the joys divine that flow
> In the pure breast that burns with heav'nly love,
> Blest with sweet longings for its bliss above.[370]

This emphasis on feeling in religion, although meant by Wesley to apply to feeling supernaturally inspired, came, on the part of many of his more easily moved congregation, to mean merely emotionalism. Enthusiasm, so long derided as fanatical madness, was becoming for many the mark of the true believer. In this sense

Methodism encouraged feeling as a rule of life, though in reality it advocated neither the guide of passion nor that of reason, since both faculties had been weakened and impaired by the Fall.

Between the extremes of Methodism and deism Edward Young took the middle way of the worship of the heart, when in accord with Christian tradition, he used the concept simply to imply sincerity in religious feelings; "if wrong our hearts, our heads are right in vain." [371] "Humble Love, and not proud Reason, keeps the door of heaven." [372] God noted in men's hearts the rise and progress of their spiritual growth.[373] Young's passing reference to "man's angry heart . . . As rightly set, as are the starry spheres" [374] might seem at first glance to resemble deism, but his frequent insistence on the need of spiritual discipline and on the weakness of fallen man implied that his lines about the goodness of the human heart meant simply that man was not wholly corrupt—he was only a little off the track of righteousness.

Poetic preference for passion as a guide to man, growing ever stronger from 1733 on towards the half century mark, represented in the ethical sphere the same tendency towards an ideal of irregularity which in philosophical realms had awakened paeans over earth's myriad creatures, and in aesthetic spheres had set the untrammeled genius of the Elizabethans over the "lays of artful Addison, coldly correct."

Benevolence

It is the property of the heart of man to be diffusive;
its kind wishes spread over the face of the creation.[375]
—Spectator, *No. 601*

Eighteenth-century gentlemen who resented the harshness of Hobbes' view of human nature and the chill cynicism of Mandeville's restatement of Hobbes' creed retreated to the warmer atmosphere of human benevolence—a climate of opinion that grew ever balmier with each succeeding generation. To eighteenth-

century minds "benevolence" seemed the kindly cement that
bound society together: "To love the publick, to study universal
good, and to promote the interest of the whole world, as far as
lies within our power, is surely the height of goodness, and makes
that temper which we call divine." [376] They found the answer to
Hobbes' insistence that "benificence [sic] is all founded in weakness," [377] in Addison's dignified reassurance: "I always imagined
that kind and benevolent propensions were the original growth
of the heart of man; and however checked and overtopped by
counter inclinations that have since sprung up within us, have
still some force in the worst of tempers, and a considerable influence on the best." [378] The poets were very willing to spread the
all-embracing cloak of benevolence over the unselfish acts of mankind.[379] The benevolent man blessed with "true friendship, love,"
and wit, was certain of days of innocence and nights of peace. His
life mirrored the bounteous bloom of Nature. His means, however
small, were spent in doing good: if his money gave out, he could
still give advice: "what aid, his little wealth perchance denies, In
each hard instance his advice supplies." A cheerful and extravagant
giver, he scattered blessings with an open hand:

> Like nature's blessing to no part confin'd,
> His well-pois'd bounty reaches all mankind;
> That insolence of wealth, the pomp of state
> Which crowds the mansions of the vainly great,
> Flies far the limits of his modest gate.[380]

His not to question the needy, his only to give, and to weep with
them: "who can all grief, for his own woes, restrain, Yet melts
in gen'rous tears, at others' pain." [381]

Even so early in the period the benevolent hero showed signs of
the sensibility that was to dissolve him in many an idle tear before
the century's end.[382] As the emotional side of the theme appealed
increasingly to the poets, benevolence took on the aspect of a holiday of feeling, "heart streaming full to heart in mutual flow Of
faith and friendship, tenderness and truth." Philanthropy assured
man "extensive bliss," "the god-like happiness," "that bliss no
wealth can bribe, no power bestow." "Our appetite's indulged in

doing good," and "acts of benevolence and love Give us a touch of heaven above."

Benevolence made virtue not only possible, but instinctive, not only instinctive but pleasant. Small wonder the poets urged man to indulge

> That godlike passion! which the bounds of self
> Divinely bursting, the whole public takes
> Into the heart, enlarged, and burning high
> With the mixed ardour of unnumbered selves . . .[383]

Inward emotion should be matched with outward show, "that virtue known By the relenting look." [384] Heart gained fast on head as an indicator of man's worth. A "young Scots gentleman" sending a lady a copy of *Mustapha* could admonish:

> Nor you, if mov'd as thick'ning woes arise,
> Blush that the gen'rous tear o'erflows your eyes,
> (Expressive tears, that undisguis'd by art,
> Shew the soft nature of the gentle heart.)
> For who unmov'd, unfeeling views distress,
> Is more than mortal, or than human less.[385]

A sympathy that led men to "make the sorrows of mankind their own" was the mark of the truly human heart. Akenside rhapsodized the "fair benevolence of generous minds." [386] When a good man was harmed, Pope claimed the insult, "mine, as a friend to ev'ry worthy mind; And mine as man, who feel for all mankind." [387]

Eighteenth-century psychology had endowed man with self-love and social. The poets of benevolence seized upon man's social instinct. "The common welfare is our only task" was the text on which they preached with variations the comfortable sermon "for such by nature is the human frame, Our duty and our int'rest are the same." [388] "The poor man's call is God's command": men's kindly hearts were the Divine means of Succoring the oppressed.[389] "The flame of social love" lighted man's happiness.[390] "Social temper" and "diffusive heart" insulated man against pride and cruel wit.[391] "In faith and hope the world will disagree, But all man-

kind's concern is charity." [392] The world's society was one benevolent whole:

> What wonder therefore, since the endearing ties
> Of passion link the universal kind
> Of man so close, what wonder if to search
> This common nature through the various change
> Of sex, and age, and fortune, and the frame
> Of each peculiar, draw the busy mind
> With unresisted charms? [393]

Loud and cheerful rose the benevolent chorus. Amid the general
rejoicings Edward Young and Mary Barber raised the only critical voices. Neither had any quarrel with benevolent deeds, but
both anxiously distinguished between benevolence and charity,
and insisted on the superiority of supernatural to natural motives
as inspirers of human virtues.

To Mary Barber, the Earl of Thanet, a model of Christian charity, was far above those "vain pretenders to superior sense" that
the freethinkers set up as a benevolent ideal:

> Ye vain pretenders to superior sense,
> Ye empty boasters of benificence,
> Who in the scorners' seat, exulting sit,
> And vaunt your impious raillery for wit,
> The Gospel-Rule defective, you pretend,
> When you the social duties recommend;
> In Thanet see them heighten'd and refin'd;
> In Thanet see the friend of humankind;
> Heighten'd by faith, see ev'ry virtue's force;
> By faith, their surest sanction, noblest source.
> Loudly ye boast a more than Christian zeal;
> For Virtue's int'rest and the public weal;
> Best by effects are boastings understood;
> Come, prove your ardor for the public good!
> The mighty heroes of your tribe survey,
> Their ev'ry hidden excellence display;
> Or dead, or living, set their virtues forth;

> Let all, united, vie with Thanet's worth;
> Free-Thinkers, Moralists, on you I call,
> Can Thanet's worth be equall'd by you all? [394]

Like Mrs. Barber, Young carefully distinguished between charity and benevolence. Scorning those deists "who smile at piety;
yet boast aloud good will to man," he stood by the ideal of the
charitable Christian who

> can't a foe, though most malignant, hate,
> Because that hate would prove his greater foe.
> 'Tis hard for them (yet who so loudly boast
> Good-will to men?) to love their dearest friend;
> For may not he invade their good supreme,
> Where the least jealousy turns love to gall?
> All shines to them, that for a season shines.
> Each act, each thought, he questions, What its weight,
> Its colour what, a thousand ages hence? [395]

But Edward Young and Mary Barber were alone in their misgivings. Their fellow poets went on singing the praises of the benevolent human heart. They found real-life prototypes of their
ideal. For one general statement:

> A British noble is a dubious name,
> Of lowest infamy, or highest fame:
> Born to redress an injur'd orphan's cause,
> To smooth th' unequal frown of rigid laws . . . [396]

there were many verses that made the general specific by praising
particular instances of benevolence in contemporary life.[397] Mary
Chandler commended a friend, Mrs. Stephens, for the unconfined
goodness which "diffuses wide her favours on her kind," and an
anonymous writer celebrated "a gentleman contributor of fifty
pounds to the sufferers by the late fire at Wellingborough." [398]
Wesley wrote hymns for the Georgia Orphans and for the Charity
Children to sing in praise of their benefactors.[399] A magazine poet
remembered James Oglethorpe as the instrument through which

"Indulgent Providence" diffused its blessings, and lauded Oglethorpe's zeal in relieving the "drooping sons of want." [400]

More courtly names than these swelled the rolls of benevolence.
Richard Nash, the *arbiter elegantiarum* of Bath was the "very essence of benevolence." [401] The dictator of the fashionable world,
the incomparable Earl of Chesterfield "endow'd with vast benevolence,"

> He lives in ev'ry other's life,
> He comforts woe, composes strife,
>   Makes angry factions kiss:
> His frowns injurious pride confound:
> He smiles benevolence around,
>   And universal bliss. [402]

(Johnson, cooling his worn heels in Chesterfield's antechamber,
might have furnished interesting footnotes to the theme of his lordship's benevolence.) The Duke of Richmond merited admiration
for his ability "to calm the sadness in the mourner's breast, To
dry the tear, and ease the heart distress't." [403] Still higher in the
social scale, Queen Caroline was respectfully admonished that

> To sooth the wretched mourner's pain,
>   Pour joy into the orphan's breast;
> To loose the weeping captive's chain,
>   And calm the soul, with pangs distrest,
> Are acts which shall transmit your name
>   Forever fair above the sky,
> When all your gems shall lose their flame,
>   Your scepter rust, and beauties die! [404]

And when George II, breathing "benevolence and peace" [405] was
dutifully lauded by Colley Cibber for his "diffus'd benevolence
of pow'r," the panegyric of benevolence had reached its limit. [406]

The classic example of benevolence (highborn or low) was of
course Pope's Man of Ross. [407] In his almsgiving, his peacemaking,
his care of the orphaned, the sick and the old, the good man typified those corporal works of mercy which Christianity had long

taught man to do for love of God, and which believers in benevolence insisted that men perform for the satisfaction of their personal instinct of altruism. The Man of Ross was less emotional than his benevolent fellows in poetry, but thanks to the skilled couplets of his panegyrist he has remained the most famous of them all.

Even the great of this world did not suffice the poets as benevolent ideals. Reading the heavens in terms of Newton's law, they saw the planets themselves linked by "mutual amity," and called the whole system of the universe a "material picture of benevolence" governed by the just decrees of the "Great Philanthropist! Father of angels! but the friend of man!" [408]

Such glowing satisfaction in a benevolent universe was contagious. Even Edward Young, usually the questioning or protesting voice among the poets, chimed in with the general rejoicing that "self-love and social are the same." Though haunted by a realization of human cruelty ("man is to man the sorest, surest ill)," [409] Young continued to preach a creed of altruism. "In age, in infancy, from others' aid Is all our hope; to teach us to be kind." [410] Vice was self-love "in a mistake." "Joy scorns monopolists: it calls for two." [411] Man's selfish part must give way to his unselfish: his personal desires to his social duties. Young might not join his poetical colleagues in their faith in the essential goodness of human nature, nor agree with their view of the natural motivation of man's altruism, but he sometimes borrowed their terms of self love and social to express his admiration for men's kindly deeds.

Certainly it is one of the curious phenomena of the eighteenth century that poets who gloried in national strength, who clamored for international conquest, and waxed violently abusive in party strife, should have been so profuse in their sentiments of universal benevolence. While poetic boastings bade the Royal Navy sweep England's rivals from the waterways of the world, poetic rhapsodies radiating sweetness and light, invited all to bask in the warmth of British benevolence:

> 'Tis scarce begun; ambition smiles
> At the poor limits of the British isles;

She o'er the globe expatiates unconfin'd,
Expands with Christian charity the mind,
And pants to be the friend of all mankind.[412]

As the eighteenth century progressed, the strong and persistent
theme of benevolence grew ever stronger and more popular, increasing with each generation its stress on the pleasure of doing
good and its substitution of a subjective motive of personal satisfaction for an objective standard of virtue.

Man and Beast

*I say, then to return to my subject, that there is no ap-
pearance to induce a man to believe that beasts should,
by a natural and forced inclination, do the same things
that we do by our choice, and industry. We ought from
like effects to conclude like faculties, and from greater
effects greater faculties; and consequently confess that
the same reasoning, and the same ways by which we
operate, are common with them, or that they have
others that are better.*[413]

—*Montaigne*, Apologie of Raymonde
Seybonde

If *vivere secundum naturam* meant "follow instinct," then ob-
viously animals, undeterred by the pale cast of thought would be
the most perfect exponents of the code. Many an eighteenth-century Englishman followed his trust in instinct to its logical conclusion—a recognition of the superiority of the animal kingdom.
Various influences of the early part of the century tended to lower
man's status and to raise that of the animal. Men knew well the
traditions of naturalism restated in such classic expressions as
Montaigne's *Apologie of Raymonde Seybonde*. They remembered
Hobbes' contrast between the generous concord of beasts and the

selfish quarrels of men. They had inherited from the seventeenth century a certain reaction against the Cartesian beast machine, a reaction which tended to put men and beasts into the same category (either by insisting that beasts do reason, or by declaring that if the beast is a machine, then man also is a mechanism). Their own favorite concept of the chain of being kept forcing man to realize that despite his midway place in the chain he was no more and no less essential to the whole than the lowliest of his fellow links:

> From Nature's chain whatever link you strike,
> Tenth or ten thousandth, breaks the chain alike.[414]

Literary sources as well as philosophical added something to the problem of the relationship of man and beast. Aesop's *Fables*, animal allegories, Plutarch's *Craftiness of Animals*, Pliny's *Natural History* continued to edify the eighteenth century, as they had amazed preceding generations, with their wonderful tales of animal cunning and of brute cleverness. The animal creation's stock was soaring.

The poets readily admitted that animals were happier, wiser and better than men. "Behold! ye pilgrims of this earth, behold! See all but man with unearned pleasure gay." [415] The wording was Thomson's, but the sentiment was almost universal. The animals ranged the fields and woods "in happy indolence," while "laborious man" toiled to earn his bread.[416] Man in pride of reason scorned creatures without it, yet "proud Man! search nature, and you'll see An insect's happier far than thee." [417] A survey of creation only served to point the moral, "how happy all things living, but a man." [418] The dreary round of human sorrows blackly contrasted the unclouded happiness of the animal world.

> Boast then no more, vain fav'rite of the sky,
> Thy brow more lofty, and thy birth more high;
> That God-like reason on thy soul does shine,
> From heav'n thy race, thy origin divine!
> What crawl the earth, or wing the upper air,
> Wanting thy glories do not feel thy care?

Have no distress to moan, no wants to weep,
Chearful their day, and undisturb'd their sleep;
While we, alas, with all our pride and pow'r,
Dread the return of ev'ry fearful hour,
Which may defeat our hope, or peace destroy,
And rob weak man of ev'ry fleeting joy.[419]

The instinctive cleverness of the beasts fascinated the poets.
Animal wisdom put to shame man's labored learning. An echo of
the controversies of the Cartesians and their opponents woke
momentarily in a compliment to a dog:

Hy to the Woods! and Cunning Tray
Will wag his tail, and know your heart,
Spite of the doctrine of DesCarte,
Who writes, that barking nothing means,
And that all beasts are mere machines.[420]

A tribute to a dead lap-dog touched on the problem of reason, or
lack of it, in brutes:

Her acting principle think what you please on;
At least 'twas next to,—if it was not—reason.
Whether her soul belong'd to man or beast,
Let others with Pythagoras contest.
This I'll affirm; were all dumb brutes like her,
To most that talk, the silent I'd prefer.[421]

Man might learn from the animals friendship, loyalty, patience,
perseverence, public spirit, industry. The beast knew and kept his
sphere: man alone insisted on wandering afar, with unhappy re-
sults to himself and to society: [422] "prompted by instinct's never-
erring power, Each creature knows its proper aliment." Docile
and happy, the beasts put to shame the erring race of man:

All species, form'd beneath the solar beam,
That numberless adorn our future theme,—
Fed in thy bounty, fashion'd in thy skill,
Cloth'd in thy love, instructed in thy will,
Safe in thy conduct, their unerring guide,

> All—save the child of ignorance and pride—
> The paths of Beauty and of Truth pursue,
> And teach proud man those lectures which ensue.[423]

Following their natural instincts, the animals achieved a perfection which man, for all his reasoning powers, had sought in vain.[424] Ingratitude, avarice, cruelty to his own (vices unknown to the brute creation) marred man's record. "Man meditating prey on humankind" was the worst of savages.[425] "Beasts kill for hunger, men for pay" [426] was the animal's reproach to that worst of animals—man:

> For Man's chief prey is Man; not so we find,
> The brute creation in their various kind.
> Wolves cherish wolves; and bears will bears defend;
> The lion to the lion is a friend.
> They have no jilt, nor false deluding fair,
> Nor bigot, nor a libertine is there.
> But man has all; he's now a rake, a sot,
> A zealot now; and now the Lord knows what:
> A foe to all, scarce to himself a friend,
> His own tormentor to his very end.[427]

After the series of charges laid at man's door, what wonder a poet begged:

> Oh man, degenerate man! offend no more!
> Go, learn of brutes, thy Maker to adore!
> Shall these, thro' ev'ry tribe, his bounty own,
> Of all his works, ungrateful thou alone! [428]

Poetic support of the superiority of the animals was almost unanimous. The lord of creation was dethroned with loud and vigorous approval and there seemed none to lament his fall.

But man had still a few defenders. Led by the redoubtable rebel, Edward Young, the insurgents attempted to hold for man his traditional place of honor. They cited in his defence his power of laughter, his commanding position in the creation, his eternal destiny.[429] The lesser voices spoke briefly: the burden of the case rested with

Young. Nor did the author of the *Night Thoughts* shirk his responsibility. He never swerved from his position of man's defender. All his comparisons between man and brute were to the disadvantage of the beast. For man to "live the brute" was for him to betray his nature:

> Lorenzo! blush at fondness for a life,
> Which sends celestial souls on errands vile,
> To cater for the sense; and serve at boards,
> Which every ranger of the wilds, perhaps
> Each reptile, justly claims our upper hand.[430]

Man's reason might lag in contrast with swift animal instinct, but in the end "the present is the scanty realm of Sense; The future, Reason's empire unconfined." [431] Brute knowledge was of the moment, man's for eternity:

> Reason progressive, Instinct is complete;
> Swift Instinct leaps; slow Reason feebly climbs.
> Brutes soon their zenith reach; their little all
> Flows in at once; in ages they no more
> Could know, or do, or covet, or enjoy.
> Were man to live coeval with the sun,
> The patriarch-pupil would be learning still;
> Yet, dying, leave his lesson half unlearn'd.[432]

No more need man puzzle over the superior happiness of the brute creation: he need only realize that his present discontent was the promise of a transcendent future:

> Is Heaven, then, kinder to thy flocks than thee?
> Not so; thy pasture richer, but remote;
> In part, remote; for that remoter part
> Man bleats from instinct, though perhaps, debauch'd
> By sense, his reason sleeps, nor dreams the cause.
> The cause how obvious, when his reason wakes!
> His grief is but his grandeur in disguise;
> And discontent is immortality.[433]

There the case rested. Let the proponents of animal happiness de-plore man's sorrows as they would: Young had for them the in-exorable answer:

> His grief is but his grandeur in disguise;
> And discontent is immortality.

It was inevitable that the weakening of the barrier between man and brute, added to an ever-growing faith in innate human be-nevolence, should encourage a spirit of humanitarianism towards beasts, a spirit that became increasingly emotional as the century wore on. Even as early as the period between 1725 and 1750 the reader may find here and there among the verses gentle languish-ings over the hardships of horses, of birds, and even of plants.[434] But since the best of the humanitarian spirit was not to be represented by such passing sentimentalities, one must turn to James Thom-son, the most influential exponent of kindness to animals, for a fair expression of the sentiment.

Thomson's all-embracing humanitarianism [435] extended to the young fish too early caught, to the fly meshed in the spider's web, to the worm twisting on the angler's hook. He looked with sympa-thetic eyes on the "labourer-ox" standing in the snow, the robin, driven indoors by winter cold, the sheep frightened at the shear-ing, the nightingale caged by "tyrant man." Thomson lamented the flowers dying in the "parching beam" of the summer noonday, and the bees driven out of their hives by sulphur. His benevolence reached even to the beasts of the far-off tropics, and regretted that the "never-resting race of man" had brought into disgraceful servitude the gentle might of the elephant. The hunt, which to the squire-poet Somervile was a chase though bloody "yet without guilt," was to Thomson a "falsely cheerful, barbarous game of death," which murdered alike the "timid hare," the harmless birds, and the noble stag. His sympathy with the hunted stood out in every line of his famous description of the cornered stag. In all his discussions of beasts Thomson was consistently on the side of the neglected, the mistreated, the hunted creatures of the animal kingdom.

An emotional sympathy with suffering, rather than a philosophical conviction of animal merit motivated his pleas for kindness to animals. His humanitarianism, like that of his fellow poets, seemed to stem rather from his overflowing benevolence, than from any reasoning about the relative positions of man and beast.

It is pleasant to remember that Thomson did not plead his cause in vain. The humanitarianism he preached bore practical fruit during the latter half of the eighteenth century in the form of legislation designed to protect beasts from man's cruelty. If credit for the growth of such a spirit belongs to any one Englishman, it belongs to James Thomson, whose prestige and popularity helped to spread the creed of kindness to animals in which the good-natured poet had so strongly believed.

PART THREE

Epilogue

Epilogue

THE main currents of primitivism have swirled and eddied by us, carrying with them the pensive poet dreaming of the Islands of the Blest, and the Opposition verseman swearing at Sir Robert, the weary bard longing for pastoral peace, and the philosophical poet pondering the *vivere secundum naturam*. In that welter of current and counter current the major poets of the period may seem to have become lost: it is not at all desirable that they should so remain. The reader interested in primitivism will endure dingdong verse and third rate hack work in order to establish the main outlines of the trend, but his ultimate goal is the discovery of the positions held by important poets on the question of primitivism. He is interested to know wherein their work was one with the opinions of their generation, and wherein it ran counter to those opinions.

Between the years 1725 and 1750, the names that mean most to the general reader are those of Pope, Thomson, Collins, Gray, Akenside, Young, and the Wartons. Pope stood for the regular and neo-classical strains in primitivism, Collins, Gray and the Wartons represented the irregular and the pre-romantic elements: neither side encompassed all or even most of the phases of the subject. Apart from both groups, but having something in common with each were the great primitivists, Thomson, Akenside, and Young.

As a primitivist, Pope represented the calm reasonableness, the interest in philosophical themes, the elegant accuracy in expression which epitomize the much-maligned term "neo-classical." He depicted with classic accuracy the state of Nature, the noble Indian, the chain of being. He found the universal machine good, and rejoicing in its perfect balance of parts, he fixed forever the creed of eighteenth-century optimism in the terse summary, "Whatever is, is right." Others might fight out the old battle of Nature and art, of reason and passion, but Pope at this period in his poetry, preserved the golden mean in his opinions on aesthetics and on morals. He satirized the formal garden, yet advised art in landscaping, complimented the rule of reason, yet remembered, "Reason the card, but Passion is the gale."

While the philosophical primitivism of Pope was rooted fast in reason, order and regularity, the emotional primitivism of the Wartons and their fellow-pre-romantics was bound up with an aesthetic ideal of the irregular. Pope disposed of the poor Indian in reasonable couplets: Joseph Warton rhapsodized him in odes. Pope sought a pleasant Horatian retreat: Warton longed for the wild reaches of primitive forests.

The Wartons and William Collins repeated frequently and fervently the favorite themes of the pre-romantic primitivists, but Thomas Gray, easily the best known and most often quoted of the group, played small part in the popularizing of primitivistic themes. Others at this period sang praises of the noble savage, of pleasing terror, of irregular genius, but Gray's voice was seldom heard amid the tributes. His great work in enriching and poetizing such topics was done after 1750. Up to the mid-century mild expressions of sympathy for the poor and gentle sentiments of Miltonic meditation were his only contribution to the cause of primitivism.

The other pre-romanticists were more outspoken than the bard of the *Elegy*. Collins' primitivism ran to enthusiasm for aesthetic ideals of irregularity, for the poet's "divine excess" and for Shakespeare's artless genius. The Wartons, usually considered together as a unified poetic group, differed a little in their treatments of primitivism. The elder Thomas Warton writing in the early years of the century was more conservative than his sons. He shared their delight in pleasing glooms, but lacked their sympathy for the noble savage, for hard primitivism, or for aesthetic freedom.

The younger Thomas Warton, ranging more widely among primitivistic themes, filled his meditations with grottoes, witches, ruins and melancholy, and championed aesthetic irregularity by bold preference for Spenser's faery way of writing over the polished elegance of Pope. Joseph Warton, easily the most radical primitivist of his family, and in some ways of his generation, rushed happily to extremes. His song of the golden age begged men to return to its primitive living conditions. He defended the noble savage with tears and threats, and desired most democratically to share the good barbarian's mode of life. On aesthetic subjects he was standard bearer for ideals of freedom and irregularity, for the pinetopt precipice and Shakespeare's untaught muse, for poetic fury and a hybrid Fancy, half classic nymph, half noble savage.

With Pope at one extreme of the scale of primitivism, and Joseph Warton at the other, by 1750 the scale was already heavily weighted in Warton's favor. But Pope and the pre-romantics, however important, did not consider at length any phase of primitivism. The detailed discussions of the theme belonged to Thomson, Akenside and Young. By 1745 Thomson had made his last revision of the *Seasons*, Young had written the last of his *Night Thoughts*, Akenside had published that version of the *Pleasures of the Imagination* which was to remain for over a decade a summary of his aesthetic judgments. These poems, major and mature works of major poets, covered in varying ways almost everything that any poet major or minor had to say on primitivism during the second quarter of the eighteenth century.

How did these three react to primitivism?

Akenside, easily the most limited in his response, had little interest in chronological or in cultural primitivism. A tribute to the fallen grandeur of Italy, a jibe at luxury as corrupter of human hearts, a gentle sigh for Miltonic solitudes and Horatian retreats, and he was done with the search for the good life in distant places or in distant times.

The philosophical and aesthetic aspects of Nature as norm were more to Akenside's taste than dreams of a golden age. Awed by the diversity of a bountiful creation, he rejoiced with true eighteenth-century optimism that the universal design was for the good of all, and accepted with reasonable eighteenth-century resignation the human limitations which barred man from understanding all the infinitely various links of the chain of being. Braver than many of his contemporaries, Akenside tried to face the problem of moral evil by explaining man's errors as the result of false representations of the fancy which led him to see things mistakenly, and as a consequence, to choose wrongly.

In matters of aesthetics Akenside was most completely a primitivist. Forever idealizing irregularity, he loved alike the "dread prophetic heat" of poetic inspiration and the untrodden paths of "nature and the muse." "Stupendous solitudes" roused in him a "noble horror," and sable woods a deep "religious awe." He hailed Shakespeare as a genius beyond the "nice touches of the critics' file," a genius inspired by the strange, the wild, the terrible aspects of the external world.

He eulogized taste, that gift ever dear to the hearts of defenders of genius. His simple swain smiled to see in Nature the reflection of the "form of beauty smiling at his heart." Taste, that strong, internal power, enabled all men to love knowledge and to appreciate Nature. Truth touched man's understanding as sound his ears. But taste alone was not enough (Akenside was too good a follower of Shaftesbury to go to that extreme); man's internal power had to be trained to ever greater skill in perceiving the true and the beautiful.

Akenside's speculations about taste were his only extended discussions of human nature. He upheld briefly and equally the rival claims of reason and passion, admired man's natural benevolence, took man's side in the quarrel between man and beast, but his favorite themes of speculation were aesthetic rather than psychological or moral.

Unlike Akenside with his relatively narrow interests, James Thomson was the most complete exponent of the greatest varieties of primitivistic themes. Thanks to his superior skill his passages of primitivism were often the best expressions of what his contemporaries were laboriously trying to make poetic. He brought to chronological and cultural primitivism his love for classical times and climates, his interest in far-off lands, and his concept of a world originally innocent and happy. As a cultural primitivist he loved the same ideals of innocence and bliss that had blessed the fabled golden age. The gentle savage (victim of European guile), the easy comfort of "Bear me, Pomona," the hardy simplicity of his

Laplanders were all part of his cultural primitivism that swung evenly between hard and soft extremes.

Like other men of his generation Thomson recreated the pastoral charm of Arcadian scenes. "The monarch swain" slumbering in the downy moss, the "drowsy shepherd As he lies reclined . . . beneath the floating shade Of willows grey," "the impatient husbandman" breaking the first furrow, the sower stalking "with measured step" were, as he drew them, idyllic versions of everyday people. His pictures of harvest joys, rustic dances, storytelling by the village fire were incidents of rural life seen through the pleasant haze of literary tradition. Literary also were Thomson's scenes of retirement, his retreat from town smoke to dewy fields after the fashion of Horace, his invocation to "mildly pleasing Solitude" in the manner of Milton. But Thomson now and then could rend the golden veil of illusion: his laments for the snowbound swain and the flood-ruined countryman belonged to the world of harsh reality.

Underneath Thomson's pictures of the golden age and of country paradises lay an ideal of universal harmony and regularity. Beneath his discussions of Nature as norm lay the very different ideal of the endless variety of the universe. Thomson loved the infinite diversity of the chain of being. Despite his momentary, and in his age unique, horror of the microscopic varieties of creatures he praised again and again other kinds of diversity, the profusion of the flowers of the field, the birds in the hedgerows, the stars in the heavens. While he admired the limitless variety of the chain of being, Thomson shared the distrust of his generation about the upper reaches of the chain. Fearful of those metaphysical mysteries about which science was silent, Thomson confined his researches into the nature of things to the realm of the tangible. In this respect he was the antithesis of Young, whose great delight was in soaring from earth to the limitless reaches of space, and beyond space itself to the trackless regions of the spirit.

Even stronger than Thomson's pleasure in the book of Nature was his optimism. His satisfaction with things as they were was part of his love for external Nature. Her beauties sang the praises of God to his ears. Her immense plan, beyond the contemplation of mere human minds, seemed to him designed for the ultimate good of all. Like his contemporaries Thomson stressed human limitations, unlike them he linked a creed of optimism with the beauties of the external world, with the suggestion of a Creator immanent in His creation, and with a strong personal sense of a Universal Love that followed and encompassed man to the farthest corners of the world.

That same admiration for the diversity of the universe inspired many of Thomson's aesthetic opinions. "Who can paint like Nature?" was his challenge, as it was the challenge of all the poets who turned from formal landscapes to Nature's unadorned beauties. He joyed in the fair profusion of the flowering countryside, the bright hues of the birds, the lavish charms of the seasons. His tropic lands were "a gay profusion of luxurious bliss," his native countryside, "far-diffused around One boundless blush, one white-empurpled shower."

Beauties of Nature more grand and more terrible than the gentle prettiness of spring flowers kindled Thomson to celebrate "the clouds, commixed With stars swift-gliding," "the shadowy gale," wild coastlines, craggy cliffs, the sea in storm. Looking at the gloom of winter he could reflect:

> The mighty tempest, and the hoary waste
> Abrupt and deep, stretched o'er the buried earth,
> Awake to solemn thought . . .

That solemn thought arising from contemplation of Nature's awe-inspiring magnificence was to fire more and more poets as the eighteenth century progressed, and as writers realized ever more clearly that the great and the terrible in the external world were fit stimulus for the creative imagination.

It was principally in connection with external Nature that Thomson felt the charm of irregularity. On literary themes he was content with the significant query "Is not wild Shakespeare thine and Nature's boast?" and with a tribute to inspiration in terms of the raptured glance and poetic ecstasy of soul.

In ethics Thomson admired at once ideals of order and of diversity. He respected the rigor of the ancients, Socrates' love of "Reason's holy law" and Lycurgus' iron rule; he commended science as a conqueror of superstitious terrors, and solitude as a calming influence on passion. But Thomson loved also benevolence, a benevolence profuse as Nature's generosity, a benevolence expansive enough to encompass all mankind. Benevolent himself, Thomson mourned the hardships of the poor and the imprisoned. His sympathy extended to all the persecuted creatures of the animal kingdom, the frightened sheep, the forlorn nightingale, the hunted hare (or stag, or elephant) the ox in the cold, the robin in the snow, the flowers in the scorching sun. Neither Young nor Akenside gave much space to humanitarian sentiments; on this theme Thomson had the field to himself.

Edward Young was the stormy petrel of primitivism. Giving the catchwords of primitivism a radically different meaning, he surpassed all other poets in the unusual quality of his opinions and in the length at which he expressed them. The key to Young's difference lay in his religious beliefs. His concept of human dignity was based on the Christian doctrine of the worth of the individual soul. Other poets carried over a deistic point of view into their verses on man and on creation. Underlying all their talk of the chain of being, of man's limitations, of the variety of creation, and the essential equality of a seraph and a clod, lay the attitude that made man a neutral link in an infinite chain, that threw his eternity into doubt, his soul into question, his God into a far-off First Cause and universal handyman. Young wedded to deistic terms an attitude which was the antithesis of deism. Following the Christian tradition of the importance of the individual human soul, Young as it were, released man from his midway link and set him free to compass creation, confident that the soul of man outweighed the planets and the stars together.

In the course of the sermon that was Young's *Night Thoughts*, chronological and cultural primitivism offered him texts for his discourse. He reminded Lorenzo that "man of the world" was a term of reproach "in ancient days and Christian," and that the virtues of the ancient worthies put to shame the crimes of modern pagans. He attacked the spiritual ills of luxury with as much fervor as Pope had damned its political evils. He praised retirement as man's liberator from fogs of sense and passion, from worldly ambition and foolish desires. The graveyard details of his melancholy retreats had all the traditional trappings, the knell, the shroud, the ruined shade, but even to the death motif Young brought his own larger sweep of vision, picturing the earth itself as a grave, and death as the master of the universe: "Death, great proprietor of all, 'tis thine To tread out empire and to quench the stars." But chronological and cultural primitivism were of only passing interest to Young. His longest, most frequent and most fervent discussions were on philosophical and moral themes.

In the Platonic tradition he marveled at the diverse chain of being created by "Godhead streaming through a thousand worlds." He offered the interdependence of the links as proof for the existence of God. He congratulated man as the "connexion exquisite" that held together the mortal and immortal parts of the chain. To other writers the chain had been a symbol of human limitation, to Young it was a proof of man's superior destiny. "Grant a make [sic] part mortal, part immortal," or the chain must break: man's half-way link was his passport to immortality.

Just as Young had his own interpretation for the chain of being, so he had his particular opinion of the book of Nature. No other poet of his time so rhapsodized Nature's volume. The endless variety of worlds whirling through space kindled his imagination: the beauty of the celestial bodies delighted his soul. He felt, as many had felt, that the knowledge needful to man was spread out before him, common to all as the unhedged common field. But Young did more—he insisted that the bounds of man's knowledge were limitless as the starry heavens, that man's mission was to know, and that the object of his knowledge was infinite. Other poets had charted cosmic journeys, usually for the purpose of admiring the intricate universe which science had explained, but none had rejoiced as did Young that "the soul of man was made to walk the skies."

Young took the whole concept of the book of Nature which deism had used to turn men from formal religion and set it against the deists, making Nature attest to the existence of a personal God, the immortality of the human soul, the existence of future rewards for man. To him the "Scripture authentic" of Nature was a volume that declared to all men the evil of scepticism, the might of the Creator, the eternity to come.

What little Young had to say on optimism deviated from the usual array of optimistic opinions. To others worldly ills seemed necessary parts of a universal scheme; to Young they were necessary steps in the perfecting of the individual soul. Vividly conscious of the evils of his time ("Sighs had sooner fail than cause to sigh"), Young put the blame for earthly evils upon man's shoulders and justified God's allowing affliction on the grounds that pain was essential to the perfecting of the human spirit.

When he left philosophical themes for aesthetic, Young's interest flagged. His sole literary judgments in *Night Thoughts* were occasional censurings of genius and wit as contrary to reason and to the laws of sense. (In the light of his enthusiasm for the freedom of the human soul, and in the light of his later *Conjectures* Young's distrust of lawless genius comes as something of a surprise.)

Ethical subjects drew him most often. He praised the passions (notably as indications of man's immortality) but he saved his eloquence for his most favored of all themes—reason. For Young the supreme guide in human life was a disciplined intellect. Reason, the "heaven-lighted lamp in man" illumined the endless quest of the human spirit. It was the source of man's best and most lasting joys, the sure way to wisdom: "what reason bids, God bids." It helped him to contemplate divine things, gave him assurance of truth in love, relief from sorrow, security in hope of a future reward.

Since he delighted in reason, Young strongly supported the cause of man's superiority to the beast. Unlike the majority of his poetic contemporaries, Young consistently drew the dividing line between the animal kingdom and the human. "Reason is man's peculiar, sense the brute's." Reason was capable of infinite progress; sense quickly reached the limit of its perfection. Passion was brutish (the term with Young was always one of contempt): Reason was of the divine. Animal happiness was for a day: man's discontent and hardship were the price he paid for immortality. His grief was but "his grandeur in disguise."

Apart from the primitivistic currents of his time, in direct opposition to many of them, Young was the most individual of the poets. Full of gloomy and terrible scenes, yet above terror and disdainful of mere gloom; lover of the stars, yet weighing the spangled firmament as less than a human soul; defender of reason the principle of restraint, yet eloquent advocate of the free questing of the human spirit, Young illustrated in his own themes the principles that he placed as guides in human life. First, reason—never satisfied in pursuit of wisdom: then the passions, "stretched out like eagles" in pursuit of knowledge—both insatiable in their quest, both looking for final satisfaction to the Truth and Goodness of another world.

PART FOUR

Notes

Bibliography

Index

Abbreviations

USED IN THE NOTES

In first footnote references the titles of the works are cited in full: subsequent references are given either in easily recognizable short titles or, as in the works listed below, in abbreviations. The procedure of using abbreviations was necessary because of the immense number of references which otherwise would have overburdened the book.

Anderson	Robert Anderson, *Works of the British Poets*
A.S.	Moses Browne, *Angling Sports*
C.I.	James Thomson, *Castle of Indolence*
C.C.S.	Allan Ramsay, *A Choice Collection of English and Scotch Songs*
Chal.	Alexander Chalmers, *Works of the English Poets*
Dods.	Robert Dodsley, *A Collection of Poems*
Eiren.	T. Curteis, *Eirenodia*
E.M.	Alexander Pope, *Essay on Man*
G.M.	*Gentleman's Magazine*
Lib.	James Thomson, *Liberty*
L.M.	*London Magazine*
Meta.	Elizabeth Thomas, *Metamorphosis of the Town*
M. Rev.	*Monthly Review*
Nichols	John Nichols, *Select Collection of Poems*
N.S.	J. T. Desaguliers, *The New System of the Universe*
N.T.	Edward Young, *Night Thoughts*
O. and E.	Thomas Nugent, *Odes and Epistles*
Pleasures	Mark Akenside, *Pleasures of the Imagination*
P.M.	Thomas Warton, *Pleasures of Melancholy*
Un.	Henry Baker, *The Universe*
Un. Mag.	*Universal Magazine*

MISCELLANY TITLES

A.L.	*The Altar of Love*
B. and V.	*Bacchus and Venus*
Bath Misc.	*The Bath Miscellany for the Year 1740*
Can.	*Candour*
C. and S.	*Clio and Strephon*

Carib.	*Caribbeana*
C.C.	*A Complete Collection* of all the Verses, Essays [etc.] which have been occasioned by the Publication of three volumes of Miscellanies by Pope and Co.
C.C. Med.	*Charing Cross Medley*
C.C.P.	*A Choice Collection of Poetry by the Most Ingenious Men of the Age*
Ch. P.	*The Christian Poet*
C. Misc.	*The Cuckold's Miscellany*
C.O.	*The Court Oracle*
Com. Tales	*The Comedians Tales*
C. Bach. S.	*A Collection of Bacchanalian Songs*
C.P.	*Court Poems*
C.P.A.	*A Collection of Poems.* By the Author of the Cambridge Ladies
C.P.O.	*A Collection of Poems;* consisting of Odes, Tales, etc.
C.P. Va. and P.	*A Collection of Pieces in Verse and Prose* which have been publish'd on the occasion of the Dunciad
Desc. B.	*A Description of Bath*
D.M.	*Delights of the Muses*
Epis.	*An Epistle from the late Lord B . . . . . to the Duke of W . . . .*
Es. C.	*An Essay on Conversation*
Fab.	*Fables and Other Short Poems*
F.P.	*The Flower Piece*
F.V.	*The Fall of Virtue*
Grub.	*Grubiana*
Har. Hor.	*Harlequin Horace*
H-S.	*The Honey-Suckle*
Lash.	*Lashley's York Miscellany*
Lov. P.	*The Lover's Pacquet*
Mem. Soc. Grub.	*Memoirs of the Society of Grub Street*
Misc.	*Miscellanea*
Miscellanies	*Miscellanies: the Last Volume*
Misc. New.	*A Miscellaneous Collection of Original Poems . . .* "By Thomas Newcomb"
Misc. O.P.	*Miscellanies consisting chiefly of Original Pieces in Prose and Verse*
Misc. P.S.H.	*A Miscellany of Poems by Several Hands*
Misc. Sav.	*Miscellaneous Poems and Translations by Several Hands.* Publish'd by Richard Savage
Misc. S.P.	*Miscellanies by Swift and Pope*
New Min.	*The New Ministry*
New Misc.	*A New Miscellany*

New Misc. '34	*New Miscellany for the Year 1734*
New Misc. '38	*A New Miscellany for the Year 1738*
P. Af. S.	*Poems on Affairs of State*
P.E. and L.	*Poems in English and Latin on the Archers and Royal-Company of Archers*
P.W.	*The Poetical Works of J.S.D.D.D.S.P.D.*
Rob. Pane.	*Robin's Panegyrick*
Scar. Misc.	*The Scarborough Miscellany*
S.P. Ire.	*Select Poems from Ireland*
S.T.	*The Stamford Toasts*
Sum. Misc.	*The Summer Miscellany*
Swift.	*Swifteana*
Tun. '30	*Tunbrigialia for the Year 1730*
Tun. '40	*Tunbrigialia or The Tunbridge Miscellany, for the Years 1737, 1738, 1739* [published 1740]
Ver.	*Verres and His Scribblers*
Win. Med.	*The Windsor Medley*

Notes

(The section on chronological primitivism includes notes 1–105: that on cultural primitivism begins again with note 1 and continues through note 308.)

PART ONE, CHAPTER I

1. For the background of chronological primitivism, see such standard treatments of the subject as, A. O. Lovejoy, "Foreword," in *Primitivism and the Idea of Progress in English Popular Literature of the Eighteenth Century* by Lois Whitney (1934), pp. xi–xx, and A. O. Lovejoy and George Boas, "Prolegomena," in a *Documentary History of Primitivism*, I, 1–23 (1935). Hereafter these works will be referred to as, L. Whitney, *Prim.*, and A. O. Lovejoy, *Doc. Hist.*

2. See the section on reason and passion in part 2 of this study for further evidence of the poets' interest in this quarrel.

3. Robert Nugent, "Epistle to Cornwallis," in *Odes and Epistles*, p. 36; John or Charles Wesley, "An Elegy," in *The Poetical Works of John and Charles Wesley*, III, 111; John Bancks, "Lycon," in *Miscellaneous Works in Verse and Prose of John Bancks*, p. 21; *The Fall of Virtue* (1738), p. 3.

4. "Spring," in *The London Magazine*, VII, 143 (1738); piece quoted, Elizabeth Rowe, "Soliloquy," in *The Miscellaneous Works in Prose and Verse of Mrs. Elizabeth Rowe*, p. 190.

5. "Jove Eleutherio," in *Dodsley's Miscellany*, III, 42–43; passage quoted, Walter Harte, "An Essay on Reason," in *Chalmers*, XVI, 352.

6. Robert Blair, *The Grave*, p. 23.

7. J. or C. Wesley, "Misery," in *Works*, I, 61.

8. R. Nugent, "Epistle to Cornwallis," in *O. and E.*, p. 40.

9. Margaret Brandwen, *Early Eighteenth Century Ideas of the Origins of Society* (Columbia University M.A. Essay, 1943). For a discussion of the patriarchal theory see pp. 9–11: the reference to Bolingbroke's use of the theory is on p. 17, to Defoe, p. 30.

10. Another description of the pastoral charm of the age is by Moses Browne, "Essay on the Universe," in *Poems on Various Subjects*, p. 334.

11. James Thomson, "Castle of Indolence," I, st. 37, in *The Poetical Works of James Thomson* (Oxford Edition of Standard Authors, 1908). All references to Thomson's poems are to this edition of his works. Hereafter only the name of the poem will be given, with stanza

NOTES 215

references for the "Castle of Indolence" and line references for the
other poems.

12. Ibid., st. 25.

13. Alexander Pope, "Essay on Man," III, 147–268, in *The Complete
Works of Alexander Pope* (Student's Cambridge Edition, 1903). All
references to Pope are taken from this edition. Hereafter references to
him will simply give the title of the poem, and the line numbers of the
passages referred to.

14. Professor Lovejoy points out that Empedocles, *Fragments*, 130,
with its kindly picture of men and animals influenced later writers,
notably Pope. "Passed on to later Greek and Roman and so to modern
writers, the Empedoclean picture of man's former amicable relations
with the animals became a part of the literary convention of chronological primitivism; e.g. almost the whole of Pope's description of the
state of Nature (Essay on Man, III, 147–60) is devoted to this theme,
and some of the couplets might serve for free translations of some of
Empedocles's lines." The quotation is from A. O. Lovejoy, *Doc. Hist.*,
I, 34.

15. Pope, *E.M.*, III, 147 ff.

16. The confusion about "Nature" underlay their philosophical,
aesthetic and moral problems. The interest in naturally benevolent human nature underlay their interest in the noble savage, in benevolence,
in the controversy concerning the relative superiority of man to beast,
and in the quarrel over reason and passion as guides to life.

17. William Whitehead, "An Ode to a Gentleman's Tent Garden,"
in *Dods.*, II, 261–62.

18. Allan Ramsay, "To the Musick Club," in *Works*, III, 49, goes
back to Old Testament times to remark the harmony of human speech
before the building of the tower of Babel.

19. "An Epigram," in *Grubiana* (1732), p. 76; *F.V.* (1738), pp. 9–10;
"Manners Make the Man," in *The Honey-Suckle* (1734), p. 226.

20. The poem has no name, merely an explanation that it was found
in *Fog's Journal*, Sept. 17, 1733: it is printed in *The Poetical Works of
J.S.D.D.D.S.P.D.* (1736), p. 261.

21. J. or C. Wesley, see passages from poems in *Works*, I, 342; II,
327, 326, 480, 345.

22. Ibid., II, 121–22.

23. Ibid., II, 351, 58; I, 369.

24. Ibid., I, 299.

25. "Damon to Philemon," in *Miscellaneous Poems and Translations
by Several Hands* (1726), p. 135; J. Bancks, "Lycon," in *Works*, p. 21;
William Hamilton, "To the Countess of Eglentoun, with the Gentle
Shepherd," in *Poems on Several Occasions*, p. 24; Sneyd Davies,
"Epithalamium," in *Dods.*, V, 102; A. Ramsay, "On the Marriage of

Alexander Brodie . . . and Mrs. Mary Sleigh," in *C.C.S.*, II, 112; quoted is A. Ramsay, "The Modern Marriage Question," in *C.C.S.*, II, 192.

26. "Ambition and Content," in *Gentleman's Magazine*, VII, 244 (1737); William Somervile, "Hobbinol," in *The Poetical Works of William Somervile*, p. 155; John Armstrong, "Art of Preserving Health," in *The Poetical Works of Dr. Armstrong*, p. 21; R. Blair, *The Grave*, p. 20; James Hammond, "Elegy 7," in *Chal.* XI, 592.

27. "The Golden Age," in *L.M.*, IV, 328 (1745).

28. "The Happiness of a Country Life," in *L.M.*, VI, 388 (1737).

29. Thomson, *Spring*, p. 48, note to 1. 271. This passage is part of a 281 line passage included in editions of *Spring* from 1728–1738: note also ibid., 257, and 250 ff.

30. William Meston, "Old Mother Grim's Tales, Tale 1," in *The Poetical Works of the Ingenious and Learned William Meston*, p. 70.

31. "Regulus," in *The Flower-Piece* (1731), p. 222; "Jovi Eleutherio," in *Dods.*, III, 44; Soame Jenyns, "An Epistle Written in the Country," in *Chal.*, XVII, 395; *F.V.* (1738), p. 1; "The Tears of Old May Day," in *Dods.*, IV, 169.

32. "Jovi Eleutherio," in *Dods.*, III, 423.

33. J. Hammond, "Elegy 2," in *Chal.*, XVII, 590.

34. Thomson, *Spr.*, 272–308. Note also his account of the deluge and of the consequent harshness of the earth's climate, ibid., 309–42. For a discussion of Thomson's use of Burnet here and elsewhere in the Seasons, see Alan Dugald McKillop, *The Background of Thomson's Seasons* (1942), pp. 97–106.

35. Joseph Warton, "The Enthusiast," in *Chal.*, XVIII, 160.

36. *War with Priestcraft*, p. 10. The author footnotes his own assertion that the learned agree that the ancients were wiser than the moderns with the remark, "Sir William Temple and most learned men own that the learning of the moderns falls far short of the ancients . . ."; Thomson has the best tributes to ancient wisdom; note his praises of Greek art and science, *C.I.*, II, st. 50; *Liberty*, II, 18–20; 86–99; 175–79; I, 233–34; 252–56; III, 508–11; *Spr.*, 52–66; Mark Akenside, "Ode 18," p. 192, in *The Poetical Works of Mark Akenside* (1857): (all references to Akenside are from this work. Line references are given for the "Pleasures of the Imagination," page references for the other poems), p. 298, has a tribute to the Pantheon; "The Gout," in *L.M.*, III, 660 (1734); "The Involuntary Sinners," in *F.P.* (1731), p. 231; Jonathan Swift, "Cadenus and Vanessa," in *The Aldine Edition of the British Poets*, II, 197; *Essay on Conversation* (1737), p. 19; Edward Young, "Night Thoughts," IX, 992; 970–1016. All quotations from the "Night Thoughts" are taken from *Young's Night Thoughts* (1853); hereafter references to this poem will be made as *N.T.* plus line references.

37. Aaron Hill, "Tears of the Muses," in *The Works of the late Aaron Hill, Esq.*, IV, 179. The reference to wrestling occurs in a passage by M. Browne, "Reflections made upon Viewing of Two Prints . . . ," in *Poems*, p. 199.
38. "An Epistle to Mr. Pope," in *G.M.*, VI, 745 (1736).
39. "Pegasus in Grub-Street," in *Memoirs of the Society of Grub Street* (1737), p. 250; J. T. Desaguliers, *The Newtonian System of the World, the Best Model of Government*, p. 1.
40. "Codrus and Caesar," in *A Miscellany of Original Poems* (1731), p. 263; "The Power of Gold," in *A Collection of Poems* (1731), p. 1.
41. Jonathan Swift, "Cadenus and Vanessa," in *Works*, p. 208.
42. "On Liberty," in *Stamford Toasts* (1726), p. 34.
43. Lord Lyttleton, "To the Rev. Dr. Ascough at Oxford," in *Dods.*, II, 25–26; "Answer to Mr. Maevius," in *Mem. Soc. Grob.* (1737), p. 251.
44. Jonathan Smedley, "Apollo's Edict," in *Gulliveriana*, p. 52.
45. J. Bancks, "Fame," in *Works*, II, 177.
46. Thomson, *Lib.*, II, 272–311; J. Smedley, "L——t's Lamentation," in *Gulliv.*, p. 332; ibid., "The Wish," p. 328; Edward Ward, *Durgen*, p. 46.
47. "Q. Horatii Flaccii ad Curionem epistola: or, an epistle from Horace in Elizium, [sic] to Curio in England faithfully translated into English from the Elizean copy," in *Misc. O.P.* (1740), p. 52.
48. Thomson, *Winter*, 539–49; J. Smedley, "The Complaint," in *Gulliv.*, p. 34. The latter is the passage quoted.
49. W. Whitehead, "The Danger of Writing Verse," in *Chal.*, XVII, 200.
50. Ibid.
51. Akenside, "Pleasures of the Imagination," II, 16 ff., in *Works*. Hereafter to be referred to as *Pleasures*.
52. Thomas Warton (Jr.), "Newmarket," in *Chal.*, XVIII, 121.
53. Ibid.
54. Ibid.
55. Lord Lyttleton, "An Epistle to Mr. Pope from a Young Gentleman at Rome," in *A Collection of Pieces in Verse and Prose which have been publish'd on the occasion of the Dunciad* (1732), pp. 4–5; 35–36.
56. Other poetic tributes to Roman greatness: "Regulus," in *F.P.* (1731), p. 217; "Palenodia," in *Misc. Sav.* (1726), p. 237; "On Ancient Medals," in *The Student*, II, 230 (1750). Thomson praises Greece in *Lib.*, II, 421–90, 394–408; I, 108–12 (quoted in text); IV, 188–91, 305–308.
57. Ibid., I, 89–92; 75–81, line quoted, 77; 216–17, line quoted, 218.
58. Ibid., 259–85, quoted, 259–63; in like spirit of lament are Thomson's desolate descriptions of modern Italy, ibid., 15–340, 372–75.
59. John Dyer, "The Ruins of Rome," in *Chal.*, XIII, 227.
60. Ibid.

61. Ibid., 227–28.

62. Joseph Trapp, "Virgil's Tomb," in *Dods.*, IV, 112.

63. Ibid., 113; 111 is another good example of the melancholy tone of the piece. Equally desolate is Akenside's description, *Pleasures*, I, 70.

64. Trapp inherited a family as well as a national distrust of Catholicism. His father had been awarded the degree of D.D. from Oxford for his "Popery truly stated and briefly confuted" (1726), and his "The Church of England defended against the Church of Rome in Answer to a Late Sophistical and Insolent Popish Book" (1727).

65. Particularly enthusiastic in its satisfaction with national prosperity in contrast to foreign poverty is the passage by R. Nugent, "Epistle to Cornwallis," in *O. and E.*, p. 53.

66. Gilbert West, "The Institution of the Order of the Garter," in *Dods.*, II, 155.

67. Samuel Boyse, *Retirement*, p. 12.

68. T. Warton (Jr.), "Newmarket," in *Chal.*, XVIII, 120.

69. "Omne ruit in pejus," in *H-S.* (1734), p. 250.

70. Hildebrand Jacob, "Epistle 7," in *The Works of Hildebrand Jacob, Esq.*, p. 120.

71. Ibid., p. 121.

72. Young, "Love of Fame," in *The Poetical Works of Edward Young* (1859), II, 84. Hereafter references to this and to poems by Young other than the *Night Thoughts* will be referred to simply by title and page number. All such references will be to this edition.

73. William Mason, "Isis," in *Chal.*, XVIII, 326.

74. David Mallet, "Verses Occasioned by Dr. Frazer's Rebuilding Part of the University of Aberdeen," in *The Works of David Mallet*, p. 84.

75. E. Ward, *Durgen*, p. 12.

76. "Manners Make the Man," in *H-S.* (1734), p. 222.

77. Thomson, "To the Memory of Mr. Congreve," 136–47.

78. Thomson, *C.I.*, II, st. 23.

79. W. Meston, "The Contrast Reversed; and Set in a True Light," in *Works*, p. 167.

80. Thomas Cooke, "Epistle the Third," in *Mr. Cooke's Original Poems*, p. 72.

81. S. Davies, "Rhapsody, To Milton," in *Nicoll*, VI, 123; A. Ramsay regrets the "lear'd days of Gawn Dunkell," in *Familiar Epistles*, Answer I, in *Works*, III, 32.

82. Mary Davys, "The Modern Poet," in *The Works of Mrs. Davys*, p. 277.

83. Henry Carey, "Of Stage Tyrants," in *The Poems of Henry Carey*, p. 106; "A Satirical Poem on the Beggars' Opera," in *A Collection of Poems* (1733), p. 6; "A Prologue to the University and Ladies of Cambridge," in ibid., p. 42.

NOTES 219

84. J. Bancks, "Of Tragedy," in *Works*, p. 44; Leonard Welsted, *Of False Fame*, p. 10; "To Mr. Keen on the New Play-House," in *Caribbeana*, I, 381 (1741).
85. Pope, "Second Satire of the Second Book of Horace," 97 f.; "Modern Politeness," in *G.M.*, V, 678 (1735); "The Progress of Deformity . . ." in *Altar of Love* (1727), p. 111.
86. M. Browne, "Times and Manners," in *Poems*, p. 189.
87. Ibid., "English Ale," p. 235; "An Invitation to a Country Walk," in *L.M.*, X, 458 (1741).
88. "A Panegyric on Ale," in *The Student* (1750), p. 67; "Roast Beef of Old England," in *A Choice Collection of Poetry* (1738), pp. 84–85; the passage quoted is from "An Invitation to a Country Walk," in *L.M.*, X, 458 (1741).
89. Elizabeth Thomas, *Metamorphosis of the Town*, pp. 7 and 26; *Harlequin Horace* (1731), p. 28; Matthew Green, "The Spleen" in *Chal.*, XV, 165; Pope, *The First Epistle of the First Book of Horace*, 97–100, complains about the speech of modern men and recommends to them the "good old song" of their ancestors with a fine disregard for the linguistic differences which would have made medieval speech unintelligible to eighteenth-century gentlemen:

And say, to which shall our applause belong,
This new court jargon, or the good old song?
The modern language of corrupted peers,
Or what was spoke at Cressy and Poitiers?

90. "A Satire on the Times," in *Lovers' Pacquet* (1733), p. 16.
91. "The Danger of Knighthood," in ibid. (1733), p. 7; "The Bishop and the Shepherd," in *Cuckold's Miscellany* (1735), p. 48; Young, *Love of Fame*, p. 101; Lord Lansdowne, "Occasion'd by the foregoing Verses," in *Works*, p. 20.
92. "An Ode to the People of Great Britain," in *Dods.*, III, 19; quoted is J. Brown, "An Essay on Satire," in *Dods.*, III, 313.
93. "A Satire on the Times," in *Lov. P.* (1733), p. 19; quoted—Christopher Pitt, "On the Masquerades," in *Chal.*, XII, 379.
94. Various laments for modern ignorance and wickedness occur in: "The Heroines, or Modern Memoirs, By the Same," [Mr. Graves] in *Dods.*, IV, 328; Thomson, "Britannia," 1–3; "To the V. B——," in *C.P.D.* (1731), p. 3; W. Meston, "Tale 7," in *Works*, p. 97; W. Somervile, "Hobbinol," in *Works*, p. 165; Paul Whitehead, "Honour," in *Chal.*, XVI, 220–21; "On Thought," in *Delights of the Muses* (1738), p. 223; Thomson, "A Poem to the Memory of Mr. Congreve," 20–24.
95. Walter Paget, *A Voyage to Ipswich*, p. 20; Pope, *Satire 2* (of Dr. John Donne versified), 113 f. W. Hamilton, "To the Countess of Egerton . . . ," in *Poems*, p. 29; "Penhurst," in *Dods.*, IV, 52.
96. "On Marriage," in *D.M.* (1738), p. 171.

97. "Rival Wives," in *New Miscellany* (1738), pp. 55 and 52.
98. "On Poverty," in *Misc. Sav.* (1726), p. 230.
99. Ibid.
100. Ibid.; see also p. 233.
101. Pope, *Epilogue to the Satires*, dialogue I, 159 f.
102. Besides those passages mentioned later, other notations of England's former grandeur occur in: Samuel Johnson, "London," in *The Poems of Samuel Johnson*, ll. 99–117; 248–344; 25–32; references to Scotland's former greatness occur in *On the Scarcity of the Copper Coin* (1739), p. 15; "On the Royal Company of Archers shooting for the Bowl," in *Poems English and Latin on the Archers* (1726), p. 28, "The Answer," in ibid., p. 34; W. Hamilton, "Horace, Book 1, Epistle 18 imitated," in *Poems*, p. 161; Tobias Smollett, "The Tears of Scotland," in *Plays and Poems*, pp. 238–39; W. Somervile, "Fable 7," in *Works*, p. 50; T. Cooke, "The Knight of Bath," in *Poems*, p. 19; ibid., "Essay on Antient and Modern Britain," p. 12; ibid., p. 10; Lord Lansdowne, "Ode on the Present Corruption of Mankind," in *The Genuine Works in Verse and Prose of the Right Hon. George Granville, Lord Lansdowne*, p. 141; "An Ode to the People of Great Britain," in *Dods.*, III, 20.
103. "Rival Wives," in *New Misc.* (1738), p. 57.
104. T. Cooke, "Essay on Antient and Modern Britain," in *Works*, p. 12.
105. Pope, *Epilogue to the Satires*, dialogue II, 248–53.
106. Ibid.

PART ONE, CHAPTER 2

1. A. O. Lovejoy, *Doc. Hist.*, I, 1–17.
2. "Five Acres and Independence," from the title of the book by Maurice Grenville Kains, *Five Acres and Independence* (1941).
3. Michel de Montaigne, "Of Cannibals," in *Works*, translated by William Hazlitt (1853), p. 89.
4. A. O. Lovejoy, *Doc. Hist.*, I, 287–367.
5. Tacitus—e.g. his praise of Teutonic respect for the marriage contract in *Germania*, Sections 17 and 19; and of their hospitality, ibid., Section 21.
6. Montaigne, "Of Cannibals," in *Works*, pp. 89–93.
7. E.g. Dryden's *Indian Queen* and Dryden and Howard's *Conquest of Granada*.
8. Captain James Cook—circumnavigator who made three important voyages of exploration to the South Seas. Among other things he explored the east coast of Australia and the Sandwich Islands and discovered New Hebrides and New Caledonia. He was killed in Hawaii

by natives in 1779. Accounts of his voyages were published 1773–1780. Captain Wallis—circled the world between 1766–1768.

9. Omai—a native of Ulaietia brought to England by Captain Furneaux; after a two year visit to England he returned with Captain Cook on the latter's third voyage. See C. B. Tinker, *Nature's Simple Plan* (1922), pp. 8–12; 27–28; 75–89. Labrador Esquimaux—brought to England by Captain George Cartwright; see C. B. Tinker, *Nature's Simple Plan*, pp. 25–27.

10. Joseph Addison, *Spectator*, No. 50.

11. A. O. Lovejoy, *Doc. Hist.*, I, 7–11, cultural primitivism; 11–14, nature as norm; 17–18, primitivism and the appraisal of human nature; 19–22, animalitarianism. Hoxie Neale Fairchild, *The Noble Savage* (1928), pp. 1–22. C. B. Tinker, "The noble savage was the offspring of the rationalism of the Deist philosophers who, in their attack upon the Christian doctrine of the fall of man, had idealized the child of nature," in *Nature's Simple Plan*, pp. 88–89; L. Whitney, *Prim.*, pp. 7–41.

12. Pope, *Essay on Man*, I, 11.

13. Earl of Shaftesbury, "Moralists," in *Works*, II, 345.

14. A. O. Lovejoy, *Great Chain of Being* (1936), Chapter 6. Hereafter this work will be referred to as *Chain*. George Boas, *The Happy Beast in French Thought of the Seventeenth Century* (1933) offers a discussion of the conflict; Hester Hastings, *Man and Beast in French Thought of the Eighteenth Century* (1936) gives the humanitarian rather than the philosophical aspects; H. C. Rosenfield, "Un Chapitre de l'Histoire de l'Animal Machine," in *Revue de la Litterature Comparée*, XVII, 461–87 (1937) outlines the conflict on this topic between Descartes and More; Albert G. A. Balz, "Cartesian Doctrine and the Animal Soul," in *Studies in the History of Ideas* (1935), pp. 117–71 outlines the philosophical objections to the beast machine.

15. "The Story of Inkle and Yarico. From the 11th Spectator," in *L.M.*, III, 257 ff. (1734).

16. Stephen Duck, "Avaro and Amanda," in *Poems on Several Occasions*, pp. 82 and 89.

17. Richard Savage, "Of Public Spirit," in *The Poetical Works of Richard Savage*, p. 154; "To the Rt. Honourable Lord Baltimore," in *G.M.*, VII, 760 (1737); like in sympathy to these expressions of interest in Indian welfare are: Thomson, *Summer*, 850–55; 747–59; ibid., *Lib.*, IV, 912–21; R. Nugent, "Epistle to Chesterfield," in *O. and E.*, p. 63; A. Ramsay, "The Rise and Fall of Stocks," in *Works*, II, 325; "The Morning Star," in *L.M.*, IX, 186 (1740); J. Warton, "Ode on Mr. West's Translation of Pindar," in *Chal.*, XVIII, 169.

18. "Fidenia," in *L.M.*, XIII, 147 (1744).

19. Ibid.

20. "The Happy Savage," in *G.M.*, II, 718 (1732).

21. J. Warton, "The Dying Indian," in *Chal.*, XVIII, 170.
22. Ibid., "The Revenge of America."
23. Ibid., "The Enthusiast," p. 161.
24. Thomson, *Sum.*, 663–747.
25. Ibid., 822 ff.; 1619 ff.—a long passage included in editions 1727–1738, but omitted from the 1744 edition.
26. J. Armstrong, "Art of Preserving Health," in *Works*, pp. 22 ff.; W. Somervile, "Fable 14," in *Works*, p. 82, has an interesting picture of balmy and luxurious Southern seas.
27. M. Browne, "The Dedication," in *Angling Sports*, p. xi; in a classical mood also is the passage by William Bowman, "Jesus Grove," in *Poems on Several Occasions*, p. 3.
28. "The Pleasures of Jamaica," in *G.M.*, VIII, 158 (1737); "India," in *L.M.*, IV, 94–95 (1735); ibid., p. 94 is the passage quoted.
29. Omitted.
30. Omitted.
31. Thomson, *Win.*, 414–23.
32. Ibid., *Lib.*, IV, 374–79.
33. Ibid., *Autumn*, 870–74.
34. Ibid., *Lib.*, IV, 330–35.
35. Ibid., *Win.*, 845–50.
36. Jabez Hughes, "Horace Book 3, Ode 24," in *Miscellanies in Verse and Prose*, p. 31.
37. W. Hamilton, "The Corycian Swain," in *Poems*, p. 247.
38. "Verses written by a Highlander the day before he was taken," in *G.M.*, XIII, 322–23 (1743); Thomas Warton (Jr.), "Pleasures of Melancholy," in *Chal.*, XVIII, 97, 218; D. Mallet, "Amyntor and Theodora," in *The Works of David Mallet, Esq.*, pp. 119–20; see also his description of the people of this primitive region in the "Preface" to the poem, p. 113; William Collins, "Ode on the Popular Superstitions of the Highlands," in *The Poems of William Collins*, p. 745; "An Epistle of a Swiss Soldier," in *Dods.*, III, 54; J. Armstrong, "The Art of Preserving Health," in *Works*, p. 22.
39. D. Mallet, "Amyntor and Theodora," in *Works*, p. 119.
40. T. Wharton (Jr.), "P.M.," in *Chal.*, XVIII, 97.
41. Ibid.
42. "Verses written by a Highlander on the day before he was taken," in *G.M.*, XIII, 745 (1743).
43. W. Collins, "Ode on the Popular Superstitions of the Highlands," in *Poems*, p. 745.
44. Theocritus, *Idyl* 7.
45. For background material on the pastoral see: Mary Loretto Lilly, *The Georgic, A Contribution to the Study of the Virgilian Type of Didactic Poetry* (1919); Marion K. Bragg, *The Formal Eclogue*

in Eighteenth Century England (1926); Dwight L. Durling, *Georgic Tradition in English Poetry* (1935).

46. Ibid.

47. Richard Steele, *Guardian*, No. 22.

48. The following are some of the descriptions of the bliss of idyllic country life: Thomson, *C.I.*, II, st. 56; William Dunkin, "Boetoia," in *Select Poetical Works of the Late William Dunkin, D.D.*, pp. 133–34; Lord Lyttleton, "Progress of Love, Eclogue 4," in *Dods.*, II, p. 15; ibid., "Eclogue 2," p. 5; "In Praise of a Country Life," in *L.M.*, XVII, 184 (1748); Thomson, *Sum.*, 493–505; J. Dyer, "The Country Walk," in *Chal.*, XIII, 250; W. Somervile, "The Chase," in *Works*, p. 242; J. Dyer, "The Country Walk," in *Chal.*, XIII, 251; "The Trophy," in *Dods.*, III, 245–46; S. Boyse, *Retirement*, p. 2; "Rural Happiness," in *The Student*, II, 277 (1750); John Gay, "Introduction to the Fables, the Shepherd and the Philosopher," in *The Poetical Works of John Gay*, p. 49; W. Somervile, "Hobbinol," in *Works*, p. 152.

49. Lord Lyttleton, "Eclogue 4," in *Dods.*, II, 15; the passage quoted is from "The Country," in *Misc. Sav.* (1726), p. 199.

50. W. Collins, "Eclogue I," in *Poems*, p. 43; "On the Happiness of a Shepherd," in *L.M.*, X, 199 (1741); "Description of Spring," in *G.M.*, II, 669 (1732).

51. "The Country," in *Misc. Sav.* (1736), p. 200.

52. "The Honey-Suckle and the Bee," in *H-S.* (1734), p. 257; "On the Pleasures of the Country," in *L.M.*, IX, 451 (1740); "The Happy Man," in *L.M.*, IV, 624 (1735).

53. H. Carey, "The Happy Rustics," in *Poems*, p. 176; David Lewis, "Pastoral," in *Miscellany of Poems by Several Hands*, (1731), p. 120.

54. Ibid.; S. Dixon, "A Pastoral," in *Poems on Several Occasions*, p. 22; "A Morning Piece," in *The Student*, I, 274 (1750); Thomson, *Sum.*, 1664–1670; "The Peasant," in *L.M.*, XV, 641 (1746); A poem without a title in *G.M.*, XV, 161 (1745).

55. "Reflections occasioned by a Comparison between the Sacred Pastoral of Solomon and that of Virgil," in *Misc. Sav.* (1726), p. 35.

56. Thomson, *Sum.*, 1664–70.

57. Ibid., 281–87; 62–80; 220–40 have further pleasant country pictures.

58. Ibid., *Spr.*, 34–49.

59. Ibid., *Sum.*, 343–47.

60. Ibid., 352–422. Note also Thomson's pictures of the harvests, *Aut.*, 151–76, and of the harvest dance, ibid., 1220–34.

61. Ibid., *Win.*, 617–29; 83–93.

62. Examples of idyllic atmosphere are to be found in Thomson's *C.I.*, I, stanzas 1, 14, 15, 26; II, stanzas 1, 26, 55.

63. Ibid., I, st. 17.

64. Ibid., I, st. 6.
65. Ibid., I, st. 2.
66. Ibid.
67. Ibid., I, st. 4.
68. Johnson, *Rambler*, no. 7.
69. E.g. Virgil, Horace, Martial, Seneca, Cicero.
70. Addison, *Spectator*, No. 264.
71. Johnson, *Rambler*, No. 135.
72. Seneca, *Moral Epistles*, No. 68.
73. Virgil, "The Second Pastoral, or Alexis," ll. 1135–36, in *The Poetical Works of John Dryden* (Student's Cambridge Edition, 1909). All quotations from Virgil used in this thesis are from this source.
74. W. Somervile, "To Mr. Addison," in *Works*, p. 266; Mary Barber, "Written from Dublin to a Lady in the Country," in *Poems on Several Occasions*, p. 101; S. Dixon, "To Silvio," in *Poems*, p. 11; Lord Lyttleton, "Eclogue I," in *Dods.*, II, 2; William Shenstone, "On a Small Building in the Gothic Taste," in *Dods.*, IV, 347.
75. Thomas FitzGerald, "An Ode," in *Poems on Several Occasions*, p. 64.
76. S. Dixon, "To Silvio," in *Poems*, p. 12; H. Carey, "Retirement," in *Poems*, p. 122.
77. Ibid.
78. S. Jenyns, "To a Lady," in *Dods.*, III, 132; it appears also in *L.M.*, XVII, 191.
79. E. Rowe, "To Chloe," in *Works*, p. 84; like in spirit to the passage quoted is the anonymous poem "The Country Life," in *H–S.* (1734), p. 29.
80. T. Warton, "On a May Morning," in *Poems on Several Occasions*, pp. 95–96.
81. "The Annual Recess," in *L.M.*, III, 661 (1734).
82. J. Dyer, "Grongar Hills," in *Chal.*, XIII, 224.
83. A. Ramsay, "Mercury in Quest of Peace," in *Works*, III, 143 f.
84. "A Dream," in *C.P.A.* (1733), p. 75; "Man's Happiness," in *L.M.*, VIII, 41 (1739); John Winstanley, "A Thought in the Pleasant Grove at Cabragh," in *Poems Written Occasionally by John Winstanley*, p. 185; S. Dixon, "Retirement," in *Poems*, p. 143; R. Nugent, "Epistle to Chesterfield," in *O. and E.*, p. 70; Thomson, *C.I.*, I, st. 13; "Reflections Occasion'd by a Comparison between the Sacred Pastoral of Solomon and that of Virgil," in *Misc. Sav.* (1726), pp. 33–34.
85. William Broome, "An Epistle to My Friend, Mr. Elijah Fenton," in *Poems on Several Occasions*, p. 55.
86. "An Ode," in *L.M.*, II, 298 (1733).
87. Johnson, "London," in *Poems*, ll. 43–47; note also ll. 5–9 and 155–162 in the same poem.

88. W. Collins, "Ode to Simplicity," in *Poems*, p. 81.
89. "Studley Park," in *Scarborough Miscellany* (1732), p. 45; similar in sentiment: "A Song by the Late Mr. W.H.," in *Universal Magazine*, I, 138 (1747); Lord Lyttleton, "To My Lord ——," in *Dods.*, II, 41; J. Armstrong, "Art of Preserving Health," in *Works*, pp. 33–34; "True Pleasure always to be found," in *L.M.*, III, 599 (1734); Lord Lyttleton, "To Mr. Poyntz," in *Dods.*, II, 32; "The Country Gentleman," in *L.M.*, IX, 42 (1740); "Erasto's Recantation," in *Misc. Sav.* (1726), p. 235; W. Shenstone, "The Progress of Taste," in *Chal.*, XIII, 316; William Melmoth, "Active and Retired Life," in *Dods.*, I, 211–12; Lord Lansdowne, "An Imitation of the Second Chorus in the Second Act of Seneca's Thyestes," in *Works*, p. 17.
90. W. Melmoth, "Of the Active and Retired Life," in *Dods.*, I, 211–12.
91. "Palinodia," in *Misc. Sav.* (1726), p. 240.
92. Thomson, *C.I.*, I, st. 17.
93. Ibid., "To the Rev. Patrick Murdock," 1 ff.
94. Ibid., *Win.*, 632–37.
95. Ibid., *Lib.*, IV, 530–31; similar, ibid., *Win.*, 423–31.
96. J. or C. Wesley, "Primitive Christianity," in *Works*, V, 482.
97. Ibid., I, 251; IV, 279; 65; V, 83, 216.
98. Young, *Love of Fame*, p. 72.
99. Young, *N.T.*, V, 310–21; single line quoted, 316; "we see" etc. is from ibid., 163–70.
100. D. Mallet, "The Excursion," in *Works*, p. 71.
101. Horace, "Satires, Book 2, 6" in Horace, *Satires, Epistles and Ars Poetica*, with an English translation by H. Rushton Fairclough (the Loeb Classical Library, 1932). All quotations from Horace's *Satires* are from this source. All quotations from his odes are from Horace, *Odes and Epodes*, with an English translation by C. E. Bennett (the Loeb Classical Library, 1932).
102. In the *Works* of Pope (Students' Cambridge Edition) this poem is attributed to both Swift and Pope. In *P.W.* it is attributed to Swift. Pope, *Horace, Satire 6, Book 2, Imitated*, 128–32: Swift, "Horace Liber II, Satire 6 part of it imitated," in *P.W.* (1736), p. 64.
103. Swift, "Horace Liber II, Satire 6 part of it imitated," in *P.W.* (1736), p. 64.
104. Virgil, *Georgics II*, 668–69. The translation used is that of John Dryden.
105. "The Country," in *Misc. Sav.* (1726), p. 206; other poems that express similar sentiments are: "To Mr. Thomson On Hearing Lady xxxx Commend his Seasons," in *G.M.*, VI, 141 (1736); T. Cooke, "Ode the First," in *Poems*, p. 99; J. Hammond, "Elegy 11," in *Chal.*, XI, 593; "Written to the Rt. Honourable the Late Robert Lord Petre," in *L.M.*,

XIV, 147 (1745); "Two Epistles to Mr. Pope, concerning the Authors of the Age," in *C.P. Vs. and Pr.* (1732), p. 25; "Remainder of the Bouts Rimez from vol. 7," in *G.M.*, VIII, 103 (1738); "The Wish," in *L.M.*, I, 415 (1732).

106. Akenside, "Odes, I, Preface," in *Works*, p. 142.

107. Ibid., *Pleasures*, I, 590–95.

108. "To Mercator, on a Country Life," in *L.M.*, XI, 304 (1742); M. Barber, "To a Lady, who invited the Author into the Country," in *Poems*, p. 137; "D—— Hall," in *L.M.*, IV, 330 (1735); "To Mr. Charles Lucy," in *L.M.*, VII, 460 (1738); "The Country Gentleman," in *G.M.*, II, 1074 (1732); "The Country Life," in *H-S.* (1734), p. 27; "An Invitation to the Country," in *G.M.*, IX, 266 (1739); W. Paget, *A Voyage to Ipswich*, p.e.; "Rural Happiness," in *L.M.*, XI, 618 (1742); J. Winstanley, "Upon Harristown," in *Poems*, p. 294; "Bro—ne Cliff," in *L.M.*, XIV, 253 (1744); J. Smedley, "A letter to Mr. Ambrose Philips," in *Gulliv.*, p. 101; "D—— Hall," in *L.M.*, IV, 330 (1735); W. Paget, *A Voyage to Ipswich*, p. 18.

109. "To the Honourable Sir William Brewer, Bar. by Mr. Victor," in *Misc. Sav.* (1726), p. 287.

110. "Verses sent in a Letter to a Friend," in *L.M.*, XII, 43 (1743).

111. "Epistle to a Friend in the Country in the Long Vacation," in *D.M.* (1738), p. 28.

112. H. Carey, "Mrs. Stuart's Retirement, in *Poems*, p. 121.

113. W. Hamilton, "The Flowers," in *Poems*, p. 103; minor passages with nature detail are "An Invitation to the Country," in *G.M.*, XII, 272 (1742); "The Vernal Invitation to Miss Jenny xxxx," in *G.M.*, XX, 181 (1750).

114. Thomson, *Spr.*, 101–106.

115. J. Smedley, "To a Clergyman, residing in a beautiful Vale in Norfolk, on his resolving to live in London," in *Gulliv.*, p. 107.

116. Mary Chandler, "My Wish," in *A Description of Bath*, p. 65.

117. M. Green, "The Spleen," in *Chal.*, XV, 168.

118. "The Wish," in *L.M.*, IV, 502 (1735) also specifies two hundred pounds yearly.

119. "Man's Happiness," in *L.M.*, VIII, 41 (1739); "The Female Wish," in *L.M.*, II, 419 (1733); "The Choice," in *G.M.*, VI, 680 (1736); "A Little Wish in Imitation of the Great Mr. Philips," in *L.M.*, V, 40 (1737); "A Prayer," in *G.M.*, XII, 384 (1742); "The Retir'd Patriot," in *Un. Mag.*, IV, 129 (1749); "Richmond Gardens," in *L.M.*, VII, 147 (1738); "The Wish," in *The Student*, II, 397 (1750); "O rus, quando ego te aspiciam?" in *G.M.*, XV, 213 (1745).

120. J. Winstanley, "On the Folly of Scribbling for Fame," in *Poems*, p. 2; S. Dixon, "The Wish," in *Poems*, p. 185.

121. M. Browne, "Essay on the Universe," in *Poems*, p. 185.

122. M. Chandler, "To Mrs. Jacob," in *Bath*, p. 73.

123. Ibid.

124. W. Broome, "The Seat of War in Flanders," in *Poems*, p. 70.

125. J. Smedley, "A Christmas Invitation to the Rt. Honourable the Lord Carteret, Lord Lieutenant of Ireland," in *Gulliv.*, p. 91.

126. "Richmond Gardens," in *L.M.*, VII, 147 (1738).

127. "Song 37," in *Bacchus and Venus* (1737), p. 29.

128. "Plaistow," in *L.M.*, III, 41 (1734).

129. *Spectator*, No. 387.

130. For a general background, see Amy Louise Reed, *The Background of Gray's Elegy, A Study in the Taste for Melancholy 1700–1751* (1924) and Eleanor Sickels, *The Gloomy Egoist, Moods and Themes of Melancholy from Gray to Keats* (1932), particularly chapter 1, "Compounded of many Simples," pp. 1–39; (pp. 27–38 deal with black melancholy).

131. "Il Penseroso, Solitude is Sometimes Best Society," in *Misc. Sav.* (1726), p. 161; W. Bowman, "Night," in *Poems*, p. 39; Young, *N.T.*, V, 178–93; "Penhurst-Coventry," in *Dods.*, IV, p. 51; H. Jacob, "Hymn to the Goddess of Silence," in *Works*, p. 38; "Answer to an Epistle to a Friend in the Country," in *H-S.* (1734), p. 311; "An Ode," in *D.M.* (1738), p. 40; "To Miss L—— from the Country," in *Lon. Mag.*, XI, 406 (1742); T. Warton (Jr.), "The Triumph of Isis," in *Chal.*, XVIII, 4; William Pattison, "The Morning Contemplation," in *Anderson*, p. 566.

132. J. or C. Wesley, "Solitude," in *Works*, I, 6; Mr. Tickell, "The Prospect of Peace," in *Dods.*, I, 14; Young, *Love of Fame*, p. 111; Akenside, "To the Honorable Charles Townshend," in *Works*, p. 239; W. Pattison, "The Morning Contemplation," in *And.*, p. 566; J. or C. Wesley, "Eupolis' Hymn to the Creator," in *Works*, I, 4; Thomson, *Hymn on Solitude*, 1; "An Ode to Solitude," in *L.M.*, XVIII, 611 (1749); W. Pattison, "The College Life To a Friend," in *And.*, p. 555; S. Duck, "Truth and Falsehood," in *Poems*, p. 110; Thomson, *Aut.*, 963–69; ibid., *Sum.*, 1379–1400; ibid., *To the Memory of Lord Talbot*, 214–21; E. Rowe, "The Vision," in *Works*, p. 1; Mr. Tickell, "The Prospect of Peace," in *Dods.*, I, 14.

133. "Poverty," in *G.M.*, XVIII, 88 (1748); "Palinodia," in *Misc. Sav.* (1726), p. 236.

134. R. Savage, "The Wanderer," in *The Poetical Works of Richard Savage*, p. 65. Other invocations to solitude and contemplation: W. Hamilton, "To the Countess of Egerton . . ." in *Poems*, p. 26; M. Browne, "Essay on the Universe," in *Poems*, p. 306; "Studley-Park," in *Scar. Misc.* (1732), p. 43; W. Shenstone, "The Enchantress," in *Poems on Various Occasions*, p. 58; Richard Glover, "Poem on Sir Isaac Newton," in *Chal.*, XVII, 13; T. Warton, "Retirement," in

Poems, p. 13; ibid., "Ode," p. 133; "An Ode to the Right Honourable the Lord Lonsdale," in *Dods.,* II, 213; D. Mallet, "A Fragment," in *Works,* p. 52; M. Browne, "Epistle 3," in *Poems,* p. 217; J. Dyer, "Grongar Hill," in *Chal.,* XIII, 233; W. Bowman, "Night," in *Poems,* p. 42.

135. Pope, *Satire 4,* 184–88.

136. Mary Masters, "An Answer to Mr. G's Invitation to the Fields and Groves," in *Poems on Several Occasions,* p. 118. Other complaints: S. Dixon, "The Shepherd's Daughter," in *Poems,* pp. 198–99; "The Country," in *Misc. Sav.* (1726), p. 197; "Richmond," in *D.M.* (1738), pp. 38–39; S. Duck, "Richmond Park," in *Poems,* p. 58; John Dalton, *Epistle to Lord B.,* in *Pearch,* I, 65; Lord Lyttleton, "A Monody," in *Dods.,* II, 69; "On Dorchester-Walk," in *L.M.,* II, 89 (1733).

137. "The Retirement," in *L.M.,* I, 200 (1732).

138. "Ode by a Young Gentleman of Fifteen since dead," in *G.M.,* XII, 271 (1742).

139. W. Shenstone, "In a shady Valley," in *Dods.,* IV, 346; "Horace Book 2, Ode 6 imitated by Mr. Marriot," in *Dods.,* IV, 280; T. Cooke, "Epistle the Third," in *Poems,* p. 73; E. Rowe, "To Mr. Thomson," in *Works,* p. 162.

140. Aubin, "Grottoes, Geology and the Gothic Revival," in *Studies in Philology,* XXXI, 408–17 (1934). T. Warton, "Ode written in a Grotto," in *Poems,* pp. 116–17, links grottoes with classic nymphs and with folk lore.

141. Mr. Grainger, "Solitude," in *Dods.,* IV, 233.

142. "Ode by a Young Gentleman of Fifteen, since dead," in *G.M.,* XII, 271; other grotto refuges are in J. Gay's "Panthea," in *Poetical Miscellanies,* p. 10 (1729), and W. Broome's "The Seat of War in Flanders," in *Poems,* p. 71.

143. Thomson, *Aut.,* 1032–36.

144. B. Sprague Allen, *Tides in English Taste,* II (1937); grottoes are discussed pp. 133–38; the references to Queen Caroline's Hermitage and to her Merlin's Cave at Richmond are pp. 135–37.

145. "Verses written by a Hermit," in *L.M.,* II, 252 (1738); also praising a hermitage is "An Inscription on the Cell" (on Lord Westmoreland's Hermitage) in *Dods.,* IV, 259.

146. "Written Extempore in Sir John Barrington's Hermitage in the Isle of Wight," in *L.M.,* XV, 257 (1746).

147. "To the Rev. Mr. R—— on his Hermitage," in *G.M.,* XVII, 391 (1747).

148. "The Cave of Pope," in *Dods.,* III, 331.

149. M. Browne, "To her Majesty on her Grotto," in *Poems,* p. 391; the lines quoted are from this poem; other tributes include: "On the Bustoes in the Royal Hermitage," in *L.M.,* III, 35 (1734); "On the

Queen's Grotto," in *G.M.*, III, 369 (1733); "On Her Majesty and the Bustoes in the Royal Grotto," in *G.M.*, III, 541 (1733).

150. "The Wish," in *L.M.*, VI, 96 (1737).

151. Ibid.

152. "The Pleasures of Bewdley," in *G.M.*, XV, 438 (1745).

153. "A Poem on Sir Isaac Newton," in *L.M.*, III, 491 (1734).

154. Ibid.

155. Ibid.

156. W. Melmoth, "Of the Active and Retired Life," in *Dods.*, I, 208; W. Shenstone, "Judgment of Hercules," in *Chal.*, XIII, 309; M. Browne, "To Mr. Thomson," in *Poems*, p. 269; "A Fit of the Spleen," in *L.M.*, VI, 159 (1737); "Il Penseroso," in *Misc. Sav.* (1726), p. 161.

157. "The Invitation to a Poetical Friend in Devonshire," in *G.M.*, III, 147 (1733). Also in "An Epistle from a Gentleman to his Friend in the Country," in *The Bee*, No. 12, Apr. 21–28, 1733.

158. J. Dyer, "R.R.," in *Chal.*, XIII, 226.

159. W. Bowman, "Jesus Grove," in *Poems*, p. 6; W. Hamilton, "Contemplation," in *Poems*, p. 6; "The Country," in *Misc. Sav.* (1726), p. 202; E. Carter, "Ode to Wisdom," in *Poems on Several Occasions*, p. 85; W. Hamilton, "Horace, Ode 24 imitated," in *Poems*, p. 137.

160. W. Hamilton, "Contemplation," in *Poems*, p. 6.

161. W. Bowman, "Night," in *Poems*, p. 32; E. Carter, "Ode to Wisdom," in *Poems*, p. 85; "Pre-Existence," in *Dods.*, I, 166.

162. T. Warton (Jr.), "P.M.," in *Chal.*, XVIII, 96; like in spirit is the passage on pp. 96–97 of the same poem.

163. "An Evening Hymn," in *Misc. Sav.* (1726), p. 266.

164. T. Warton (Jr.), "Triumph of Isis," in *Chal.*, XVIII, 90.

165. Thomson, *Aut.*, 1004–15.

166. R. Savage, "The Wanderer," in *Works*, p. 63.

167. S. Duck, "On Richmond Park and the Royal Gardens," in *Poems*, p. 52.

168. "A Rural Lay," in *L.M.*, I, 411 (1732); W. Bowman, "Jesus Grove," in *Poems*, p. 21.

169. M. Masters, "To Clemene," in *Poems*, p. 35.

170. Rev. Mr. Merrick, "Ode to Fancy," in *Dods.*, IV, 183.

171. J. Warton, "Verses Occasioned by Mr. West's Translation of Pindar," in *Chal.*, XVIII, 169.

172. "An Inscription," in *Dods.*, III, 194.

173. W. Pattison, "The College Life," in *And.*, p. 556; R. Savage, "The Wanderer," in *Works*, p. 100; "An Imitation of the Fourth Ode of Anacreon," in *H-S.* (1734), p. 9.

174. Thomson, *Aut.*, 1235–77.

175. Ibid., *Sum.*, 458–75. It was Thomson also who declared in *Aut.*, 1003, "The desolated prospect thrills the soul."

176. "Il Penseroso," in *Misc. Sav.* (1726), p. 162.

177. "The Spring," in *C.C.P.* (1738), II, 3.

178. D. Mallet, "Excursion," in *Works*, p. 77.

179. Thomas Gray, "Ode to Spring," in *The Poems of Gray and Collins*, ed. by Austin Lane Poole (1917), ll. 10 ff.

180. Ibid.

181. "The Squire of Dames," in *Dods.*, IV, 121.

182. M. Chandler, *Bath*, p. 16; Mr. Duncombe, "Ode to Health," in *Dods.*, IV, 269.

183. "A Sapphic Ode," in *L.M.*, XVI, 383.

184. T. Warton (Jr.), "P.M.," in *Chal.*, XVIII, 96; ibid., 95. Dr. Grainger in "Solitude, an Ode," in *Dods.*, IV, 229, placed solitude against a background of nodding towers, trackless deserts and mountain tops.

185. W. Collins, "Ode to Evening," in *Poems*, p. 100.

186. "On Poverty," in *Misc. Sav.* (1726), p. 225; W. Pattison, "Rosamund to Henry," in *And.*, p. 560; "On the death of the Rev. Alured Clarke late dean of Exeter," in *G.M.*, XIII, 268.

187. S. Rowe, "Soliloquy 8," in *Works*, p. 182.

188. Mr. Grainger, "Solitude," in *Dods.*, IV, 234.

189. "Her Answer," in *G.M.*, IX, 435.

190. "A Winter's Day," in *Misc. Sav.* (1726), p. 309.

191. Ibid.; similar to this piece in their mingling of gloom and contemplation are: E. Rowe, "Despair," in *Works*, p. 71; W. Collins, "The Passions," in *Poems*, p. 110; W. Bowman, "A Pastoral in Imitation of Virgil's Alexis," in *Poems*, p. 84; J. Hammond, "Elegy 6," in *Chal.*, XI, 590; "On the Death of Mr. Richard P——r late of Oxford," in *L.M.*, XI, 210.

192. John Gilbert Cooper, "The Estimate of Life," in *Dods.*, III, 210; W. Bowman, "Night," in *Poems*, p. 51.

193. J. Warton, "Ode to Solitude," in *Chal.*, XVIII, 168.

194. W. Bowman, "Night," in *Poems*, p. 67.

195. "The Wish," in *G.M.*, VII, 115 (1737).

196. R. Dodsley, "The Guardian Angel," in *Muse in Livery*, p. 60; T. Warton also hails the "awful gloom" of a grotto in "Ode written in a Grotto," in *Poems*, p. 118.

197. T. Warton (Jr.), "P.M.," in *Chal.* XVIII, 96.

198. J. Warton, "The Enthusiast," in *Chal.*, XVIII, 161; similar to this in their grim mood of meditation are: Akenside, *Pleasures*, II, 187–212; Mr. Vansittart, "The Pleasures of Poetry," in *Dods.*, III, 214.

199. "The Vision," in *H-S.*, (1734), p. 163; similar—"Calliope," in *D.M.* (1738), p. 130.

200. "A Night-Piece," in *G.M.*, XV, 661 (1745).

201. Young, *N.T.*, II, 621–26.

202. Gray, "Elegy," in *Poems*, ll. 13–16.
203. Mr. Tickell, "On the Death of Addison," in *Dods.*, I, 23.
204. "Written on a Brick in the Ruins of Holy-Abbey on Holy Island," in *L.M.*, XIII, 461 (1744).
205. Ibid.
206. Ibid.
207. Rev. Mr. Merrick, "Ode to Fancy," in *Dods.*, IV, 182.
208. W. Hamilton, "Contemplation," in *Poems*, p. 20.
209. Mr. Grainger, "Solitude," in *Dods.*, IV, 235.
210. No title, in *G.M.*, IX, 599 (1739).
211. T. Warton (Jr.), "P.M.," in *Chal.*, XVIII, 95; a parody on gloom and death is to be found in the poem "New Night Thoughts on Death, A Parody, By Mr. Wh——," in *G.M.*, XVII, 444 (1746).
212. Spectator, No. 494.
213. For a description of the disappearance of the yeomanry, see Arnold Toynbee, *Lectures on the Industrial Revolution of the Eighteenth Century in England* (1927); A. S. Turbeville, *Johnson's England*, I (1933); A. E. Dobbs, *Education and Social Movements* (1919).
214. About 1700 poor relief cost £400,000 yearly; in 1750 the cost had risen to £700,000; see A. S. Turbeville, *Johnson's England*, I, 301–311; Sidney and Beatrice Webb, *English Local Government: English Poor Law History*, Part 1, "The Old Poor Law" (1927), give an exhaustive account of experiments in caring for the poor in England. See particularly "Methods of Poor Relief," pp. 212–21.
215. Henry Fielding, *A Proposal for Making Effective Provision for the Poor* (1753), p. 28, mentions this evil. Between 1727 and 1751 consumption of spirits rose from three and one half million gallons yearly to eleven million. See Edward A. Whitney, "Humanitarianism and Romanticism," in *Huntington Library Quarterly*, II, 159–78 (1939).
216. John Milton, "Comus," 319–26, in *The Complete Poetical Works of John Milton* (Student's Cambridge Edition, 1924). All quotations from Milton's poetry used in this study are from this source. Hereafter only title and line reference will be given.
217. Sir Charles Hanbury Williams, "Sir Charles Hanbury Williams to Sir Hans Sloane," in *The Works of the Right Honourable Sir Charles Hanbury Williams, K.B.*, p. 128; "The Art of Trimming," in *C. Misc.* (1735), p. 34; H. Jacob, "Ode 7," in *Works*, p. 56; W. Collins, "Eclogue 2," in *Poems*, p. 49. "Address to Poverty," in *G.B.*, XI, 495 (1741); "A Rural Ode," in *L.M.*, X, 251 (1741).
218. "Rural Happiness," in *The Student*, II, 274 (1750).
219. John Bancks, "Tranquillity and Happiness," in *Works*, p. 351.
220. D. Mallet, "A Fragment," in *Works*, pp. 49–50; A. Glover, "Leonidas," in *Chal.*, XVII, p. 107; J. Armstrong, "Art of Preserving

Health," in *Works*, p. 14; "A Rhapsody on Country Life," in *Un. Mag.*, II, 132; R. Nugent, "An Epistle to the Rt. Honourable the Earl of Chesterfield," in *O. and E.*, p. 61; S. Duck, "On Poverty," in *Poems*, p. 5. This is in marked contrast to his first poem "The Threshers' Labor" with its picture of country living taken from reality rather than from literature.

221. "A Letter to a Friend," in *G.M.*, V, 327 (1735); Shepherds are idyllically presented in the following: J. or C. Wesley, *Works*, IV, 106, 118, 123; H. Jacob, "Song 3," in *Works*, p. 127; T. Curteis, *Eiren.*, p. 26.

222. J. Armstrong, "Art of Preserving Health," in *Works*, p. 30; an anonymous miscellany writer contributes a similar picture of the poor man's health in "On Health," in *G.M.*, IX, 547.

223. J. Winstanley, "A Rural Ode," in *Poems*, p. 142.

224. Thomson, *Aut.*, 173–310.

225. A. Ramsay, "Song 45," in *C.C.S.*, II, 47–48.

226. Ibid., p. 48.

227. Young, *Ocean*, p. 179; similar in sentiment; W. Somervile, "Epitaph on Hugh Lumber, Husbandman," in *Works*, p. 272, and his "Mahomet," in *Works*, p. 133.

228. Johnson, "The Vanity of Human Wishes," in *Poems*, ll. 31–36.

229. J. Warton, "Ode to a Lady who Hates the Country," in *Chal.*, XVIII, 168.

230. H. Carey, "The True Tarr," in *Poems*, p. 116; see also his "The Sailor's Rant," ibid., p. 168.

231. A. Ramsay, "The King and the Miller," in *C.C.S.*, II, 115.

232. H. Carey, "Morning Cries," in *Poems*, p. 133. Pieces similar in tone: A. Ramsay, "The Happy Clown," in *C.C.S.*, I, 196–97; ibid., "Song 44," II, 43, "The Hay-Maker's Song," p. 128; J. Gay, "Fable 2, 6," in *Works*, p. 162.

233. A. Ramsay, "The Cobler's [sic] Happiness," in *C.C.S.*, II, 249.

234. H. Carey, "The Surly Peasant," in *Works*, p. 134.

235. W. Shenstone, "The Schoolmistress," in *Chal.*, XIII, 327.

236. A. Ramsay, "The Happy Beggars," in *C.C.S.*, II, 148.

237. "Song 49," in *B. and V.* (1737), p. 54: also ibid., p. 43.

238. Passing praises of the country occur in: A. Ramsay, "The High-land Laddie," in *Works*, II, 256 f.; H. Carey, "The Disparity of Youth and Age," in *Poems*, p. 134; M. Browne, "Eclogue 4," in *A.S.*, p. 46.

239. W. Dunkin, "Lover's Web," in *Works*, pp. 312–13.

240. W. Hamilton, "Miss and the Butterfly," in *Poems*, p. 48; H. Jacob, "Ode 7," in *Works*, p. 55; Lord Lyttleton, "Eclogue 1," in *Dods.*, II, 4; "Country Innocence," in *L.M.*, VIII, 251 (1939).

241. A. Ramsay, "Song," in *C.C.S.*, I, 177; similar to this are: "Coun-

NOTES

try Innocence," in *L.M.*, VIII (1739), p. 200; A. Ramsay, "The Milking Pail," in *C.C.S.*, II, 224.

242. A. Ramsay, "Song 69," in *C.C.S.*, II, 72. "William and Dorothy of Datchet," in *Windsor Medley* (1731), p. 6, has a similar message.

243. "The Rural Lass," in *G.M.*, XX, 517 (1750).

244. A. Ramsay, "Love Inviting Reason," in *C.C.S.*, II, 75 laments the corruption of once charming "Annie" by town follies. "Lavinia" is mourned in "A Modern Truth," in *G.M.*, XI, 48 (1741); other pieces on the theme include: "A Song," in *H-S.* (1734), p. 77; A. Ramsay, "The Highland Lassie," in *C.C.S.*, I, 157; "Fanny," in *L.M.*, XVI, 430 (1747); "The City Ladies and the Country Lass," in *Grub.* (1732), p. 69; "Country Innocence," in *L.M.*, VIII, 251-52 (1739); "Rural Happiness," in *The Student*, II, 274 (1750); Mr. Boyce, "The Non-Pareil," in *Un Mag.*, IV, 280 (1749); ibid., "The Rural Beauty," 186.

245. "To Sally at the Chop-House," in *L.M.*, I, 483 (1732).

246. *Spectator*, No. 30.

247. Ibid.

248. Shaftesbury, "Moralists," in *Works*, II, 376.

249. Young, *Love of Fame*, p. 116.

250. 1726-27-28: average annual export = £7,891,739; 1749-50-51: average annual export = £12,599,122. See George L. Craik, *The History of British Commerce* II, chap. 9 (1844) for further details; the statistics quoted are on pp. 163, 185, 186, 201-202.

251. Daniel Defoe, *The Complete English Tradesman* (1725), pp. 70-71.

252. John Chamberlayne, *Magnae Britannize Notitia; or the Present State of Great Britain* (37th edition) (1748), p. 38.

253. Fielding, *An Enquiry into the Causes of the late Increase in Robbers* (1751), pp. xxii-xxiii.

254. Ibid., pp. 6-7.

255. Thomson, *C.I.*, I, stanzas, 53, 54, 55.

256. Ibid., st. 19.

257. Thomson, *Lib.*, III, 357 ff.

258. Ibid., *Britannia*, 251-58; like in tone to these Thomas passages are: *Verres and His Scribblers* (1732), p. 54; Akenside, *Pleasures*, I, 417-25; ibid., "Ode," p. 222; J. Gay, "Fable 2, 10," in *Works*, p. 183.

259. Pope, *Moral Essay's Epistle 3*, 342 ff.

260. Ibid.

261. Ibid., 39-48.

262. Young, *N.T.*, V, 965.

263. Ibid., VI, 494-505.

264. Ibid., IV, 350.

265. Ibid., *Love of Fame*, p. 132.

266. Ibid., *N.T.*, VI, 216–20; other condemnations of wealth and of its useless pursuit are: ibid., *Ocean*, p. 173; ibid., *N.T.*, V, 957–1000; "On Happiness," in *Misc. Sav.* (1726), p. 108; "Contentment," in *Dods.*, III, 111; W. Pattison, "The Morning Contemplation," in *And.*, p. 567; W. Hamilton, "Ode on The New Year," in *Poems*, p. 45.

267. Fielding, *A Proposal for Making an Effectual Provision for the Poor* (1753), p. 10.

268. *Spectator*, No. 232.

269. Ibid.

270. Fielding, *A Proposal* . . . , pp. 48–49.

271. Ibid.

272. T. Smollett, "Advice," in *Plays and Poems*, p. 213.

273. Ibid.

274. Rev. Dr. Brown, "Honour," in *Dods.*, III, 273; see also: W. Somervile, "The Chase," in *Works*, p. 195; W. Hamilton, "On the New Year," in *Poems*, p. 43.

275. Thomson, *Win.*, 322; the whole passage runs, 322–47; ibid., 337 ff.

276. W. Whitehead, "To the Hon. xxx," in *Dods.*, II, 252.

277. Akenside, "Ode 11, Bk. 2," in *Works*, p. 225. The whole poem, pp. 220–26 is on the theme.

278. Thomson, *Win.*, 286–321.

279. Ibid., *Aut.*, 339–59; quoted 341–59.

280. M. Masters, "The Defence of Myself," in *Poems*, p. 26.

281. R. Nugent, "Epistle to Cornwallis," in *O. and E.*, p. 45.

282. J. or C. Wesley, "Isiah 52," in *Works*, IV, 314.

283. "Luxury and Want," in *G.M.*, XVIII, 87.

284. "On Poverty," in *Misc. Sav.* (1726), p. 227.

285. "Gin," in *L.M.*, III, 663.

286. Richard Steele, *Guardian*, No. 26.

287. "An injur'd shade" protests insults to his poverty in *S.T.* (1726), pp. 12–14; "A hopeless wretch" laments his "narrow fate" an "boundless mind" in D. Dodsley's "Guardian Angel," in *Muse*, p. 61.

288. Johnson, *London*, l. 177.

289. Ibid., ll. 159 ff.; see also 79–82.

290. Gray, "Elegy," in *Poems*, ll. 29–32.

291. T. Smollett, "Advice," in *Plays and Poems*, p. 205.

292. Juvenal, "Satires, 8," in *Juvenal and Persius* with an English translation by G. G. Ramsay (The Loeb Classical Library, 1924).

293. Steele, *Tatler*, No. 69.

294. Johnson, *Rambler*, No. 58.

295. Pope, *E.M.*, IV, 248.

296. James Bramston, *Seasonable Reproof*, p. 15.

297. "A Song," in *Tunbrigialia* (1730), p. 45.

298. H. Jacob, "Chiron to Achilles," in *Works*, p. 134.

299. "A Right Honourable Dialogue," in *Summer Miscellany* (1742), p. 21; "The Vanity of Birth," in *Un. Mag.*, I, p. 84 (1747); "Manners Make the Man," in *H-S.* (1734), p. 224; D. Lewis, "Translated from the Antient British," in *Poems*, p. 53.

299a. P. Whitehead, "Honor," in *Chal.*, XVI, 219.

300. Pope, *E.M.*, IV, 215 ff.

301. Ibid., 247 f.; "Vir bonus et Rex Est Quis?," in *L.M.*, IX, 348 (1740); A. Ramsay, "Content," in *Works*, I, 150; J. Hughes, "Song from the Same," in *Miscellanies*, p. 142.

302. "On the True Nobility," in *L.M.*, X (1741), pp. 48–49; "Virtue is the only True Happiness and Nobility," in *L.M.*, X, 49 (1741); "Manners Make the Man," in *H-S.* (1734), p. 231; J. Hughes, "Song from the Same," in *Miscellanies*, p. 141.

303. Pope, *E.M.*, IV, 203–204.

304. Young, *Love of Fame*, p. 68.

305. Ibid.

306. Ibid., *N.T.*, VI, 333–35; 494–541.

307. Ibid., VIII, 432–38.

308. Pope, *E.M.*, IV, 247–48.

PART TWO

1. Marjorie Hope Nicolson, "A World in the Moon," in *Smith College Studies in Modern Languages*, XVI (1935); "The Microscope and the English Imagination," in *Smith College Studies in Modern Languages*, XVII (1936).

2. Shaftesbury, "Moralists," in Works, II, 366.

3. *Spectator*, No. 421.

4. Blaise Pascal, "Thoughts," translated by W. F. Trotter, in *The Harvard Classics*, XLVIII, 26 (1910).

5. Shaftesbury, "Moralists," in *Works*, II, 370.

6. *Spectator*, No. 543.

7. Richard Cumberland, *A Treatise on the Laws of Nature* (1727), p. 67.

8. A. O. Lovejoy, *Chain*, see p. 52 for a definition of the *plenum formarum;* for the later development of the concept see Chapters 4, 5, and 7.

9. *Spectator*, No. 11; Locke quoted by Addison.

10. *Spectator*, No. 519.

11. "On the Queen's Grotto," in *G.M.*, III, 430 (1733).

12. "Upon Sir Isaac Newton's Principles of Natural Philosophy," in *L.M.*, XII, 353 (1735).

13. "A Poem on Sir Isaac Newton," in *L.M.*, XII, 491 (1734).

14. "On the Queen's Grotto," in *G.M.*, III, 430 (1733).

15. J. Bancks, "To Mr. Mitchell," in *Works*, II, 60; "Mrs. Pilkington to the Rev. Dr. Hales," in *G.M.*, XVIII, 566 (1748); "Philosophy," in *L.M.*, XVI, 188 (1747). James Thomson describes the prism of light in his description of the gems which sunlight helps to form, *Sum.*, 104–70; J. Bancks, "Mons. Voltaire to the Marchioness du Ch*t," in *Works*, II, 245.

16. Akenside, *Pleasures*, II, 127–28.

17. "Philosophy," in *L.M.*, XVI, 188 (1747).

18. Henry Brooke, "Universal Beauty," in *Chal.*, XVII, 351.

19. Ibid., 348; other poems that mention the chain: S. Boyse, *The Deity*, p. 6; Young, *N.T.*, IX, 1450–58 uses the chain as a proof for the existence of God; J. or C. Wesley, "God's Greatness," in *Works*, I, 144; Thomson, *Lib.*, III, 67–70 regrets Pythagoras had not evisioned the chain as a "rising whole."

20. Young, *N.T.*, IV, 683.

21. Pope, *E.M.*, IV, 334.

22. Henry Baker, *The Universe*, p. 33.

23. Pope, *E.M.*, II, 3–4.

24. *Spectator*, No. 10.

25. Pope, *E.M.*, II, 31 ff.

26. Other reminders to man may be found in Akenside, "Ode 7," in *Works*, p. 160; "On Thought," in *D.M.* (1738), p. 217.

27. Young, *N.T.*, I, 73–75. See also ibid., VI, 723–34 wherein Young uses man's middle place as proof of his immortality, and *N.T.* I, 76–79, wherein he calls man "a beam ethereal."

28. H. Brooke, "Universal Beauty," in *Chal.*, XVII, 345.

29. H. Baker, *Un.*, p. 11.

30. *Spectator*, No. 9.

31. Eliza Haywood, *Female Spectator*, IV, 30 (1747).

32. Young, *N.T.*, II, 206.

33. S. Boyse, *Retirement*, p. 19; other references to the overflowing creation or to its bounteous Creator include: H. Brooke, "Universal Beauty," in *Chal.*, XVII, 347–48; Young, *N.T.*, V, 98–99; S. Jenyns, "An Essay on Virtue," in *Dods.*, III, 164–65.

34. S. Boyse, *The Deity*, p. 7. Besides the passage quoted, there is a description of the chain of being, one with a Platonic cast, in R. Nugent, "Epistle to Cornwallis," in *O. and E.*, p. 38.

35. H. Brooke, "Universal Beauty," in *Chal.*, XVII, 348.

36. Akenside, *Pleasures*, II, 307 ff.

37. "To Mr. Moses Browne, with a Present of a Microscope," in *G.M.*, IX, 546 (1739).

38. Ibid.

39. "Il Penseroso," in *Misc. P.S.* (1731), p. 164.

40. D. Mallet, "Excursion," in *Works*, I, 108.

41. H. Baker, *Un.*, p. 35.

42. Eliza Haywood, *Female Spectator*, IV, 27.

43. "The Invitation," in *L.M.*, II, 209 (1732).

44. "The Mossey Journey," in *L.M.*, II, 420 (1732).

45. "To Mr. Moses Browne, with a Present of a Microscope," in *G.M.*, IX, 546 (1739).

46. H. Brooke, "Universal Beauty," in *Chal.*, XVII, 339.

47. Thomas Sprat, *History of the Royal Society* (1722), p. 384.

48. Shaftesbury, "Moralists," in *Works*, II, 370.

49. "Poetic Epistles on Nature, Man, and Morals, Essay I, to Dr. Askew," in *Monthly Review*, III, 36 (1750).

50. "Pre-Existence," in *Dods.*, I, 164.

51. "An Epistle from a Cornish Gentleman to a Friend at Oxford," in *L.M.*, XVII, 571 (1748).

52. Young, *N.T.*, I, 286–87; see also his description of the antediluvian world, *N.T.*, IX, 124–32.

53. "On the Queen's Grotto," in *L.M.*, II, 37 (1732); there is a very similar passage in *G.M.*, III, 41 (1733); see also "Richmond Gardens," in *L.M.*, VII, 38 (1738).

54. J. Armstrong, "Art of Preserving Health," in *Works*, p. 26.

55. *F.V.* (1738), p. 4; Young in *N.T.*, IX, 153–54 wrote of the ultimate end of the world:

> Earth's actors change earth's transitory scenes
> And make creation groan with human guilt.

56. Thomson, *Spr.*, 309–18.

57. M. Browne, "Essay on the Universe," in *Poems*, p. 307. The original text has as a note "This is Descartes Theory improv'd upon by Dr. Burnet" . . . This anti-scriptural account of the original Mountains; etc. reflects very unhappily on the Scheme of the above mentioned theorist."

58. M. Chandler, *Bath*, p. 7.

59. Edwin Arthur Burtt, *The Metaphysical Foundations of Modern Physical Science* (1925).

60. H. Brooke, "Universal Beauty," in *Chal.*, XVII, 347; quoted, ibid., 349.

61. "A Poem on the Divine Attributes," in *G.M.*, VII, 370 (1737).

62. Young, *N.T.*, II, 295–304.

63. "The Prospect," in *G.M.*, XIII, 608 (1743); Young, *N.T.*, IX, 940–66.

64. H. Brooke, "Universal Beauty," in *Chal.*, XVII, 347.

65. "Epitaph," in *Miscellanies of Swift and Pope* (1732), p. 64. Other readers of the book of Nature were; "Scipio" "By no Bible taught, but nature's book," and a "rural swain" who "never read but what dame

Nature writ . . ." The first was in "A Rhapsody on Virtue and Pleasure" by T. Cooke in *Poems*, p. 55; the second was in "The Morning Star," in *L.M.*, IX, 186 (1740).

66. "On Her Majesty and the Bustoes," in *G.M.*, III, 541 (1733).

67. "A Poem on Life, Death, Judgment and Hell," in *G.M.*, V, 396 (1735); "The Prayer of the Archbishop of Cambray, author of Telemachus paraphras'd," in *L.M.*, XVII, 280 (1748); W. Somervile, "The Chase," in *Works*, p. 234.

68. W. Pattison, "The Morning Contemplation," in *And.*, p. 566; R. Savage, "The Wanderer," in *Works*, p. 120.

69. "The Prospect," in *G.M.*, XIII, 608 (1743).

70. Thomson, *Aut.*, 1306–10.

71. Ibid., 1352–66.

72. Young, *N.T.*, IX, 615–19.

73. Ibid., 1399; VI, 673; VIII, 590.

74. Ibid., IX, 1295–97; long passage quoted is ibid., 636–42.

75. Ibid., 647, 648; 1659–73.

76. Francis Hutcheson, *An Inquiry into the Original of our Ideas of Beauty and Virtue* (1726), p. 70.

77. A. O. Lovejoy, "Optimism and Romanticism," in *PMLA*, XLII, 921–45.

78. Young, *N.T.*, I, 283–84.

79. Pope, *E.M.*, I, 60.

80. For an account of the rise in English commercial enterprise during this period, see G. A. Craik, *The History of British Commerce* (1897), II, Chapter 9.

81. *Tatler*, No. 130.

82. Thomson, *Sum.*, 1453–56; 136–39.

83. Colley Cibber, "Ode for New Year's Day," in *G.M.*, II, 580 (1732). The same page carries a burlesque of Cibber's poem:

> Your ancient Ballad-makers read,
>   And mark the fool you most admire;
> The present shall the past exceed,
>   And yield enjoyment to desire.

84. "England," in *L.M.*, IV, 95 (1735); "The Present State of Great Britain," in *G.M.*, XIII, 269 (1743); "Ode for the New Year," in *L.M.*, III, 36 (1734).

85. "Smyrna Coffee-House," in *L.M.*, III, 487 (1734).

86. C. Cibber, "Ode for the New Year," in *G.M.*, IV, 41 (1734).

87. "The Present State of Great Britain," in *G.M.*, XIII, 269 (1743).

88. Young, *N.T.*, I, 242–56; a like catalogue is in ibid., VIII, 101–18. A minor protest against one of Nature's harmful productions, the savage rocks against which mariners are shipwrecked occurs in "Sang 21" by A. Ramsay, in *C.C.S.*, II, 23.

89. R. Savage, "Wanderer," in *Works,* p. 105. Thomson in *Win.*, 1041–69 explained that in the "second Spring" men should at last discover how sufferings not understood by them were for the good of the whole creation.

90. Pope, *E.M.,* I, 29–34. Similar passages occur in the same work, I, 85 ff., 190 ff., 205 ff.; also in III, 79 ff.

91. Akenside, *Pleasures,* II, 448–51; like sentiments are in the same work, ll. 242–54. In ibid., III, 18–62 Akenside attributes vice to false representations of fancy.

92. Thomson, *Sum.,* 318–23.

93. Akenside, "On the Winter Solstice," in *Works,* pp. 145 f.

94. W. Paget, *A Voyage to Ipswich,* p. 25.

95. Akenside, "For the Winter Solstice," in *Works,* p. 148.

96. S. Boyse, *The Deity,* p. 51.

97. "Some Lines occasion'd by a series of Theological Enquiries," in *G.M.,* XVI, 216 (1746).

98. J. Gay, "Fable 13, book 2," in *Works,* p. 202.

99. Pope, *E.M.,* I, 165; II, 285–90 (the latter is the passage quoted).

100. Young, *N.T.,* IX, 406–12.

101. Ibid., 495–500.

102. W. Paget, *A Voyage to Ipswich,* p. 27.

103. "On the Deist's Scheme of Fitness," in *G.M.,* V, 553 (1735).

104. Pope, *E.M.,* I, 289–94.

105. Thomson, *Spr.,* 871–903; *Sum.,* 185–90.

106. Ibid., 13; ibid., *Hymn to the Seasons,* 82.

107. Ibid., 111–16.

108. Ibid., *Spr.,* 904–16 in editions 1728–38; dropped 1744.

109. J. T. Desaguliers, *N.S.,* p. 25.

110. Pope, *E.M.,* III, 113–16; see also ibid., II, 249–72; and J. Gay, "Fable 43, book 1," in *Works,* p. 123.

111. A. Hill, "The Picture of Love, in *Misc. Sav.* (1726), p. 202.

112. D. Mallet, "Amyntor and Theodora," in *Works,* I, 126.

113. H. Baker, *Un.,* p. 34.

114. "To Mr. Hervey on his Meditations," in *G.M.,* XIX, 422 (1749).

115. S. Boyse, *The Deity,* pp. 7, 41.

116. "To the Reverend Mr. Whitefield," in *L.M.,* VIII, 257 (1739).

117. "Directions how to make and preach a sermon that shall please," in *G.M.,* XVI, 490 (1746).

118. Young, *N.T.,* V, 225–33.

119. H. Baker, *Un.,* p. 14.

120. "Poetic Essays on Nature, Man, and Morals, Essay I, to Dr. Askew of Newcastle," in *Monthly Review,* III, 35 (1750).

121. *The World,* No. 15.

122. Pope, *Moral Essays, Epistle IV,* 117–20.

123. Francis Bacon, "Of Gardens," in *Essays* (selected and edited by R. F. Jones), p. 131 (1937).

124. Milton, *Paradise Lost*, IV, 390–91; 206 ff.

125. Ibid., 241–43.

126. Stephen Switzer, *Iconographia Rustica*, p. 346 (1718).

127. Edmund Spenser, "The Faerie Queene," III, 6, 29, 30, in *The Complete Works of Edmund Spenser* (Student's Cambridge Edition), 1908. All quotations from Spenser are from this source.

128. Shakespeare, *Winter's Tale*, IV, 4.

129. Abraham Cowley, "The Garden," in *Eighteenth Century Garden Essays* (1908), p. 73; Andrew Marvell, "The Mower Against Gardens," in ibid., pp. 169 f.

130. Sir Thomas Browne, "The Garden of Cyrus," in ibid., p. 89.

131. John Evelyn, excerpt from his "Diary" in ibid., p. 202.

132. Sir William Temple, "Upon the Gardens of Epicurus," in ibid., pp. 5 ff., 50.

133. Pope, *The Guardian*, No. 173.

134. Shaftesbury, "Moralists," in *Works*, II, 393–94.

135. *Spectator*, No. 477.

136. Ibid., Nos. 411, 412, 414, 589, 477.

137. "Wentonia," in *Miscellanea*, p. 28 (1727); similar in sentiment; J. Winstanley, "Upon Harristown," in *Poems*, p. 294; "To the Author the Poem on Lord C—b—m's Gardens," in *G.M.*, XIII, 134 (1743); Mr. Price, "To Lady Ernle," in *L.M.*, V, 513 (1738); Mr. Lockman, "The Pleasures of the Spring Gardens, Vauxhall," in *L.M.*, VI, 217 (1737); "To Nathanael Paylor . . . ," in *G.M.*, II, 126 (1732); Lord Lyttleton, "Written at Mr. Pope's House at Twickenham," in *Dods.*, II, 56; "Hymn 5," in *G.M.*, XVII, 40 (1747); "Hampstead," in *D.M.* (1738), p. 72; "Triumph of Nature," in *G.M.*, XII, 380 (1742); mention of art and nature in grottoes; "To Mrs. M.L. on her Grotto," in *G.M.*, II, 370 (1732); Stephen Duck, "On the Queen's Grotto," in *G.M.*, II, 1121 (1732); "On the Queen's Mount in Kensington," in *G.M.*, III, 206 (1733).

138. "On the Queen's Grotto," in *L.M.*, I, 481 (1732); T. FitzGerald, "Chearfulness," in *Poems*, p. 43; "A Song," in *Un. Mag.*, III, 85 (1748); Thomson, C.I., II, st. 28; M. Chandler, *Bath*, p. 18; S. Boyse, *Retirement*, p. 11; Henry Jones, "To a Young Lady on her Grotto," in *Poems on Several Occasions*, p. 127; R. Savage, "Of Public Spirit," in *Works*, p. 149; "Vecta," in *G.M.*, X, 310 (1740).

139. M. Chandler, "On Mr. B.'s Garden," in *Bath*, p. 71; W. Harte, "Essay on Satire," in *Chal.*, XVI, 350; Lord Lyttleton, "To Mr. West at Wickham," in *Dods.*, II, 57; "To Miss ——," in *The Student*, II, 65 (1750); "Buckingham-House," in *Clio and Strephon*, p. 18 (1732); Lady Mary Wortley Montague, "An Epistle to Lord B.," in *Dods.*, I,

109; Thomson, *Aut.*, 72–79; verses which speak of the richness or variety of art—"A Description of Powis Gardens at Redcastle," in *G.M.*, XVIII, 373 (1748); "Lane-borough Park," in *C.C.P.* (1738), p. 117; "To a Lady," in *L.M.*, XVII, 191 (1748); Mr. Tickell, "Kensington Gardens," in *Dods.*, I, 42; John Dalton, "Epistle to the Countess of Hertford," in *Pearch*, I, 5; G. West, "Ode on the Institution of the Order of the Garter," in *Dods.*, II, 162.

140. A. Hill, "The Choice," in *Misc. Sav.* (1726), p. 163.

141. J. Armstrong, "Art of Preserving Health," in *Works*, p. 33.

142. W. Pattison, "On a Painted Lady," in *And.*, p. 275; J. Dalton, "Epistle to the Rt. Hon. the Countess of Hertford," in *Pearch*, I, 70–71; "To the Rev. Mr. L. Seaman," in *G.M.*, XVI, 100 (1746); a prose note to "Loch Rian," in *G.M.*, XII, 269 (1742) praised the mixture of art and Nature in the place: "Dawley Farm," in *G.M.*, I, 262 (1731) was apparently an expression of admiration for a ferme ornee, "Politely furnish'd, regularly grand": "A Poem," in *G.M.*, XI, 661 (1741); John Dalton, "Epistle to the Countess of Hertford," in *Pearch*, I, 74; "Richmond Gardens," in *L.M.*, VII, 38 (1738).

143. S. Duck, "Richmond Park," in *Poems*, p. 58.

144. Thomson, *Aut.*, 1043–47.

145. "An Epistle to Lord B.," in *Dods.*, I, 109.

146. Mr. Tickell, "Kensington Gardens," in *Dods.*, I, 42.

147. Mr. Wyld, "Lane-borough Park," in *C.C.P.* (1738), p. 117.

148. Bevil Higgons, *A Poem on the Glorious Peace of Utrecht*, p. 6.

149. "The Spring Morning," in *L.M.*, XIII, 98 (1744); "The Character and Speech of Cosroes the Mede," in *G.M.*, X, 404 (1740); Mr. Lewis, "A Description of Maryland," in *G.M.*, III, 209 (1733); "Spring," in *L.M.*, VII, 143 (1738); "To a Friend upon Illness," in *L.M.*, VII, 460 (1738); "A Hymn to the Creator," in *Misc. Sav.* (1726), p. 142; W. Whitehead, "An Ode to a Gentleman . . . ," in *Dods.*, II, 261; "A Reflection on the Year 1720," in *The Student*, I, 35 (1750); "A Journey to Nottingham," in *G.M.*, XIII, 491 (1743); J. Armstrong, "Art of Preserving Health," in *Works*, p. 21; S. Duck, "Richmond Park," *Poems*, p. 55; "Remainder of an Epistle from the Cape of Good Hope," in *G.M.*, VIII, 370 (1738); "To a Friend in the Country," in *L.M.*, XII, 43 (1743); "On the May Morning," in *Un. Mag.*, IV, 226 (1749).

150. W. Bowman, "Night," in *Poems*, p. 33.

151. Mr. Gazley, "Stokes-Bay," in *L.M.*, VIII, 201 (1739).

152. "To Nathanael Paylor," in *G.M.*, II, 1026 (1732); "Spring," in *L.M.*, VII, 143 [it is also in *G.M.*, II, 1026 (1732)]; W. Pattison, "The Morning Contemplation," in *And.*, p. 567; "A petition to His Grace the Duke of Grafton," in *Swifteana* (1727), p. 91; "To Mr. Browne," in *G.M.*, IX, 546 (1739).

153. W. Hamilton, "Ode 1," in *Poems*, p. 31; similar: Mr. R. Lewis,

"A Journey from Patopsko to Annapolis," in *L.M.*, II, 204 (1732); W. Hamilton, "The Episode of the Thistle," in *Poems*, p. 105.

154. "An Epistle to Myrtillo," in *L.M.*, IX, 345 (1740).

155. Mr. Christopher Pitt, "An Epistle to Mr. Spence," in *The Student*, I, 314 (1750).

156. "Triumph of Nature," in *G.M.*, XII, 435 (1742).

157. T. Warton, "On a May Morning," in *Poems*, pp. 96–97.

158. W. Dunkin, "The Lover's Web," in *Works*, p. 237; "The Moral Alchymist," in *G.M.*, XII, 45 (1742); "The Triumphs of Nature," in *G.M.*, XII, 324 (1742); "Siris," in *G.M.*, XV, 160 (1745); "Inscription on a Grotto," in *The Student*, I, 36 (1750); Christopher Pitt, "Epistle to Mr. Spence," in *Chal.*, XII, 399; T. Warton (Jr.), "Newmarket," in *Chal.*, XVIII, 120; "Epistle to a Learned Friend," in *G.M.*, XVII, 95 (1747); "A Pindaric Ode," in *L.M.*, XIII, 460 (1744); "Il Penseroso," in *Misc. Sav.* (1726), p. 162; G. West, "Education," in *Chal.*, XIII, 182; H. Travers, "An Epistle from the Isle of Ely," in *Miscellaneous Poems and Translations* (1740), p. 2; "An Epistle upon an Epistle from a Certain Doctor to a Certain Great Lord," in *Select Poems from Ireland* (1730), p. 20; "An Essay on Time," in *L.M.*, XIX, 375 (1750) is different in that it makes "regular nature" the superior of art. Beautifully wild grottoes: "On the Royal Grotto," in *G.M.*, III, 369 (1733); "On the Bustoes in Her Majesty's Grotto," in *G.M.*, III, 431 (1733).

159. "The Landskip," in *L.M.*, XVII, 134–35 (1748).

160. Thomson, *Spr.*, 468–70.

161. Ibid., 504–507.

162. "Description of the Spring, a Journey from Patapsco in Maryland to Annapolis," in *G.M.*, II, 669 (1732); "To a Lady," in *L.M.*, XVII, 181 (1748).

163. T. Warton, "Against Dress," in *Poems*, p. 108.

164. W. Hamilton, "Contemplation," in *Poems*, p. 14.

165. J. Warton, "The Enthusiast," in *Chal.*, XVIII, 160.

166. *Spectator*, No. 412.

167. Ibid.

168. Mr. Bazley, "Stoke's Bay," in *L.M.*, VII, 201 (1739); "A Poem," in *G.M.*, XI, 661–62 (1741); "The Happiness of a Country Life," in *L.M.*, VI, 329 (1737).

169. Mr. Mason, "Ode to a Water Nymph," in *Dods.*, III, 283, 282; "Stoke's Bay," in *G.M.*, IX, 263 (1739).

170. "Stoke's Bay," in *G.M.*, IX, 263 (1739).

171. "A Poem," in *G.M.*, XI, 661 (1741).

172. D. Mallet, "A Fragment," in *Works*, p. 49.

173. J. Warton, "The Enthusiast," in *Chal.*, XVIII, 159.

174. Thomson, *Win.*, 57–71; long storm scene, 118–200; 817 ff. description of the wild Tartar coast.

175. Ibid., 118–19; 195–200.

176. Ibid., *Aut.*, 777–835; (see McKillop, *The Background of Thomson's Seasons,* pp. 86–87 for a discussion of the background of Thomson's roll call of the mountains).

177. Ibid., *Win.*, 25–27.

178. William Bowman, "Night," in *Poems,* p. 54.

179. D. Mallet, "The Excursion," in *Works,* I, 78; Akenside, *Pleasures,* II, 274–76; "The Nocturnal Excursion of Fancy," in *G.M.,* XVII, 102 (1746); "To M. Vaughan," by Mr. Coventry, in *Dods.,* IV, 61.

180. "A Winter's Day," in *G.M.,* X, 256 (1750).

181. D. Mallet, "Amyntor and Theodora," in *Works,* I, 141.

182. *Spectator,* No. 412.

183. Thomson, *Aut.*, 1327–30.

184. "The Cornish Mount," in *G.M.,* X, 256 (1750).

185. Akenside, *Pleasures,* III, 282–89.

186. J. Armstrong, "Art of Preserving Health," in *Works,* pp. 12–13; similar: G. West, "Education," in *Chal.,* XIII, 185; Thomson, *Sum.,* 642.

187. Robert A. Aubin, "Grottoes, Geology, and the Gothic Revival," in *Studies in Philology,* XXXI, 408–17 (1934); ibid., "Some Augustan Gothicists," in *Harvard Studies in Philology,* XVII, 15–27 (1935); A. O. Lovejoy, "The First Gothic Revival," in *Modern Language Notes,* XLVII, 419–46 (1932).
Passages linking awe or horror with death: "A Winter's Day," in *G.M.,* X, 256 (1750); "On the Death of a Friend," in *L.M.,* I, 33 (1732); R. Nugent, "An Elegy," in *O. and E.,* p. 25; J. Winstanley, "An Address to the Sepulchre of the late Prince George of Denmark," in *Poems,* p. 69; R. Blair, *The Grave,* p. 1; Mr. Tickell, "To the Right Honourable the Earl of Warwick . . . on the Death of Mr. Addison," in *Dods.,* I, 22.

188. J. Armstrong, "Art of Preserving Health," in *Works,* p. 24; similar: D. Mallet, "The Excursion," in *Works,* I, 82.

189. Batty Langley, as quoted by A. O. Lovejoy, in his article "The First Gothic Revival," in *MLN,* XLVII, 432 (1932).

190. J. Warton, "Epistle from Thomas Hearne Antiquary, to the Author of the Companion to the Oxford Guide," in *Chal.,* XVIII, 170.

191. "Epistle to a Learned Friend Going to Travel," in *G.M.,* XVII, 95 (1747).

192. G. West, "The Institution of the Order of the Garter," in *Dods.,* II, 112.

193. "Sarum," in *G.M.,* X, 255 (1750).

194. Most passages make "Gothic" mean wild and irregular. A few use it to mean rude, uncouth: Mr. Tickell, "On Queen Caroline's rebuilding the Lodgings of the Black Prince," in *Nicoll,* IV, 316; Pope, *Dunciad,* I, 125–26; "To the Rev. Mr. Lionel Seaman, M.A.," in *G.M.,*

XVI, 100 (1746). Some use "Gothic" to mean regular: G. West, "Ode on the Institution of the Garter," in Dods., II, 165; Mr. Smart, "The Fair Recluse," in The Student, II, 316 (1750).

195. T. Warton (Jr.), "Temple of Isis," in Chal., XVIII, 90; Mr. Marriot, "Ode to Fancy," in Dods., IV, 291.

196. "Studley-Royal," in G.M., II, 1122 (1732).

197. "Studley-Park," in Scar. Misc. (1732), p. 45; an imaginary abbey, as picturesque as Fountain, is described by R. Savage in "Wanderer," in Works, p. 97.

198. "The Glories of Bury," in G.M., III, 657 (1733).

199. J. Dyer, "Grongar Hill," in Chal., XIII, 223; S. Boyse, Retirement, p. 9; The Stamford Toasts (1726), p. 1; H. Travers, "Epistle from the Isle of Ely," in Poems, p. 18; "Written Extempore in the Castle of Edinburgy," in L.M., XIII, 61 (1744); "To Mr. Henry B—g—ll at Kensington," in L.M., X, 406 (1741); "A Journey to Nottingham," in G.M., XIII, 492 (1743); "Sarum," in G.M., X, 255 (1740).

200. Sneyd Davies, "A Voyage to Tintern Abbey," in Nicoll, VI, 127, 126.

201. M. Browne, "Epistle 4," in Poems, p. 222; Foreign ruins: Rome— J. Dyer, "R.R.," in Chal., XIII, 224; J. Warton, "Ode to a Gentleman on his Travels," in Chal., XVIII, 165; Persepolis, T. Warton (Jr.), "P.M.," in Chal., XVIII, 219.

202. "The Prospect," in G.M., XIII, 608 (1743).

203. "The Glories of Bury," in G.M., III, 657 (1733).

204. Spectator, No. 160.

205. Charles Gildon, "The Complete Art of Poetry, dialogue II," in Critical Essays of the Eighteenth Century, 1700–1725, edited by Willard Hagley Durham (1915), p. 27. Hereafter this work will be referred to as Durham.

206. George Farquahar, "A Discourse upon Comedy," in Durham, p. 262.

207. Spectator, No. 592.

208. "Prologue spoken at the Theater Royal . . . ," in L.M., III, 250 (1739).

209. "On Shakespeare's Monument at Stratford on Avon," in Dods., II, 300.

210. W. Collins, "Epistle to Hanmer," in Poems, p. 65. For evidence of seventeenth-century veneration for Jonson, see Gerald Eades Bentley, Shakespeare and Jonson, their reputations in the Seventeenth Century compared (1945).

211. Ibid., p. 66.

212. Akenside, "Ode 1, Remonstrances of Shakespeare," in Works, p. 197.

213. "Shakespeare's Ghost," in L.M., XIX, 279 (1750).

214. Thomson, *Sum.*, 1457.

215. W. Collins, "Ode to Fear," in *Poems*, pp. 722–23; the passage quoted is Ibid., "Ode on the Popular Superstitions of the Highlands," in *Poems*, p. 746.

216. Akenside, *Pleasures*, III, 546–55; another compliment to Shakespeare's fancy occurs in ibid., I, 109–18.

217. J. Warton, "The Enthusiast," in *Chal.*, XVIII, 161.

218. "The Progress of Poetry," in *F.P.* (1731), p. 134.

219. Horace, "Ars Poetica," in *Horace, Satires, Epistles and Ars Poetica*, with an English translation by H. Rushton Fairclough (Loeb Classical Library), 1932, p. 485.

220. John Dennis, "The Impartial Critick," in *Critical Essays of the Seventeenth Century*, edited by J. E. Spingarn (1908–1909) III, 194 (henceforth to be referred to as *Spingarn*); Pope, *Essay on Criticism*, 89.

221. Pope, *Essay on Criticism*, 140; C. Gildon, "The Complete Art of Poetry," in *Durham*, p. 23.

222. Ben Jonson, "Timber," in *Spingarn*, I, 20.

223. Milton, "Preface to Logic," in *The Works of John Milton* (Columbia University Press, 1935) XI, 15.

224. C. Gildon, "The Complete Art of Poetry," in *Durham*, pp. 52–53.

225. Sir William Davenant, "Preface to Gondibert," in *Spingarn*, II, 24–25.

226. T. Warton, "To Mr. Addison," in *Poems*, p. 169; "A Hymn to the Laureat," in *G.M.*, I, 21 (1731); "To Mr. P—pe," in *L.M.*, II, 301 (1733); R. Nugent, "An Ode to Bavius," in *O. and E.*, p. 14.

227. Rev. Mr. Thomson, "A Character of Mr. Pope's Writings," in *Dods.*, III, 326; "Musaeus," in *Dods.*, III, 294; R. Savage, "The Wanderer," in *Works*, p. 72.

228. "In Praise of Chaucer," in *G.M.*, X, 31 (1730); J. Hughes, "Upon Reading Mr. Dryden's Fables," in *Miscellanies*, p. 95; Mr. Concanen, "To Aaron Hill, Esq.," in *Misc. Sav.* (1726), p. 180; "On the Controversy between Mr. Pope and Mr. Theobald," in *New Miscellany* (1736), p. 47, speaks of Pope's and Theobald's quarreling as to "Who best could blanch dark Shakespeare's blotted page."

229. W. Somervile, "To Allen Ramsay," in *Works*, p. 262; similar in sentiment are: Mr. Somervile, "Epistle to Mr. Thomson," in *The Student*, II, 354 (1750); Akenside, "Ode 16," in *Works*, p. 187; W. Pattison, "To Mr. Hodges . . . ," in *And.*, p. 574; "From a Poetical Epistle on Design and Beauty," in *G.M.*, IV, 94 (1734); S. Boyse, *Retirement*, p. 7; *Harlequin Horace*, pp. 2, 14; J. Armstrong, "Of Benevolence," in *Works*, p. 70 wishes to please the polished few: not many, he admits, will read his works or will care for them.

230. "An Epistle to Myrtillo," in *L.M.*, IX, 345 (1740).

231. "From a Friend in the Country to a Young Gentleman in Town," in *L.M.*, V, 156 (1736).

232. Ben Jonson, "Timber," in *Spingarn*, I, 54.

233. Plato, "Ion," in *The Dialogues of Plato*, selections from the translation of Benjamin Jowett (1929), p. 127. All quotations from Plato used in this dissertation are from this source.

234. *Spectator*, No. 592.

235. "To His Grace John Duke of Bedford," in *G.M.*, X, 83 (1740); A. Philips, "To Lord Carteret," in *Chal.*, XIII, 120; no title, in *L.M.*, XVI, 191 (1747); S. Dixon, "On a Dispute between two Farmers for an old Sow," in *Poems*, p. 99; M. Browne, "To Mr. Moses Browne," in *Poems*, p. 3; W. Dunkin, "The Lover's Web," in *Works*, p. 311; "On the Queen's Grotto," in *G.M.*, VIII, 41 (1733); Mr. Concanen, "A Familiar Ode for the New Year, 1728," in *F.P.* (1731), p. 43; Young, *Ocean*, p. 183; D. Mallet, in the preface to "Amyntor and Theodora," in *Works*, I, 117, says that "effectually touching the passions" is the genuine province" and "great triumph" of poetry.

236. D. Mallet, "Verses presented to the Prince of Orange," in *Works*, I, 31.

237. "The Genuine Englishman," in *L.M.*, II, 417 (1732).

238. "On Being Charged with writing incorrectly," in *Carib.*, I, 316 (1741).

239. "Postscript apologizing for the poetica licentia in the foregoing poem," in *G.M.*, VIII, 486 (1738).

240. A. Hill, "Advice to the Poets," in *Works*, p. 213; similar in sentiment is "Morning," in *The Student*, I, 234 (1750).

241. A. Ramsay, "From C.T.," in *Works*, I, 120.

242. E. Rowe, "On the Death of the honourable Mrs. Thynne," in *Works*, p. 156; J. Winstanley, "An Ode on the Death of the Rt. Honourable William Earle C——r," in *Poems*, p. 204.

243. A. Ramsay, "Tartana," in *Works*, I, 140; Young, *Love of Fame*, p. 114.

244. "An Elegiac Poem," in *G.M.*, I, 261 (1731); "To Mr. Brooke, author of Gustavus Vasa," in *L.M.*, VIII, 407 (1739); "Ode for the New Year, 1750," in *L.M.*, XIX, 39 (1750).

245. J. or C. Wesley, "True Praise," in *Works*, I, 82, 47.

246. "To Stephen Duck," in S. Duck, *Poems*, p. xl; Nicholas Munckley, "On the Death of Mrs. Rowe," in E. Rowe, *Works*, p. cxv.

247. T. Curteis, *Eiren.*, p. 36.

248. T. Warton (Jr.), "P.M.," in *Chal.*, XVIII, 96.

249. Plato, *Phaedrus*, p. 1.

250. "On Divine Poetry," in *L.M.*, I, 309 (1732).

251. C. Pitt, "The Invitation," in *The Student*, I, 316 (1750); "A Letter from a Gentleman," in *The Bee*, II, 543 (1733); the passage

quoted is Mr. Vansittart, "The Pleasures of Poverty," in *Dods.*, III, 216.
   252. M. Masters, "The Resolution broke," in *Poems*, p. 94.
   253. J. Hughes, "On Our Savior's Incarnation," in *Miscellanies*, p. 106.
   254. W. Hamilton, "Pindar's Olympia," in *Poems*, p. 188; application of the sentiment to music; Thomson, *C.I.*, I, st. 41; "Inscription on an Aeolian Harp," in *The Student*, I, 311 (1750).
   255. W. Collins, "Ode on the Poetical Character," in *Poems*, p. 83; ibid., "The Passions," pp. 108, 112; "Ode to Pity," p. 74; "The Manners," pp. 106–107; "Ode to Simplicity," p. 79.
   256. Akenside, "Remonstrance of Shakespeare," in *Works*, pp. 198–199.
   257. Ibid., *Pleasures*, I, 37–43.
   258. Ibid., "Ode 19," in *Works*, p. 170; Pleasures, III, 380 ff. (quoted).
   259. J. Warton, "Ode to Fancy," in *Chal.*, XVIII, 163.
   260. *Spectator*, No. 160.
   261. J. Warton, "Ode occasion'd by reading Mr. West's translation of Pindar," in *Chal.*, XVIII, 169.
   262. Thomas Rymer, "Tragedies of the Last Age," in *Spingarn*, II, 185.
   263. T. Warton (Jr.), "Ode to Fancy," in *Chal.*, XVIII, 164.
   264. Shaftesbury, "Advice to an Author," in *Works*, I, 333.
   265. Thomas Rymer, "Tragedies of the Last Age," in *Spingarn*, II, 183.
   266. Thomas Sprat, *The History of the Royal Society* (1722), p. 113.
   267. Addison, *Tatler*, No. 165.
   268. *Spectator*, No. 409.
   269. Shaftesbury, "Miscellaneous Reflections," in *Works*, III, 401.
   270. Frances Hutcheson, *Inquiry*, p. 92.
   271. Leonard Welsted, "A Dissertation Concerning the Perfection of the English Language," in *Durham*, p. 365.
   272. W. Collins, "Ode to Simplicity," in *Poems*, p. 81.
   273. J. Armstrong, "Of Benevolence," in *Works*, p. 67; an anonymous poem, "Fashion," in *Dods.*, III, 258, satirizes the unfortunate effects of lack of taste.
   274. Akenside, *Pleasures*, III, 526 ff., contains the reference to the swain: the long quotation is ibid., 517–23.
   275. J. Bramston, "The Man of Taste," in *Dods.*, I, 287.
   276. Milton, *Comus*, 710–14 for Comus' speech: 762–67 for the Lady's.
   277. Ibid., Shakespeare, *Troilus and Cressida*, II, 2.
   278. "Verses on I . . . ," in *Grub.* (1732), p. 8; "To the Prince of Orange on his approaching Marriage with the Princess Royal," in *G.M.*, IV, 98 (1734); "On Miss K—tch—g," in *G.M.*, IX, 267 (1739).

279. "The Character of Lady A——y," in *Grub.* (1732), p. 6.

280. Mrs. Charlotte Lennox, "The Art of Coquetry," in *G.M.*, XX, 518 (1750).

281. T. Warton, "Verses Left on a Lady's Toilette," in *Poems*, p. 176.

282. "On Thought," in *D.M.* (1738), p. 223; H. Jacob, "Charon to Achilles," in *Works*, pp. 140, 134.

283. Mr. Hatchett, "An Ode to the Hon. Master Spencer," in *L.M.*, XIX, 601 (1750).

284. A. Philips, "To Miss Georgina," in *Chal.*, XIII, 125.

285. "An Epistle to Mr. Pope," in *L.M.*, VI, 47 (1737).

286. Thomson, *Sum.*, 1758-77.

287. "To the Author of the Farmers' Letters," in *Dods.*, III, 221-22.

288. "On the Choice of a Wife," in *Misc. Sav.* (1726), p. 131; similar in sentiment; A. Ramsay, "On our Ladies . . . " in *C.C.S.*, I, 220; Lord Lyttleton, "Advice to a Lady," in *Dods.*, II, 42; "To a very Pretty Lady, on her using paint," in *L.M.*, II, 362 (1733); Young, *Love of Fame*, p. 110; "Imitation of a Greek Epigram of Cardinal Berberini . . . ," in *A.L.* (1727), p. 43; William Shenstone, "The Judgment of Hercules," in *Chal.*, XIII, 310; "To Miss Polly Ast——n in New Bond Street," in *L.M.*, XII, 460 (1743).

289. "To a very Pretty Lady on her using paint," in *L.M.*, II, 362 (1733).

290. T. Cooke, "Epigram the First," in *Poems*, p. 172; similar, his "Epigram the Third," p. 174.

291. "On a Lady . . . ," in *L.M.*, XV, 421 (1746); "To Miss G——d or P——ll——n," in *G.M.*, XX, 278 (1750); "A New Song," in *Un. Mag.*, V, 271 (1750); Akenside, "Ode 8," in *Works*, p. 216.

292. "A Love Epistle," in *G.M.*, XVI, 607 (1746); similar, "To the Memory of a Mother," in *G.M.*, X, 518 (1740); "An Apology for Love," in *L.M.*, XVI, 432 (1747).

293. W. Hamilton, "Song," in *Poems*, p. 61.

294. "The Bachelor's Choice," in *Tun.* (1730), p. 20; "Love's Motive," in ibid., p. 19; "On Miss Evans," in ibid, p. 3.

295. A. Ramsay, "The Lass of Peattie's Mill," in *C.C.S.*, I, 1-2.

296. M. Green, "The Spleen," in *Chal.*, XV, 168; similar, A. Ramsay, "Keitha," in *Works*, II, 180.

297. Lord Lyttleton, "To My Lord . . . . . . ," in *Dods.*, II, 39; W. Collins, "The Manners," in *Poems*, p. 105; J. or C. Wesley, "For Christian Friends," in *Works*, V, 404; Lord Lyttleton, "Verses to be Written under a picture of Mr. Poyntz," in *Dods.*, II, 34-35; "Satire in the Manner of Persius," in *S.P. Ire.* (1730), p. 9; "The Man of Sense," in *L.M.*, II, 207 (1733).

298. D. Mallet, "The Excursion," in *Works*, p. 80: see also "On the

Death of Roundale Lloyd, M.S.," in *G.M.*, V, 103 (1735); J. Bancks, "Every Man in His Way," in *Works*, p. 172.

299. W. Hamilton, "Epitaph on Sir James Sooty," in *Poems*, p. 84.

300. E. Rowe, "On the Death of Mr. Thomas Rowe," in *Works*, p. 112; W. Whitehead, "On Ridicule," in *Chal.*, XVII, 206; "The Rose-Bud," in *G.M.*, IX, 267 (1739).

301. G. West, "On the Institution of the Order of the Garter," in *Dods.*, II, 136.

302. Young, *Love of Fame*, p. 145.

303. Ibid., *N.T.*, II, 111–22; V, 43–46, 110.

304. F. Hutcheson, *Inquiry*, p. 193.

305. Thomas Hobbes, "Leviathan," in *The English Works of Thomas Hobbes of Malmesbury*, III, 113 (1839).

306. Henry More, *Enchiridion Ethicum*, the English Translation of 1690. Facsimile Text Society (1930), pp. 6, 16, 28.

307. John Locke, *Essay Concerning Human Understanding*, pp. 290–91 (1912).

308. M. Browne, "The Christian Hero," in *Poems*, p. 423; W. Bowman, "Night," in *Poems*, p. 62; "The Divine Presence," in *L.M.*, XVII, 182 (1748); "A Prologue to the University of Cambridge," in *C.P.A.* (1733), p. 30.

309. J. or C. Wesley, "In Desertion and Temptation," in *Works*, I, 132; ibid., I, 84, 82.

310. Ibid., 49; similar, II, 253.

311. "Richmond Gardens," in *L.M.*, VII, 91 (1738).

312. W. Paget, *A Voyage to Ipswich*, p. 33; The Fall of Virtue, p. 13, the latter is the passage quoted.

313. "To the Rev. Mr. Pyle . . . ," in *L.M.*, IV, 384 (1735); Akenside, "Ode 11," in *Works*, pp. 171 ff. explained that love engendered sloth; "To the Rev. Mr. Whitefield," in *L.M.*, VIII, 356 (1730).

314. W. Broome, "Epistle to Fenton," in *Poems*, p. 51.

315. Young, *N.T.*, VIII, 315; similar: ibid., 546–47.

316. Ibid., IX, 1655–57.

317. Ibid., III, 330–46.

318. "To the Hon. Miss A——t," in *G.M.*, IX, 210 (1730); "Her Answer," in *G.M.*, IX, 435 (1739); "To Carolina," in *G.M.*, XI, 548 (1741).

319. R. Savage, "To John Powell," in *L.M.*, XI, 454 (1742); the passage quoted is Lady Mary Wortley Montague, "A Receipt to Cure the Vapours," in *Dods.*, I, 114.

320. W. Shenstone, "Judgment of Hercules," in *Chal.*, XIII, 308; "To the Rev'd. Mr. L——ther —dg— on his marriage," in *G.M.*, XX, 327 (1750); Thomson, "Epitaph on Miss Elizabeth Stanley," 13–16; "True Happiness," in *L.M.*, III, 260 (1734); "Song," in *L.M.*, XIII, 462 (1744);

"To the Rev. Mr. ———," in *L.M.*, VIII, 148 (1739); "Essay on Truth," in *The Champion* (1740), p. 69; R. Dodsley, "The Advice," in *Muse*, p. 734; "On Dr. Tyndale," in *D.M.* (1738), p. 84; Lord Lyttleton, "To the Rev. Dr. Asycough," in *Dods.*, II, 26–27; "To the Rev. Mr. Whitefield," in *L.M.*, VIII, 385 (1739).

321. "The Balance," in *G.M.*, X, 139 (1740).

322. R. Nugent, "Epistle to Chesterfield," in *O. and E.*, p. 64; T. Curteis, *Eiren.*, pp. 52, 50; A. Ramsay, "Content," in *Works*, I, 145; J. Bancks, "Tranquillity and Happiness," in *Works*, p. 352; R. Savage, "The Wanderer," in *Works*, p. 74.

323. Pope, Horace, Satire 2, Book 2, 61 f.; similar, R. Nugent, "To the Earl of Chesterfield," in *O. and E.*, p. 17.

324. "Life burthensome, because we know not how to use it," in *Dods.*, III, 56; similar, R. Savage, "The Gentleman," in *G.M.*, IV, 694 (1734); "Happiness and Grandeur never Companions," in *L.M.*, VIII, 660 (1739).

325. Mrs. Grierson, "Upon my Son's Speaking Latin in School," in M. Barber, *Poems*, p. 89; W. Paget, *A Voyage to Ipswich*, p. 38.

326. H. Travers, "Verses upon the Death of a Learned Young Lady," in *Poems*, p. 58.

327. J. Gay, "Fable 14, Book 2," in *Works*, p. 197; M. Browne, "An Essay on the Universe," in *Poems*, p. 292.

328. J. Bancks, "An Ode to Mr. Bellamy," in *Poems*, II, 81.

329. Pope, *E.M.*, II, 13, 54 ff.; Young, *N.T.*, II, 524–25; "Verses to Peter Delme, Esq.," in *Newcomb Miscellany* (1740), p. 8; R. Nugent, "Epistle to Chesterfield," in *O. and E.*, p. 68; Young, *N.T.*, VIII, 159–160; "To A ------- H -------, Esq.," in *C. Misc.* (1740), p. 40; T. Warton, "An Epistle to Dr. Young," in *Poems*, p. 3; "Decorum," in *G.M.*, IX, 597 (1739); "To the Rt. Hon. George Lyttleton, Esq.," in *G.M.*, XVIII, 520 (1748); J. Warton, "Ode to Superstition," in *Chal.*, XVIII, 165; "The Pleasures of Reflection," in *L.M.*, XII, 354 (1743); H. Jacob, "Chiron to Achilles," in *Works*, p. 136; John Dalton, *Epistle to Lord B.*, p. 58; R. Nugent, "An Epistle to the Rt. Hon. the Lord Viscount Cornbury," in *O. and E.*, p. 32; "Reflections . . . Virgil," in *Misc. Sav.* (1726), p. 36; "To Sylvius," in *G.M.*, XIX, 38 (1749); M. Browne, "Essay on the Universe," in *Poems*, p. 359.

330. "The Judgment of Hercules," in *L.M.*, XVIII, 88 (1749); quoted is a passage from "Essay on Truth," in *The Champion* (1740), p. 68.

331. "Essay on Truth," in *The Champion* (1740), p. 68.

332. W. Hamilton, "A Soliloquy in Imitation of Hamlet," in *Poems*, p. 96.

333. Thomson, *Win.*, 441–43; 439–40.

334. Young, *Love of Fame*, p. 70; ibid., *N.T.*, VIII, 1160–81.

335. Ibid., *N.T.*, VIII, 826–31.

336. Ibid., VI, 248–55.

337. "Another," in *Carib.*, I, 254; "The Abess and the Nun," in *A Collection of Poems, Odes and Tales . . ."* (1731), p. 23; Young, *Love of Fame*, p. 141; Lord Hervey, "Roxana to Usbeck," in *Dods.*, IV, 100; J. Hammond, "Elegy 7," in *Chal.*, XI, 592; "On a Picture of a Fair Libertine," in *H-S.* (1734), p. 291; Lord Lansdowne, "Chloe," in *Works*, p. 60.

338. R. Savage, "The Bastard," in *Works*, p. 123.

339. Lord Lansdowne, "Song to the Same," in *Works*, p. 106.

340. "Essay on Satire," in *C.P. Pr. and Vs.* (1733), p. 34.

341. J. Gay, "Fable 32, Book 1," in *Works*, p. 106; "To Miss —— on her Constant reading the Weekly Miscellanies," in *L.M.*, II, 361 (1733).

342. "In Laudem Ignorantiae," in *L.M.*, I, 365 (1732).

343. Ibid.

344. G. West, "Education," in *Chal.*, XIII, 183. (Note that it is not instinct but "Squire Locke" that defies custom.) "Custom," in *Un. Mag.*, I, 233 (1747).

345. "On Castle Building," in *G.M.*, XV, 213 (1745); H. Jacob, "Bedlam," in *Works*, p. 14; implies that the mad are happier so, since "returning Reason finds 'em poor."

346. Thomson, *C.I.*, I, st. 48. A minor description of man's originally untainted state prior to his attaining the use of reason may be found in Mr. Blythe, "A Soliloquy," in *G.M.*, V, 48 (1736).

347. "Against our modern freethinkers," in *G.M.*, XVI, 491 (1746).

348. Young, *N.T.*, VIII, 283–300.

349. J. or C. Wesley, "Another 13," in *Works*, V, 158; "To the Author of the Essay on Reason," in *L.M.*, IV, 152 (1735).

350. "Verses occasion'd by reading the Essay on Man, first part," in *L.M.*, II, 153–54 (1732).

351. Thomson, *Lib.*, III, 208–212; "Lord H–rv–y, to Mr. S. L——x," in *Win. Med.* (1731), pp. 3–4.

352. H. Travers, "To the Fair Unknown," in *Miscellaneous Poems and Translations* (1740), p. 359.

353. "No real happiness below," in *L.M.*, VIII, 408 (1739).

354. "On the Death of T. Rustat," in *G.M.*, XI, 493 (1741).

355. Young, *N.T.*, V, 251–54.

356. Ibid., VII, 490–96.

357. Ibid., 515–20.

358. Ibid., 524–44.

359. The passage quoted is from "Soliloquy on Religion," in *Un. Mag.*, VII, 332 (1750); similar references to the naturally good heart of man include, "The Origin and Duration of Love," in *Un. Mag.*, II, 37 (1748); "On a Grave Stone in a Country Churchyard," in *The Stu-*

dent, II, 230 (1750); R. Nugent, "An Ode to H.R.H. on his Birthday," in *O. and E.*, p. 19; S. Duck, "Avaro and Amanda," in *Poems*, p. 62.
  360. Ibid.
  361. D. Lewis, "Paraphrase on the 7th Psalm," in *Poems*, p. 250.
  362. "Answer," in *L.M.*, VI, 701 (1737); H. Greville, "The Moral Alchymist," in *G.M.*, XII, 45 (1742).
  363. John Dryden, *Religio Laici*, l. 432, in *The Poetical Works of John Dryden* (Student's Cambridge Edition, 1909).
  364. Pope, *Universal Prayer*, st. 8; Thomson, *Lib.*, III, 53 ff.
  365. J. or C. Wesley, "The Backslider's Confession," in *Works*, I, 320; see also ibid., II, 6; VI, 6; I, 14; III, 109; IV, 36.
  366. Ibid., VIII, 80.
  367. Ibid., I, 35; see also I, 166.
  368. Ibid., I, 210.
  369. Ibid., 76.
  370. "On inward feelings; or the happy experiences of devout souls," in *G.M.*, IX, 491 (1739). Similar reference to the "mighty grace" that transforms the soul is made in "On Mr. Whitefield's Preaching," in *G.M.*, IX, 281 (1739).
  371. Young, *N.T.*, VI, 281.
  372. Ibid., IX, 1858–59.
  373. Ibid., VIII, 47–49.
  374. Ibid., IX, 710–16.
  375. *Spectator*, No. 601.
  376. Shaftesbury, "A Letter Concerning Enthusiasm," in *Works*, I, 37.
  377. Addison, *Spectator*. No. 588, from his discussion of and attack on Hobbes and Lucretius.
  378. Ibid.
  379. A. Ramsay, "Answer to Mr. Somervile's Epistle," in *Works*, III, 89; W. Paget, *A Voyage to Ipswich*, p. 10; Thomson, *Spr.*, 7–10; H. Brooke, "Universal Beauty," in *Chal.*, XVII, 36; R. Savage, "The Friend," in *G.M.*, VI, 673 (1737); S. Dixon, "To Fortune," in *Poems*, p. 155.
  380. Mr. Melmoth, "Of the Active and Retired Life," in *Dods.*, I, 206.
  381. A. Hill, "Advice to the Poets," in *Works*, II, 216.
  382. "An Address to James Oglethorpe, esq.," in *G.M.*, III, 209 (1733); other references to the joys of benevolence: M. Chandler, "To Mrs. Moor," in *Poems*, p. 61; W. Shenstone, "The Progress of Taste," in *Chal.*, XIII, 315; M. Chandler, "On Mr. B's Garden," in *Poems*, p. 71; R. Savage, "Of Public Spirit," in *Works*, p. 149; Akenside, *Pleasures*, II, 254–68; "An Epistle to his Excellency John Lord Carteret," in *F.P.* (1731), p. 91; D. Mallet, "Amyntor and Theodora," in *Works*, p. 135; T. Cooke, "A Rhapsody on Virtue and Pleasure,"

in *Poems*, p. 51; W. Somervile, "The Sweet-Scented Miser," in *Works*, p. 134.

383. Thomson, *Lib.*, III, 107–10.

384. Ibid., IV, 486–490.

385. "To a Young Lady with Mustapha," in *L.M.*, VIII, 624 (1739); a description of the benevolent heart as confiding is given in S. Dixon, "The Shepherd's Daughter," in *Poems*, p. 199.

386. A. Hill, "The Choice," in *Chal.*, XIII, 252; the passage quoted is from "A Satire in the Manner of Persius," in *S.P. Ire.* (1730), p. 2; similar in sentiment: J. or C. Wesley, "The Communion of Saints," in *Works*, I, 362; Thomson, *Win.*, 348–58; has a plea for sympathy for the thousand nameless ills that hurt men; in the 1727 edition of *Sum.*, 1169 ff., Thomson describes the unsympathetic man as the greatest wretch among human beings.

387. Pope, *Epilogue to the Satires*, dialogue 2, 203 f.

388. S. Jenyns, "An Essay on Virtue," in *Dods.*, III, 166; also Pope, *E.M.*, IV, 353 ff.

389. W. Somervile, "To Dr. Mackenzie," in *Works*, p. 270; R. Savage, "The Wanderer," in *Works*, p. 69.

390. R. Nugent, "Epistle to Cornwallis," in *O. and E.*, p. 56.

391. E. Carter, "In Diem Natalem," in *Poems*, p. 7.

392. Pope, *E.M.*, III, 317; 307–30.

393. Akenside, *Pleasures*, III, 1–7.

394. M. Barber, "To Alexander Pope, Esq. . . . ," in *Poems*, p. 180.

395. Young, *N.T.*, VIII, 1194–1202.

396. John Dalton, *Epistle to Lord B.*, p. 61.

397. Fictitious examples of benevolence: W. Somervile, "Fable 14," in *Works*, p. 93; ibid., "Mohamet Ali Beg," p. 129; R. Savage, "The Wanderer," in *Works*, p. 115; ibid., p. 114; T. Warton, "Of the Universal Love of Pleasure," in *Poems*, p. 19; Minor real life benevolent people: "A Poem by the Rev. Mr. Chamberlayne . . . ," in *G.M.*, XI, 661 (1741); J. or C. Wesley, "An Elegy," in *Works*, III, 118.

398. M. Chandler, "To Mrs. Stephens," in *Bath*, p. 52; "Sir, you are desir'd to insert the following lines in celebration of a gentleman's contribution of £50 to the sufferers of the late fire at Wellingborough," in *G.M.*, IX, 42 (1739).

399. J. or C. Wesley, "For their Benefactors," in *Works*, II, 16; ibid., "A Hymn for the Georgia Orphans," II, 16; ibid., 22.

400. "To James Oglethorpe, Esq.," in *L.M.*, III, 440 (1734).

401. No title, in *G.M.*, XIII, 99 (1743).

402. Mr. Chamberlin, "On his Excellency the Earl of Chesterfield's being appointed Lord Lieutenant of Ireland,' 'in *L.M.*, XIV, 305 (1745); "An Ode to the Earl of Chesterfield," in *G.M.*, XVIII, 251 (1748).

403. "To His Grace the Duke of Richmond," in *F.P.* (1731), p. 251.

404. Rev. Mr. Newcomb, "An Ode to the Queen," in *F.P.* (1731), p. 113.

405. C. Pitt, "An Epistle to Dr. Edward Young," in *Chal.*, XII, 372.

406. C. Cibber, "An Ode for His Majesty's Birthday," in *Mem. Soc. Grub.*, II, 167 (1737).

407. Pope, *Moral Essays, Epistle 3*, 250 ff.

408. Young, *N.T.*, IX, 699; ibid., 709; even a spring of water could teach a lesson in benevolence—see the poem by W. Somervile, "The Two Springs," in *The Champion*, II, 8 f. (1740); Young, *N.T.*, IV, 602–603. A similar attitude is expressed in Young, *Ocean*, p. 181, and in "The Storm," in *G.M.*, XVII, 95 (1747).

409. Young, *N.T.*, III, 217.

410. Ibid., I, 297–98.

411. The passages quoted are ibid., VIII, 886–87; II, 508; similar is the whole passage VIII, 873–86.

412. John Dalton, *Epistle to Lord B.*, p. 61.

413. Montaigne, "Apology of Raymonde Seybonde," in *Works*, pp. 209 f.

414. Pope, *E.M.*, I, 245–46.

415. Thomson, *C.I.*, I, st. 9.

416. "On Mr. Howard's Observatory," in *G.M.*, XX, 277 (1750).

417. "The Flea of Taste," in *H-S.* (1734), p. 141.

418. "A Comparison," in *L.M.*, XVII, 326 (1748).

419. "Verse occasion'd by the death of J.J. Esq. . . . ," in *Newcomb Miscellany* (1740), p. 254.

420. H. Jacob, "Epistle 8," in *Works*, p. 122.

421. "Epitaph on a Lap Dog," in *L.M.*, III, 215 (1734); similar— "Verses sent to a Lady with a Lap-Dog," in *L.M.*, II, 289 (1733).

422. J. Armstrong, "Art of Preserving Health," in *Works*, p. 17, is the passage quoted. Other poems in praise of animals are: "To the Same," in *Dods.*, III, 180; Lady Mary Wortley Montague, "Verses written in a Garden," in *Dods.*, IV, 192; "To the Author of the verses inscrib'd to Miss Molly H—— in W——shire," in *L.M.*, XI, 148 (1742); "The Parrot," in *Carib.*, II, 194 (1741); "The Country," in *Misc. Sav.* (1726), p. 204; J. or C. Wesley, "Affliction," in *Works*, I, 37; J. Gay, "Introduction to the Fables," in *Works*, p. 50.

423. H. Brooke, "Universal Beauty," in *Chal.*, XVII, 17.

424. "Epitaph on an old favorite dog," in *G.M.*, XVII, 145 (1747).

425. R. Savage, "The Wanderer," in *Works*, p. 95.

426. J. Gay, "Fable 10, book 1," in *Works*, p. 95.

427. "The Invective," in *H-S.* (1734), p. 157; like reproaches: H. Brooke, "Universal Beauty," in *Chal.*, XVII, 361; M. Browne, "Eclogue 3," in *A.S.*, p. 39; J. Gay, "Fable 36, book 1," in *Works*, p. 111; ibid., "Fable 15," p. 17; "Fable 30," p. 102; "Fable 17," p. 80; Lord

Lansdowne, "The Wild Boar's Defence," in *Works*, p. 112; W. Somervile, "Field Sports," in *Works*, p. 186; ibid., "The Chase," p. 196; "Fashion," in *Dods.*, III, 261; Thomson, *C.I.*, II, st. 15; ibid., *Spr.*, 343–78; T. Warton, "Newmarket," in *Chal.*, XVIII, 121.

428. S. Boyse, *Deity*, p. 41.

429. W. Whitehead, "On Ridicule," in *Chal.*, XVII, 206; Thomson, *Spr.*, 170–73; W. Somervile, "The Chase," in *Works*, p. 222 puts reason as superior to brute rage: Akenside, *Pleasures*, I, 526 ff.; W. Somervile, "The Chase," in *Works*, p. 231; "On Infidelity," in *L.M.*, II, 259 (1733); J. or C. Wesley, "Hymn 14," in *Works*, III, 86.

430. Young, *N.T.*, VII, 289–312; VII, 732–49; III, 347–50; the passage quoted is III, 474–78; IV, 545–49.

431. Ibid., VII, 1434–35.

432. Ibid., 81–88.

433. Ibid., 46–53.

434. Sentimental references to animals: "To his Excellency the Right Honourable the Lord Viscount Howe," in *Carib.*, II, 182 (1741); W. Shenstone, "A Pastoral Ballad," in *Dods.*, IV, 351; J. Warton, "Ode to a Nightingale," in *Chal.*, XVIII, 168; T. Smollett, "Burlesque Ode," in Poems and Plays, p. 249; J. Hammond, "Elegy 13," in *Chal.*, XI, 594; "On the Death of a robin accidentally slain," in *G.M.*, XI, 45 (1741); sympathy with the hunted: H. Baker, *Un.*, p. 35; W. Somervile, "The Chase," in *Works*, pp. 330; 318; Ibid., "Field Sports," p. 186; sympathy with enslaved human beings: R. Savage, "Of Public Spirit," in *Works*, p. 154; S. Duck, "Avaro and Amanda," in *Poems*, p. 77.

435. Thomson's humanitarian passages are so familiar that the reader needs no detailed references for them.

Bibliography

MISCELLANIES AND PAMPHLETS

The Altar of Love. Consisting of Poems and other Miscellanies. By the most eminent Hands. London, H. Curll, 1727.

Bacchus and Venus; or a Selection of near 200 of the most witty and diverting Songs and Catches In Love and Gallantry. London, R. Montague, 1737.

The Bath Miscellany for the Year 1740. Bath, W. Jones, 1741.

The Bays Miscellany or Colley Triumphant. Written by Scriblerus Quarlus. London, A. Moore [n.d., the copy in the Harvard Library has noted on the title page in pencil the dates 1732, 1742].

Candour: or an Occasional Essay on the Abuse of Wit and Eloquence. London, M. Watson, 1739.

Caribbeana: Containing Letters and Dissertations together with Political Essays on Various Subjects and Occasions—chiefly wrote by several hands in the West-Indies and some of them to gentlemen residing there. London, T. Osborne [etc.], 1741.

The Charing Cross Medley. London, W. James, 1732.

The Christian Poet or Divine Poems on the Four Last Things. London, 1735.

A Choice Collection of Poetry by the Most Ingenious Men of the Age. Most carefully collected from Original Manuscripts, By Joseph Yarrow, Comedian—York. London, A. Staples, 1738.

Clio and Strephon. Being the second and last part of the Platonic Lovers consisting of Love Epistles etc. by Wm. Bond, Esq.; of Bury St. Edmonds and Mrs. Martha Fowke . . . . to which is added a collection of Miscellanies by the most eminent Hands. London, E. Curll, 1732.

A Collection of Bacchanalian Songs. London, J. Stagg and T. Astley, 1729.

A Collection of Pieces in Verse and Prose which have been publish'd on the occasion of the Dunciad. By Mr. Savage. London, L. Gilliver, 1732.

A Collection of Poems. By the Author of a Poem on the Cambridge Ladies. Cambridge, W. Fenner, 1733.

A Collection of Poems; consisting of Odes, Tales, etc. as well as Originals and Translations. Dedicated to the Rt. Hon. William Pulteney, Esq. By the Author of The Duel, a Poem. London, J. Roberts, 1731.

The Comedians Tales: or Jests, Songs, and Pleasant Adventures of Several Famous Players. London, T. Warner and W. Pepper, 1729.

A Compleat Collection of all the Verses, Essays, Letters and Advertisements which have been occasioned by the Publication of three volumes of Miscellanies by Pope and Co. London, A. Moore, 1728.

The Court Oracle: A New Miscellany. London, S. Slow, 1734.

Court Poems in two Parts. By Mr. Pope, etc. London, E. Curll, 1726.

The Cuckold's Miscellany: or, a Modest Plea for Padlocks. London, W. Williams, 1735.

Delights of the Muses being a Collection of Poems never before Published. London, J. Osborn and J. Bailey, 1738.

A Description of Bath. A Poem. London, J. Leake and J. Gray, 1734.

An Epistle from the late Lord B .... *to the Duke of W* .... London, A. Moor [sic], 1730.

An Essay on Conversation: London, L. Gilliver and J. Clarke, 1737. [The copy in the New York Public Library has in long hand on the title page "By Benjamin Stillingfleet."]

Fables and Other Short Poems; Collected from the most celebrated English Authors. London, William and Cluer Dicey, 1737.

The Fall of Virtue: or the Iron-Age: a Poem. Edinburgh, A. Kincaid, 1738.

The Flower Pieces: A Collection of Miscellany Poems. By several eminent Hands. London, J. Walthoe and H. Walthoe, 1731.

Grubiana: or a compleat collection of all the Poems and Material Letters from the Grub Street Journal. London, J. Hughs, 1732.

Harlequin Horace: or the Art of Modern Poetry. London, Lawton Gilliver, 1731. [The copy in the New York Public Library has "By James Miller" written in long hand on the title page.]

The Honey-Suckle; By a Society of Gentlemen. London, Chas. Corbett, 1734.

Lashley's York Miscellany: Containing a Collection of all the Letters, Ballads, Advertisements, Paragraphs in the Newspapers, etc. that have been published by both Parties since the Contest about the late City and Country Elections first begun. York, 1734.

The Lover's Pacquet; or, the Marriage-Miscellany with the Newest Mode of Courtship, etc., etc. London, T. Reynolds, 1733.

Martyn, John and Richard Russell. *Memoirs of the Society of Grub Street.* London, J. Wilford, 1737. Two volumes.

Miscellanea in Two Volumes, Never before Published. Vol. 1. London, 1727.

A Miscellaneous Collection of Original Poems, consisting of Odes, epistles, translations etc. written chiefly on Political and Moral subjects. London, J. Wilson, 1740. [The copy in the Harvard Library has "By Thomas Newcomb M.A." written on the title page.]

Miscellaneous Poems and Translations by Several Hands. Publish'd by Richard Savage, Son of the Late Earl Rivers. London, Samuel Chapman, 1726.

Miscellanies by Swift and Pope. The Third Volume. London, B. Motte and L. Gilliver, 1732.

Miscellanies consisting chiefly of Original Pieces in Prose and Verse. By D——n S——t. Never before published in this Kingdom. London, A. Moore, 1734.

Miscellanies: the Last Volume. London, B. Motte, 1727.

A Miscellany of Poems by Several Hands. Publish'd by J. Husbands. A.M. Fellow of Pembroke College, Oxon. Oxford, Leon Lichfield, 1731.

The New Ministry. Containing a collection of all the Satyrical Poems, Songs, etc., since the Beginning of 1742. London, W. Webb, 1742.

A New Miscellany. London, A. Moore, 1736.

New Miscellany for the Year 1734. Part I–II. [The copy in the Yale Library has n.p., n.d.]

A New Miscellany for the Year 1738. London [n.d.].

On the Scarcity of the Copper Coin. A Satyr. Edinburgh, 1739.

Poems in English and Latin on the Archers and Royal-Company of Archers. By several Hands. Edinburgh, 1726.

Poems on Affairs of State. London, J. Roberts, 1733.

Poetical Miscellanies: consisting of original Poems and Translations. By the best Hands. Publish'd by Mr. J. Gay. Dublin, J. Thomson, 1729.

The Poetical Works of J.S.D.D.D.S.P.D. Consisting of Curious Miscellaneous Pieces, both Humorous and Satyrical. Reprinted from the Second Dublin Edition, with Notes and Additions [n.p.], 1736.

Robin's Panegyrick. Or, the Norfolk Miscellany. London, T. Tims [n.d.].

The Scarborough Miscellany. For the Year 1734. [N.p., n.d. on the copy in the New York Public Library.]

Select Poems from Ireland. London, T. Warner, 1730.

The Stamford Toasts: or Panegyrical Characters of the Fair-Ones Inhabiting the good Town of Stamford in Lincolnshire. With some Poetical Amusements. By Mr. Pope; not the Undertaker. E. Curll [etc.], 1726.

The Summer Miscellany; or a Present for the Country. London, T. Cooper, 1742.

Swifteana Consisting of Poems by Dean Swift and several of his Friends. Never before Printed. London [n.p.], 1727.

Tunbrigialia: or Tunbridge Miscellanies. For the Year 1730. London,
T.B., 1730.
Tunbrigilia: or The Tunbridge Miscellany, for the Years 1737, 1738,
1739. Being a Curious Collection of Miscellany Poems, &c. Ex-
hibited upon the Walks at Tunbridge Wells, in the last three
Years. By a Society of Gentlemen and Ladies. London, T. Webb,
1740.
Verres and His Scribblers; a Satire in three cantos. London, C. Browne,
1732.
War with Priestcraft; or the Freethinker's Iliad. A Burlesque Poem in
three Cantos. London, J. Roberts, 1732.
The Windsor Medley: Being a Choice Collection of several Curious
and Valuable pieces in Prose and Verse: That were handed about
in Print and Manuscript during the Stay of the Court at Windsor-
Castle last Summer. London, A. Moore, 1731.

Poets

Akenside, Mark. *The Poetical Works of Mark Akenside.* With
Memoir and Critical Dissertation by the Rev. George Gilfillan.
London, James Nesbit, 1857.
Armstrong, Dr. John. *The Economy of Love:* a Poetical Essay. A New
Edition. London, M. Cooper, 1745. [The copy in the New York
Public Library has no name printed on the title page, only a pen-
ciled "John Armstrong."]
———— *The Poetical Works of Dr. Armstrong.* Collated with the best
editions: by Thomas Park. London, J. Sharpe, 1807.
Baker, Henry. *The Universe.* A Poem Intended to Restrain the Pride
of Man. London, T. Worall, 1727.
Bancks, John. *Miscellaneous Works in Verse and Prose of John Bancks.*
London, T. Aris, 1738.
Barber, Mary. *Poems on Several Occasions.* 1734. [The copy in the
New York Public Library has no title page: this is the catalogue
listing.]
Blair, Robert. *The Grave.* A Poem. Illustrated by twelve etchings exe-
cuted by L. Schavonetti from the original inventions of William
Blake. New York, D. Appleton & Company, 1903.
Bowman, William. *Poems on Several Occasions.* London [n.p.]. 1727.
Boyse, Samuel. *The Deity:* a Poem. London, C. Corbett, 1749.
———— *Poems,* in Chalmers, *English Poets,* Vol. XIV.
———— *Retirement,* a Poem, occasioned by seeing the Palace and Park
of Yester. Edinburgh, 1735.
Bramston, James. *Poems,* in Dodsley, *A Collection of Poems,* Vol. I.

—— *Seasonable Reproof*, A Satire in the Manner of Horace. By the Author of the Man of Taste. Dublin, George Faulkner, 1736.

Brooke, Henry. *Poems*, in Chalmers, *English Poets*, Vol. XVII.

Broome, William, LL.D., Chaplain to the Right Honourable Charles Lord Cornwallis, Baron of Eye in Suffolk. *Poems on Several Occasions*. The Second Edition with large alterations and additions. London, Lintot, 1739.

Browne, Moses. *Angling Sports:* in Nine Piscatory Eclogues. A New attempt to introduce a more pleasing Variety and Mixture of Subjects and Characters into Pastoral—on the Plan of its Primitive Rules and Manners. Suited to the Entertainment of Retirement, and the Lovers of Nature in rural Scenes. Their edition corrected and very much improved. London, Edw. and Charles Dolly, 1773.

—— *Poems on various Subjects*. Many never printed before. London, Edw. Cave, 1739.

Carey, Henry. *An Ode to Mankind*. London, Dodsley, 1741.

—— *The Poems of Henry Carey*. Edited with an introduction and notes by Frederick T. Wild. London, The Scholartis Press, 1930.

Carter, Elizabeth. *Poems on Several Occasions*. The Second Edition. London, J. Rivington, 1766.

Chandler, Mary. *The Description of Bath*. A Poem. Humbly Inscrib'd to her Royal Highnes the Princess Amelia. The fourth edition. To which are added, Several Poems by the same Author. London, James Leake, 1738.

Collier, John. *The Works of Tim Bobbin, Esq*. in prose and verse, with a memoir of the author by John Corry; to which is added a rendering into simple English of the dialogue of Tummus and Mary by Elijah Ridings. Manchester [n.p.], 1862.

Collins, William. *The Poems of William Collins*. Edited with an Introductory Study by Edmund Blunden. London, Frederick Etchells and Hugh Macdonald, 1921.

Cooke, Thomas. *Mr. Cooke's Original Poems with Imitations and Translations of Several Select Passages of the Antients*. In four Parts; to which are added Proposals for perfecting the English language. London, T. Jackson and C. Bathurst, 1742.

Curteis, T. *Eirenodia:* A Poem sacred to Peace, and the Promoting of Human Happiness. By T. Curteis, Rector of Sevenoke in Kent. London, R. Wilkin, 1728.

Davys, Mary. *The Works of Mrs. Davys:* consisting of Plays, Novels, Poems, and familiar Letters—several of which never before publish'd. London, H. Woodfall, 1725.

Desaguliers, J. T. *The Newtonian System of the World, the Best Model of Government:* an Allegorical Poem. London, J. Roberts, 1728.

Dixon, Mrs. Sarah. *Poems on Several Occasions.* Canterbury, J. Albree, 1740.

Dodsley, Robert. *A Muse in Livery.* A Collection of Poems. London, J. Nourse, 1732.

Duck, Stephen. *Poems on Several Occasions.* By the Reverend Mr. Stephen Duck. With a Life of the Author, by the Rev. Joseph Spence, late Professor of Poetry in the University of Oxford. The fourth edition. London, John Livingston, 1764.

Dunkin, William. *Select Poetical Works of the late William Dunkin, D.D.* In Two Volumes. Volume II, Dublin, S. Powell, 1770.

Dyer, John. *Poems,* in Chalmers, *English Poets,* Vol. XIII.

FitzGerald, Thomas. *Poems on Several Occasions.* London, J. Watts, 1733.

Gay, John. *The Poetical Works of John Gay.* Edited with a Life and Notes by John Underhill. Volume II. New York, Charles Scribner's Sons, 1893.

Glover, Richard. *Poems,* in Chalmers, *English Poets,* Vol. XVII.

Granville, George. *The Genuine Works in Verse and Prose of the Right Hon. George Granville,* Lord Lansdowne. London, J. and R. Tonson [etc.], 1736.

Gray, Thomas. *The Poetical Works of Gray and Collins.* Edited by Austin Lane Poole. Oxford Edition. New York, Oxford University Press, 1917.

Green, Matthew. *Poems,* in Chalmers, *English Poets,* Vol. XV.

Hamilton, William. *Poems on Several Occasions.* Edinburgh, W. Gordon, 1760.

Hammond, James. *Poems,* in Chalmers, *English Poets,* Vol., XI.

Hervey, J. *A Satire in the Manner of Persius.* London, J. Clarke and T. Robinson, 1739.

Higgons, Bevil. *A Poem on the Glorious Peace of Utrecht.* London, P. Meighan, 1731.

Hill, Aaron. *Works of the late Aaron Hill, Esq.* In four Volumes. Consisting of Letters on Various Subjects, and of original Poems, moral and facetious. With an essay on the art of Acting. London [n.p.], 1753.

Hughes, Jabez. *Miscellanies in Verse and Prose.* London, John Watts, 1737.

Jacob, Hildebrand. *The Works of Hildebrand Jacob, Esq.;* containing Poems on various Subjects, and Occasions; with the Fatal Constancy, a Tragedy; and Several Pieces in Prose. London, W. Lewis, 1735.

Johnson, Samuel. *The Poems of Samuel Johnson.* Edited by David Nichol Smith and Edward L. McAdam. Oxford, The Clarendon Press, 1941.

King, William. *The Toast.* an Heroick Poem in four Books, written originally in Latin by Frederick Sheffner; now done into English, and illustrated with Notes and Observations by Peregrine O'Donald Esq. London [n.p.], 1732.

Lewis, David. *Miscellaneous Poems* by Several Hands. London, J. Watts, 1726.

Lockman, John. *An Ode for St. Cecilia's Day.* The Words by Mr. Lockman. The Musick by Mr. Boyse. 1739.

────── *An Ode to his Eminence Cardinal de Fleury.* By Mr. Lockman. Paris, Piget, 1741.

────── *An Ode to the Memory of his Grace the Duke of Buckinghamshire.* 1735.

Lyttleton, Lord. *Poems,* in Dodsley, *A Collection of Poems,* Vol. II.

Mallet, David. *The Works of David Mallet Esq.;* in three volumes. A new edition corrected. London, A. Millar and P. Vaillant, 1759.

Mason, William. *Poems,* in Dodsley, *A Collection of Poems,* Vol. III, and in Chalmers, *English Poets,* Vol. XVIII.

Masters, Mary. *Poems on Several Occasions.* London, T. Browne, 1733.

Meston, William. *The Poetical Works of the Ingenious and Learned William Meston, A.M.* Seventh edition. J. Burnett, Aberdeen, 1802.

Nugent, Robert. *Odes and Epistles.* London, R. Dodsley, 1739.

Pattison, William. *Poems,* in Anderson, *British Poets,* Vol. VIII.

Pitt, Christopher. *Poems,* in Chalmers, *English Poets,* Vol. XII.

Pope, Alexander. *The Complete Poetical Works of Alexander Pope.* Student's Cambridge Edition. New York, Houghton Mifflin Co., 1903.

Ramsay, Allan. *A Collection of Choice Songs Scots and English.* In two volumes. Glascow, John Crum, 1871.

────── *The Works of Allan Ramsay.* In three volumes. With a life of the author by George Chalmers: an essay on his genius and writings by Lord Woodhouseler. London, A. Fullarton and Co., 1851.

Rowe, Mrs. Elizabeth. *The Miscellaneous Works in Prose and Verse of Mrs. Elizabeth Rowe.* The Greater Part now first published by her Order, from her Original Manuscripts by Mr. Theophilus Rowe. London, R. Hill and R. Dodsley, 1739.

Savage, Richard. *The Poetical Works of Richard Savage* with the Life of the Author by Doctor Johnson. Cooke's Edition. London, J. Wright [n.d.].

Shenstone, William. *Poems on Various Occasions.* Written for the Entertainment of the Author, and Printed for the Amusement of a few Friends, Prejudic'd in his Favour. Oxford, Leon Lichfield, 1737. [In the copy in the Yale Library Shenstone's name does not appear on the title page.]

────── *Poems,* in Chalmers, *English Poets,* Vol. XIII.

Smedley, Jonathan. *Gulliveriana*. [The copy in the Columbia Library has the title page missing: a note in longhand says "printed 1728."]

Smollett, Tobias. *Plays and Poems*, written by T. Smollett, M.D. with memoirs of the Life and Writings of the Author. London, T. Evans, 1777.

Somervile, William. *The Poetical Works of William Somervile*, with the life of the author. Cooke's edition. London, Cooke [n.d.].

Swift, Jonathan. *Poems of Jonathan Swift*. Edited by Harold Williams. Oxford, The Clarendon Press, 1937.

Thomas, Elizabeth. *The Metamorphosis of the Town: or a View of the Present Fashions. A Tale: after the Manner of Fontaine*. London, J. Wilford, 1730.

Thomson, James. *The Complete Poetical Works of James Thomson*. Edited with notes by J. Logie Robertson. Oxford Edition. New York, Oxford University Press, 1908.

Trapp, Joseph. *Poems*, in Dodsley, *A Collection of Poems*, Vol. IV.

Travers, Henry. *Miscellaneous Poems and Translations*. York, C. Ward and B. Chandler, 1740.

Warton, Joseph. *Poems*, in Chalmers, *English Poets*, Vol. XVIII.

Warton, Thomas, the Younger. *Poems*, in Chalmers, *English Poets*, Vol. XVIII.

Warton, Thomas, the Elder. *Poems on Several Occasions*. Reproduced from the Edition of 1748. New York, The Facsimile Text Society, 1930.

Welsted, Leonard. *Of False Fame. An Epistle to the Right Honourable the Earl of Pembroke*. London, T. Cooper, 1732.

Wesley, John and Charles. *The Poetical Works of John and Charles Wesley*. Collected and Arranged by G. Osborn, D.D. London [n.p.], 1868.

West, Gilbert. *Poems*, in Chalmers, *English Poets*, Vol. XIII.

Whitehead, Paul. *Poems*, in Chalmers, *English Poets*, Vol. XVI.

Whitehead, William. *Poems*, in Chalmers, *English Poets*, Vol. XVII.

Williams, Sir Charles Hanbury. *The Works of the right Honourable Sir Charles Hanbury Williams, K.B.* ambassador to the Courts of Russia, Saxony, etc. from the originals in the possession of his grandson the Right Hon. the Earl of Essex: with notes by Horace Walpole, Earl of Orford. London, Edward Jeffery and Son, 1822.

Winstanley, John. *Poems Written Occasionally by John Winstanley; Interspers'd with Many Others, By Several Ingenious Hands*. Dublin, S. Powell, 1742.

Young, Edward. *Night Thoughts*, with Life, Critical Dissertation, and Explanatory Notes, by the Rev. George Gilfillan. London, James Nisbet and Co., 1853.

——— *The Poetical Works of Edward Young.* In two volumes. Boston, Little, Brown and Company, 1859.

Collections of Poetry

Anderson, Robert. *The Works of the British Poets.* London, J. and A. Rich, 1795.

Chalmers, Alexander. *The Works of the English Poets from Chaucer to Cowper.* London, J. Johnson, 1810.

Dodsley, Robert. *A Collection of Poems.* In six volumes. London, Dodsley, 1770.

Nichols, John. *A Select Collection of Poems.* London, J. Nichols, 1780–82.

Pearch, George. *A Collection of Poems.* London, Pearch, 1775.

Index

Adam, 4

Addison, Joseph, 30, 44, 56, 116, 136, 147, 182, 183; defence of great, artless genius, 149; estimate of Shakespeare's genius, 141-42; on taste, 157; "Pindaric manner" of gardening, 127; pleasure in "what is great, uncommon, or beautiful," 134

Advice to an Author, 157

Aesop, 190

Aesthetics, 99. *See also* Genius; Rules, the

Agincourt, 20, 26

Akenside, Mark, ix, 71, 118, 145, 155, 199, 201, 202, 205; benevolence, 184; chain of being, 104; optimism, 117-18; poetic fury, 154-55; rural retirement, Horatian, 52; summary of his primitivism, 201-2; taste, 158; tribute to Shakespeare, 144

Ancients and moderns, quarrel of the, 14-15

Ancients, 146; destroyed by luxury, 17-19; poetic fervor of, 15-17, 153; superiority as citizens, 13-14; superiority in literature, 14-17

Anne, queen of England, 20, 115

Aphra Behn, 30

Apologie of Raymonde Seybonde, 189

Arcadia, vii, 40

Aristotle, 142, 146

Armstrong, John, 34, 76, 137, 158

Art and external nature, *see* External Nature

Art, detrimental to human conduct, 163-66; necessary in human conduct, 161-63

Art of Poetry, 146

Astronomy, the new, 97

Atlantis, 2

Avalon, 29

Avaro and Amanda, 31

à Wood, Anthony, 137

Background of Thomson's Seasons, vii

Baker, Henry, 122

Barber, Mary, 185-86

Bath, 55, 187

Beast machine, 189-90

Beasts, *see* entries under Man and Beast

Beggars' Opera, 22

Benevolence, 59, 121, 166, 182-89, 205

Black Prince, 27

Boadicea, 20, 26

Boas, Frederick, ix

Boniform Faculty of the Soul, 166-67

Book of nature, 107-14, 206-7

Britannia, 84

Brooke, Henry, 101

Brown, "Capability," 125

Burnet, Thomas, bishop, 109, 140

Bury St. Edmund's, 139

Cambridge Platonists, the, 166-67, 175

Carey, Henry, 78

Caroline, queen of England, 187

Castle of Indolence, 6, 42

Cato, 27, 45

Cato, 22

Caves and mines, interest in, 58

Cave of Sleep, Spenser's, 58

Chain of being, 30, 98, 100-7, 114, 199, 203, 205, 206

Chamberlayne, John, 82-83

Chandler, Mary, 55, 186

Chaucer, Geoffrey, 147

Grottoes and grotto building, 58, 59, 60, 200

Hamilton, William, of Bangour, 53, 133, 164, 173
Happy Beast in French Thought in the Seventeenth Century, ix-x
Hebrides, 29, 36
Hector, 161
Hesiod, 3
Hermitage, Queen Caroline's, 60, 109
Hill, Aaron, 147
Hobbes, Thomas, 7, 149, 166, 168, 175, 182, 183, 189
Homer, 15
Honeycomb, Will, 81
Horace, 15, 37, 45, 50, 52, 54, 146; *see also* Rural retirement, Horatian
Horror, *see* Melancholy; Rural retirement, Miltonic; External Nature, wild and irregular
Humanitarianism, 194-95, 205
Hutcheson, Francis, 114, 157, 166

Idyl, 39
Ion, 149
Il Penseroso, 57
Il Penseroso, 44, 62, 70, 71
India, 35, 36
Indian Kings, 30
Inkle and Yarico, 31
Inquiry into the Original of our Ideas of Beauty and Virtue, 114, 166
Islands of the Blest, 29

Jamaica, 35, 36
Je ne sais quoi, 149
Johnson, Samuel, 26, 43, 44, 45, 47, 78, 90, 187
Jonson, Ben, 143, 146, 148
Juvenal, 72, 91

Kensington Gardens, 129
Kent, William, 124, 125
"Kilda's race," 37, 38

Landscapes, *see* entries under External Nature
Langley, Batty, 125
Lapland, Laplanders, 36, 203

Learning, decline of modern, 21-22
Liberty, 84
Literature, rules of, *see* entries under Rules
Locke, John, 22, 60, 61, 98, 108, 161, 167
Lovejoy, A. O., vii, ix, 96
Love of Fame, 49, 85
Luxury, evil effects of, 17-18, 74-75, 82, 201, 205-6
Lycurgus, 173, 205

Mallet, David, 50, 66, 149
Man, cause of ruin'd Nature, 108-110; effects of his Fall, 4-5, 168, 169; innately good, 174, 175; limitations of his knowledge, 201, 117-18; misfit in ordered universe, 110-11; naturally benevolent, 7, 160, 167, 182-89; place in the chain of being, 101-2, 98-99, 206
Man and beast, 160, 189-95, 202, 207
Mandeville, Bernard, 168, 175, 182
Manners, decline of modern, 23-24
Man of Ross, 187-88
Marlborough, John Churchill, duke of, 26
Masters, Mary, 64
McKillop, Alan D., viii
Melancholy, 56, 57, 62-63, 71, 200; black, 57, 67-71
Methodism, 180-81, 182
Micro-biology, 97
Microscope, 104
Milton, 20, 22, 56, 67, 72, 125, 137, 146, 152, 160
Molly Mog, 81
Montaigne, Michel de, 29, 30, 189
Moral Epistles, 45, 84
Moral evil, problem of, 115, 119-20, 201-2
Moralists, The, 82, 108
Moral sense, 161, 167

Nash, Richard, 187
Natural History, 190
Nature, 160; as guide in life, vii; as norm, 96, 201; benevolence in, 188; book of, 107-14, 203, 206-7; confusion about the term, 7; ethical